SEA POWER
IN THE
PACIFIC

SEA POWER
IN THE
PACIFIC

A history from the sixteenth century to the present day

DONALD MACINTYRE

Distributed in the United States by
CRANE, RUSSAK & COMPANY, INC.
347 Madison Avenue
New York, New York 10017

ISBN 0 213 99456 9

Printed in Great Britain by
Redwood Press Limited
Trowbridge, Wiltshire

Typesetting by
Truset (Trowbridge) Ltd.
Trowbridge, Wiltshire

CONTENTS

MAPS (261-72)

I

DEVELOPMENTS PRIOR TO EUROPEAN INTERVENTION

At what period of history the dwellers along the Pacific shores began to use the sea for travel or commerce is a matter for conjecture. For many centuries after that, lacking the ability to build ships fit to sail the open sea and all but the most primitive navigational techniques, these dwellers must have been confined to coastwise journeys in small boats. It was not until about the beginning of the Christian era that regular trade routes along the coast of Asia between Korea and Indo-China began to be developed.

The Chinese, who inhabited the greater part of this long coastline and claimed suzerainty over much of the remainder, took comparatively little interest in this development. Geography has throughout the ages made a land power of China ; successive ruling dynasties devoted most of their energies to expansion and conquest or reconquest over land routes, even when these expeditions were aimed at countries such as Korea or Indo-China with extensive sea coasts. Trade was also mainly overland by the famous Silk Route and the 'Golden Road to Samarkand' by which Marco Polo reached the court of Kublai Khan in the thirteenth century.

Sea-borne traffic to and from China was nearly always to remain chiefly in the hands of foreigners. The first to develop it were the various city-states along the shore of the Gulf of Siam, Malaysian populations with Indian culture and rulers, which became federated into the empire of Funan around the middle of the third century AD. As time went on, trading communities of foreigners, at first probably Malaysian, became established in southern Chinese ports of which Chao-Chi in the Red River delta in Tongkin was the principal *entrepôt*.

Indian penetration of Siam and Cochin-China had begun some hundreds of years earlier as a result of the coastal shipping route established by their seamen round the Bay of Bengal and thence south to the Kra Isthmus where there existed portage routes to the Gulf of Siam. By the second century they had become sufficiently skilled in navigation and ship-building to venture by ocean routes from the port of Tamralipti at the western end of the Ganges delta to the East Indies where Sumatra and part of Java had come under Hindu rule by the middle of the second century AD.

Thus when the first fully recorded voyage from Ceylon to China took place, that of the Chinese Buddhist pilgrim Fa-Hsien between 413 and 415, we find him embarking in a ship, probably Indian, carrying some two hundred persons, many of them merchants. After surviving a storm which lasted thirteen days, during which all the heavy cargo had to be jettisoned, the ship was beached for repairs either at the northern point of Sumatra or in the Nicobar Islands before resuming the voyage to reach a port called Yeh-po-ti, probably in western Java or perhaps in Borneo. There Fa-Hsien had to wait for five or six months, presumably for the onset of the south-west monsoon in July, before setting off again in another ship of similar size.

That ships were still clumsy craft with limited control under sail is indicated by the sixty to eighty days that this one was driven helplessly before the wind, while food and water were exhausted, before making a landfall on the coast of Shantung in northern China and safely reaching port. It is not surprising therefore that the greater part of the sea-borne traffic to and from China followed the coastal routes. This had the other disadvantage of exposing trading ships to attack by the cruel and rapacious pirates who swarmed throughout South-east Asian waters, particularly in the Malacca Straits, where their swift, oar-propelled *praus* would find their victims becalmed for long periods. Other much-feared pirates were the Chams, a Malayan/Polynesian people whose country, Champa, lay along the Vietnam coast to the north of Funan. To avoid capture, trading ships would usually gather in convoys for mutual protection.

Sea power can hardly be said to have existed at this period except to the extent that Funan lay athwart the main sea routes, either via the portages of the Kra Isthmus or from Sumatra and Java, and fees were exacted from passing ships in return for some protection. Important changes took place, however, during the seventh century. Funan was overrun by Khmers from the hinterland. The commercial leadership of the area was then taken by the Hindu-ruled state of Sri-Vijaya, whose principal port lay at the mouth of the Palembang river in southern Sumatra. This gradually developed into the capital of an extensive maritime empire by the absorption of two other independent ports : Malayu, on the eastern coast of the island near the entrance to the Malacca Strait, and Kedah, on the Malay Peninsula. Further expansion brought the western end of Java into the empire as well and with it control of the important Sunda Strait between the Indian Ocean and the Java Sea. With its control of all the corridors between the Indian Ocean and the South China Sea including, after reduction of Malaya to a condition of vassalage, the portage routes across the Kra Isthmus, this grew into the first empire to exercise genuine sea power in Pacific waters. Its position was much strengthened by the arrival of Arab and Persian traders from the west and a greatly expanded interest in foreign sea-borne trade by China where the T'ang Dynasty had risen to the height of its power, ruling over a united and orderly country. The primitively rigged and designed ships of that age were wholly dependent upon the seasonal monsoon winds. A ship arriving on the Sri-Vijayan coasts from the west, borne on the south-west monsoon, would require a safe haven where she could be refitted and supplied. Meanwhile the south-west winds would be failing, to be replaced by the north-east monsoon, requiring a six-month lay-over in harbour until the next seasonal shift.

Sri-Vijaya, itself primarily a militarized community, was thus able to prosper, partly in parasitic fashion by charging harbour dues and selling provisions and services and partly by ensuring the safety of trading ships through the suppression of piracy and the provision of fortified harbours behind booms of iron chains. With the establishment of these conditions the advantages of the all-sea route to and from China, cutting out the laborious portage across the Kra Isthmus, were soon apparent and by the eighth century there was a busy traffic encouraged by the vast Islamic Empire centred on Baghdad as well as by the T'ang government of China.

The principal Chinese terminus for this traffic was Canton ; but during the ninth century Arab ships pressed on northwards and an alternative port was established at Amoy where ships and traders from Korea and the Liu-chiu (Ryu-kyu) Islands also congregated.

While Sri-Vijaya was establishing its sea power in the south, the Chinese, under the firmly settled T'ang rule, were also having one of their periods of renaissance as a naval power in the East China Sea. In 610 a naval expedition was launched against the Liu-chiu Islands kingdom to enforce traditional Chinese suzerainty. A sea battle took place in which the islanders were defeated, but no permanent conquest was attempted. The main task for sea power in that distant epoch before ships became truly ocean-going, however, was the protection of ships on the coastal routes against the ubiquitous pirates. Though piracy was never eliminated from eastern seas, Sri-Vijaya at the height of its power and China during its mid-dynasty periods of firm rule succeeded in suppressing it sufficiently for sea-borne trade to flourish. Conversely, when centrally controlled sea power languished, trade virtually collapsed.

During the seventh, eighth and ninth centuries, the vastly profitable China trade was almost entirely conducted by Persians and Arabs, sailing in Arab ships ; by their non-aggressive behaviour they secured complete tolerance from the Chinese who were content to leave the traffic in their hands. Arab communities were found at all the main ports, where they enjoyed a measure of extra-territorial rights under control of their own headmen. Apart from the normal interchange of commerce, the Chinese government profited from the heavy import and export duties and the harbour dues levied.

The Arabs were well equipped for self-defence, however, and could muster a formidable fighting force if required. Thus when in 758 the first signs of a decline in the power of the T'ang emperor manifested themselves in a revolt at Canton, a powerful force of Muslim mercenaries assisted in its suppression. In the process, though, they sacked and burned Canton with the result that the terminus of the trade route reverted to the Tongkinese port of Chao-chi until 792.

For another eighty years the China trade continued to flourish mainly in the hands of the Arabs ; but during the ninth century the T'ang dynasty's hold on the sprawling Chinese Empire steadily weakened with rebellion raising its hydra-like head. With the relaxation of government control, private Chinese traders, operating large junks, began to take an increasing share of the carrying trade and there soon grew up a rivalry with the foreign communities and a hostility to them. In 878 the rebel Huang Ch'ao captured and sacked Canton. The foreign residents found themselves restricted and oppressed. Fewer and fewer Arab ships made the voyage to China until by 925 the traffic had ceased and virtually all foreign merchant communities were banished. Chinese junks and Arab ships would meet in East Indian ports and exchange their cargoes.

This could have brought even greater prosperity to Sri-Vijaya ; but with the collapse of orderly government in South China, piracy along the coasts became so rife that the volume of trade greatly diminished, bringing a serious loss of revenue to the Sri-Vijayan Empire. It was not until the Sung successors to the T'ang dynasty brought South China once again under central control in 971 that trade recovered, with Arab, Malayan, Sumatran, Javanese and Philippine Island trading communities at Canton and at Ch'üanchow (Zaitun) in Fukien, the two principal trading ports. Much of this trade was now carried in Chinese junks which were of a size to accommodate as many as two hundred people. The compass was in general use by Chinese seamen and their ships voyaged as far as Ceylon and India.

All this brought prosperity back to Sri-Vijaya, whose ports and facilities were vital to the transient shipping. Meanwhile rivals to Sri-Vijayan supremacy had not been lacking. Disputes with the powerful Chola Tamil state of South India over control of the Kra Isthmus portage routes were endemic. At the same time the central Javanese state of Mataram, which first came into prominence in the eighth century, had extended its territory to include the whole of central and eastern Java and had entered the sea-borne trade between the Moluccas to the east and Sumatra and Malaya to the west.

What grievances or warlike impulses drove this comparatively minor state to challenge the long-established Sri-Vijayan Empire is not known ; but in 992 Mataram launched a naval campaign which threatened Palembang itself and was not finally defeated until 995. It took another ten years for Sri-Vijaya to reconcentrate its forces, but then a merciless revenge was taken. An army gathered from Sumatra and its vassal states on the Malay Peninsula swept over Java, reducing the East Javan state to chaos and destroying its ports and shipping.

The next assault on Sri-Vijaya came in 1025 when the great ruler of Chola, Rajendra Choladeva I, led a fleet to attack and raid the Sumatran and West Malayan coast. The king was seized and his palace looted ; the ports of Malayu (Jambi) and Ligor (Tambalinga) in Sumatra and Kedah in Malaya were captured. Sri-Vijaya lay prostrate, but the invaders were satisfied with their destruction and loot and made no effort to establish an effective occupation of the Empire. After ravaging Atjeh (Achin) at the northern end of Sumatra they sailed back to India.

Out of the ruins an even richer Sri-Vijaya arose under its new king. By a matrimonial alliance with a princess of the house of Airlangga, the Balinese prince who was restoring and re-unifying East Java gained control of the whole of the seaways of the area at a time when they were once again thronged with traffic to and from the prosperous China of the Sungs. This traffic was subjected to a harsh control, with all foreign ships forced to pay toll under threat of outright destruction.

With such a concentration of wealth in the ruler's hands, Sri-Vijaya reached the height of its power during the eleventh and twelfth centuries. But this monopoly was about to be broken. In Java a rival maritime state was again emerging under Airlangga's successors at the very time that the demand from Europe for spices, particularly cloves and nutmegs, which grew abundantly in the Moluccas, was rapidly expanding. In 1222 a ruthless Javanese adventurer, Angrok, founded the state of Singhasari in the hinterland of the modern Surabaya. By the middle of the thirteenth century, Singhasari had spread westwards to absorb Banka Island lying athwart the entrance to Palembang, forcing a shift of the Sri-Vijayan capital to Malayu. At the other end of the great arc of rich islands, the spice centre of Ternate in the Moluccas was reduced to subservience.

The last and perhaps the greatest king of Singhasari, Kertanagara, who ruled from 1268 to 1292, spread the empire to embrace all Java, Bali and Madura. He attacked Sri-Vijaya by land and sea, capturing Malayu, occupying both sides of the strategic Sunda Straits, parts of coastal Borneo and southern Malaya and thereby challenging Sri-Vijayan control of the Malacca Straits.

A southern empire of unprecedented size and power was in the making. If unopposed, it could soon impose an impenetrable barrier across the sea-route joining the extremities of another and greater power bloc. This was the vast empire ruled over by the Great Khan of the Mongols.

During the thirteenth century the Mongols, under the leadership first of Genghis Khan and then of his grandson, Kublai Khan, had carved out an empire stretching from the Crimea in the west to China in the east where the latter established himself as the successor to the Sungs. Not content with dominion over China itself, Kublai Khan set out to restore the ancient suzerainty over other lands across the seas. The traditional payment of tribute as acknowledgement of Chinese overlordship did not satisfy the Great Khan. He demanded more real subservience marked by the personal appearance and homage of the various rulers. When this was refused, naval expeditions were launched to enforce his demands.

The first country to be so attacked was Japan. In 1274 a Mongol army of 25,000 and 15,000 Korean soldiers were embarked in 900 Korean ships and set out in November across the Straits of Tsu-shima. Having captured the island of that name on their way, they landed on Northern Kyushu. Meeting unexpectedly stiff resistance from the despised 'dwarf people', the Mongol army fell back towards its boats and re-embarked ; but before they could recross the straits a violent storm struck the fleet, scattering it and wrecking many of the ships.

Some 13,000 men were lost in this unhappy enterprise ; and over the next four years Kublai Khan renewed his efforts to secure the peaceful submission of the Japanese ruler. But when the news reached Peking that the Mongol envoys had been executed, preparations for another and larger invasion were begun. A force of 50,000 Mongol soldiers and 20,000 Koreans embarked at the Korean port of Fusan (Pusan) in 1,000 ships ; another 50,000 Mongols and 50,000 Chinese sailed from Ch'üanchow in Fukien. The two fleets made rendezvous off the Japanese coast in August 1281, only to be overwhelmed once again by a typhoon, remembered ever after in Japanese history as the *Kamikaze* (divine wind) which saved them in their hour of peril. Only a small fraction of the invading army survived the débâcle ; Kublai Khan abandoned his designs on the Japanese but they were the foundations of a lasting enmity between the two empires.

Meanwhile Kublai Khan's demands for South-East Asian rulers to make personal acts of submission at Peking had met with similar refusals, and between 1281 and 1285 Mongol expeditions by land and sea attempted to subdue Annam and Champa. These two abandoned their traditional feuding to combine against the common danger and, though the coastal areas suffered devastation, resistance in the highlands of the interior was never overcome and the Mongol armies finally withdrew without achieving their purpose. When the rulers of Annam, Champa and Cambodia later offered the traditional tribute and nominal subservience, this was accepted.

Kublai Khan's desire to bring the growing power of Singhasari under his control was based on more than a conqueror's unshakeable thirst for ever wider dominion. The sea route from China to the Persian Gulf not only carried a huge commerce of great value to China, but was also an important link between the two ends of the vast, sprawling empire ruled over by other Mongol princes. Kublai was naturally unwilling to see this empire subjected to the control of an independent power and sent envoys to Kertanagara summoning him to come to Peking, or at least to send a member of his family as a hostage.

For a number of years Kertanagara was able to avoid giving a definite answer ; but by 1289 these prevarications would no longer satisfy the increasingly uncompromising demands of the Great Khan. The cloak of subservience was thrown off, and the Chinese ambassadors were seized and sent home with their faces branded. The inevitable punitive expedition left China in 1292 and, after surprising and capturing a Javanese fleet, landed at the eastern end of Java early the next year. There they learned that Kertanagara had been assassinated by Jayakatwang, ruler of the subordinate state of Kediri who had then assumed power in his place. Prince Vijaya, Kertanagara's son-in-law and the legitimate heir, had been forced to submit and content himself with lordship of a mere district of which the village of Majapahit on the River Brantas was the centre. He had however been plotting revenge, and the appearance of the Chinese fleet and army provided his opportunity. Professing acceptance of the emperor's demands, he asked for and obtained the assistance of the Chinese army to overthrow the usurper, whose troops were quickly defeated and Jayakatwang captured in his capital.

The time had now come for Vijaya to carry out his side of the bargain and, under Chinese escort, he and his followers made for Majapahit where final arrangements for payment of tribute and the handing over of hostages were to be made. On the way, the Javanese turned treacherously on their escort and murdered the members of it. The Chinese generals had unwisely divided their force into a number of detachments and scattered them about the country. Vijaya and his followers next made a number of surprise attacks on some of these detachments. The remainder beat a retreat to the fleet and taking members of the defeated Jayakatwang's family as hostages, set sail for home.

Perhaps this was represented at Peking as a satisfactory restoration of face for the Emperor ; in any case, the uniform lack of success of Chinese naval expeditions under the Mongols against overseas tributary states had deflated Kublai's ambitions. From this time onwards, he and his successors accepted formal tributary missions making nominal submission, and Chinese expeditions to the area were henceforth commercial or diplomatic in nature.

The disorders in Eastern Java begun by Jayakatwang's revolt, and others which followed during the first thirty years of the fourteenth century, halted the Javanese take-over of Indonesia for the time being, leaving it fragmented under a number of petty rajahs. This state of affairs and the resultant absence of law and order in the Malacca Straits were described by Marco Polo, who took passage *en route* back to Venice in 1292 with a Chinese fleet of fourteen ships carrying a Mongol princess bride for the Great Khan's nephew, Argun the Ilkhan of Persia. During the voyage a necessary halt of five months to await the shift of monsoon winds was made at the port of Samudra on the northern Sumatran coast.

In 1330, however, the chaos in Eastern Java was resolved when the ruler of Majapahit raised Gaja Mada, an officer of the royal bodyguard, to the position of chief minister. As actual autocratic ruler from that time until his death in 1364, Gaja Mada concentrated his energies on a programme of expansion of Javanese power over the whole of Indonesia. Though he never succeeded in establishing a truly unified empire, Majapahit authority was accepted in Bali, Macassar, parts of Borneo and the Malay peninsula, much of Sumatra and western Java.

Gaja Mada maintained a powerful fleet and it was by sea power that Majapahit secured the submission of the numerous little states in the archipelago and the monopoly of the spice trade of the Moluccas, which brought with it immense wealth. A rajah who showed signs of opposing this control would be 'visited' by a Javanese squadron, an early example of the less reputable forms of gunboat diplomacy of a later era. With Gaja Mada's death, however, Javanese control weakened its grip, particularly in Sumatra and Malaya, and piracy grew so rife that the Straits of Malacca were virtually closed to commercial traffic.

However, a new influence had meanwhile been spreading southwards through the area : that of the Muslim traders from India who, unlike the longer established Persian and Arab Muslims, were not only filled with proselytizing fervour on behalf of Islam, but also aggressive in their demand for law and order in which to pursue their commercial aims. Of these Indian Muslims the most important were those from Gujerat, where conversion to Islam had taken place in 1325. They and others from Bengal and southern India brought to Sumatran ports the cloth products of India and goods obtainable from Europe, in exchange for cargoes of spices, pepper, sandalwood and so on. Conversion of the rulers of these ports to Mohammedanism brought political and commercial favour in its train.

The most urgent political aim of these traders was the reopening of the Straits of Malacca by the suppression of piracy. It was equally important at this time (the beginning of the fifteenth century) to China where, since 1368, the native Ming dynasty had been established in place of the Mongol descendants of Kublai Khan. By 1400, when the overland caravan routes to the west had been closed by the sweeping conquests of Tamerlane, making the re-establishment of the sea-route to Ceylon, India and the Middle East of commercial importance, the Chinese had also begun one of their periodic efforts to recall the allegiance of their overseas tributaries.

In 1403, therefore, the Emperor Yung-Lo despatched the first of a series of naval expeditions to the South China Sea under the direction of Cheng-ho, a eunuch high official of the Ming Court. By diplomacy and fair words backed by a sizeable fleet, he secured the submission of a number of states before tackling the problem of the Straits. There he found the new port of Malacca in the process of establishing itself in the face of hostility from two rival claimar.ts to suzerainty, Siam and Majapahit, and under the rule of a rebel Sumatran refugee from Majapahit Java named Parameswara. Malacca was strategically placed for control of the Straits ; the rajah was anxious to obtain Chinese recognition and protection. On this occasion the fleet included sixty-six war junks and brought an army of some 37,000 men with it. This force entered the port of Palembang and dispersed the Chinese pirates, for whom it had long been a lair, sending the pirate chief back a prisoner to China.

Two years later Cheng-ho was on the scene again on his way with a fleet to Ceylon and then to the shores of the Arabian Sea. On Cheng-ho's return Parameswara accompanied him to make a personal obeisance to the Ming Emperor, an act repeated on a number of occasions by his successors. Now that the security of the infant state had been assured, Parameswara set about soliciting the Indian traders of Pasai, Perlak and Pedir in North Sumatra to shift their headquarters to Malacca. They demanded that he should accept conversion from Hinduism to Mohammedanism. It appears that he did so. Certainly his son, who succeeded him on his death in 1414, ruled under the Muslim name of Muhammad Iskander Shah ; and thereafter, except for his immediate successor who reverted to Hinduism, he was followed by Muslim rulers. It was as a stronghold of Islam that Malacca continued to be the centre of a powerful state until 1511, drawing sustenance from the concentration of trade passing through it.

By the time the brief upsurge of Chinese interest in overseas domination died down again after 1430, Malacca had extended its rule to large areas of Sumatra and much of the Malay peninsula and had become strong enough to stand on its own feet, defying the efforts of Siam to reimpose its suzerainty. To this seething *entrepôt* flocked traders from China, the Liu-chiu islands, Tonkin and Siam to the north, the Moluccas or Spice Islands and Java in Javanese ships to the east and India to the west to exchange their goods in its highly organized market.

By levying duty on every form of trade, the Sultans amassed great wealth. The real power, however, was in the hands of the *Bendahara* or chief minister. Under him was a Minister of the Interior or *Temenggong* and the admiral of the fleet or *Laksamana*. The foreign traders were regulated by four harbour masters or *Shahbandars* selected from their own communities; one was responsible for the shipping from the north; one for Javanese and other Indonesian ships and one for traders from the Bay of Bengal, the Malabar Coast of India and northern Sumatra. The fourth took care of the Gujeratis alone, an indication of the preponderance of these traders in the port.

Such was the teeming, polyglot state of Malacca, secure and prosperous under the able *Bendahara* Tun Mutahir, ruling on behalf of the weak and degenerate Sultan Mahmud, when in 1509 there appeared a squadron of Portuguese carracks under Diogo Lopez de Sequeira. A new era in the maritime history of the Pacific was about to open.

2

PORTUGUESE ASCENDANCY

The squadron of six broad-beamed, square-rigged carracks that appeared off Malacca, with the black muzzles of their cannons emerging from the gunports along their flanks and the banner of King Manuel I of Portugal at their mastheads, had been despatched by that monarch in 1508. The existence of Malacca had become known to the Portuguese from the accounts of Arab traders and its strategic position recognized. This first expedition under Diogo Lopez de Sequeira was to convey diplomatic greetings to the ruler and arrange for Portuguese participation in the trade of the port on the same terms and conditions as other foreigners. A second squadron of six ships was to follow in the next year to take advantage of the permission confidently expected.

Sequeira had reached Cochin on the west coast of India in the autumn of 1508 and waited there until the return of the south-west monsoon to continue his voyage. In the interval his ships had been commandeered by the Portuguese viceroy of India, Francisco de Almeida, to strengthen the fleet with which, off Diu, at the western entrance of the Gulf of Cambay, he destroyed the Arab fleet sent from the Red Sea to dispute Portuguese participation in the carriage of the spice trade between India and Europe. Sequeira had then been sent on his way.

At Malacca he was at first amicably received by the *Bendahara*, Tun Mutahir, but it was not long before the Muslim trading community persuaded the *Bendahara* that these eager commercial competitors were a serious threat to the state. Weight was lent to this warning by Sequeira making known his intention of building a fort nearby. The *Bendahara* thereupon planned and launched a treacherous attack on the Portuguese. A number were made prisoner and two of the carracks were destroyed. With the remainder, Sequeira sailed for home, sending word to the new Viceroy, the great Alfonso de Albuquerque.

Albuquerque was at that time occupied with his second and final capture of Goa for which purpose he had added the second expedition for Malacca under Diogo Mendes de Vasconcellos to his force just as Almeida had done with Sequeira. Goa fell on 25 November 1510. With the north-east monsoon still holding, Vasconcellos could not yet leave for Malacca, and Albuquerque therefore informed him that he was to accompany the Viceroy on an expedition to the Red Sea to destroy an Arab fleet being fitted out there. Vasconcellos and his squadron promptly deserted, but were overtaken by Albuquerque's galleys as they were beating out of harbour and forced to return, when he and his captains were arrested and shipped off home.

Albuquerque sailed on 20 April 1511 for the Red Sea, with eighteen ships, three of which were galleys, and about 1,400 men, nearly half of them locally recruited Hindus. But when the monsoon winds on which the unhandy ships of that time had to rely for the westward voyage died away and an early seasonal shift took place, he reversed course and bore away for Malacca. In northern Sumatra he picked up some of Sequeira's men who had escaped from Malacca with the aid of a friendly Hindu. He lost one of his galleys on passage, but captured five Gujerati Muslim vessels and a large Javanese warship carrying a Sumatran rajah. With guns firing and flags and banners flaunting and amidst a blare of defiant trumpets, the Portuguese squadron anchored in the roadstead off Malacca on 1 July 1511.

Albuquerque at once demanded the release of the Portuguese captives, payment of an indemnity and the restoration of peaceful relations. Since Sequeira's departure the government of Malacca had fallen apart as a result of internal dissensions. The able *Bendahara* had been executed by the degenerate Sultan Mahmud. The Chinese and Javanese communities had been alienated by discrimination against them in favour of the Indian Muslim traders. The defences of the town had been neglected, though Malay vassals of the sultan had mobilized some twenty thousand men, armed chiefly with blowguns and poisoned darts. The Gujeratis, in the knowledge that they were likely to suffer hardest at Albuquerque's hands, had, however, taken steps to hire six hundred Turkish mercenaries and to provide muskets and cannon.

Malacca had no enclosed harbour ; the open roadstead was a safe enough anchorage in the storm-free straits and was crowded with shipping of every kind and nationality. When the Sultan failed to accede at once to Albuquerque's terms, the latter burnt every ship belonging to Gujeratis or Arabs, but spared the remainder.

The frightened Sultan released the survivors of the cruel captivity suffered by Sequeira's men ; but no indemnity would he pay, nor would he grant the Portuguese trading concessions. Albuquerque thereupon launched an attack to seize the central key-point, the fortified bridge spanning the river that bisected the town.

The Captain General believed that this would be sufficient to bring the Sultan to terms. It proved a serious under-estimation. His men duly stormed the stockades defending the bridge on either side and occupied the bridge itself. But they suffered heavy casualties from the poisoned darts of the Malays and, when the Sultan continued defiant, were soon forced to retire again having exhausted the food and munitions they had brought with them.

It was clear now to Albuquerque that only by capturing the town and establishing Portuguese sovereignty in place of the Sultan's would he be able to gain for his country a share in the teeming, profitable trade of the East Indies. As elsewhere in the East, only extermination of the implacable infidel foe would really satisfy either the followers of the Prophet or the fighting crusaders of Portugal and Spain. Invoking the principle of 'divide and rule', Albuquerque won over the disaffected Chinese and Javanese. The latter had been an important element of the defending forces ; they now stood aside. From the Chinese, the Captain General was able to obtain one of their high-charged junks on which he rigged ramparts of sail canvas as protection against the hail of poisoned darts. From this, floated up to the bridge, the Portuguese were able to dominate the defences and to re-occupy them, following which they brought up on the flood tide a number of lighters mounting cannon.

Ten days of bombardment laid in ruins the centre and rear of the town, containing the treasury and palace of the Sultan who fled with a few followers to the interior. The commercial area along the waterfront was left largely undamaged. With the aid of the Javanese fighting men, the remainder of the Muslim population was slaughtered. The Hindus and Chinese came over to the victor's side and were contentedly re-established under their own *Shahbandars*. So too, at first, were the Javanese. But Muslims and Christians were unable to exist peacefully side by side. Even before Albuquerque's departure early in 1512, the Javanese *Shahbandar*, accused of intriguing to restore Muslim rule, was tried, condemned and publicly executed.

Mortal enmity between the Portuguese and the Muslim rulers of the trading centres of Java and Sumatra was thereafter a permanent feature, while Muslim trade, carried in Gujerati, Bengali, Arab, Turkish and Persian ships, made efforts to establish a new *entrepôt* at Pasai in Sumatra. Another centre, where Chinese as well as Muslims met to trade was Brunei in north-west Borneo, where the rajah adopted the Mohammedan faith and in proselytizing fervour extended his rule over northern Borneo and the Sulu Islands. Meanwhile Albuquerque, in accordance with his system of backing sea power with secure land bases, erected a fortress on the south side of the river mouth at Malacca commanding the town and roadstead. To pay for its erection and upkeep, dues were levied on the trading communities. On his departure, Albuquerque left a fleet of fourteen vessels to command the straits and a garrison of 600 for the fort. The situation of the Portuguese was a precarious one, nevertheless, with enemies on every hand.

The next step was, inevitably, to reach out towards the source of the spice trade. The prize being sought was indeed a glittering lure, for a cargo of cloves could earn a profit of 2,500 per cent between the Moluccas and Europe while nutmeg, produced mainly in Amboyna and the Banda Islands, was equally valuable. The first expedition of three ships under Antonio d'Abreu was but partially successful. Only one ship returned, having loaded a cargo of cloves and nutmegs in the Banda Islands. But the captain of one of those lost, Francesco Serrao, rescued by a Malay pirate who took him to Amboyna, made such a reputation for himself as a *condottiere* in the service of local chieftains that the Sultan of the Spice Island of Ternate sent a ship for him. At this important centre of the spice trade he lived for some years as the Portuguese agent and concluded an alliance with the Sultan, giving the Portuguese a monopoly.

This brought the rivalry with the Javanese states to an open, armed conflict. The most important of these in Java itself was Demak, occupying the northern plains of the eastern half of the island, and exercising a powerful influence in western Java and Palembang. Portuguese intrusion into the spice trade, their ruthless means of excluding all foreign ships, as well as the stiff trading conditions imposed by them at Malacca, all operated to the detriment of Javanese prestige and prosperity. In 1513 the Sultan of Demak gathered a fleet of some one hundred ships which, having embarked an army, sailed to aid the Sultan of Malacca in his efforts to recapture the port and drive out the infidel intruders. In the sea fight that ensued the Portuguese fleet of thirteen ships under Fernando Perez de Andrade demonstrated, once and for all, the invulnerability of European cannon-mounted carracks to the assault of Malayan *praus*. The Javanese fleet was massacred. The huge shipping losses crippled both the military sea power and the commercial prosperity of the Javanese states.

Though they were for most of the time on a level of mere harassment, hostilities never entirely ceased throughout the period of Portuguese occupation of Malacca ; over the next sixty years the fever-plagued and often short-handed garrison of the fort was forced to beat off repeated direct attacks. In these, after the Javanese defeat of 1513, the ambitious Sultanate of Atjeh in northern Sumatra took the chief part, though in 1551 it was a combined fleet of the state of Johore (set up under the ex-Sultan of Malacca) and Japara (in northern Java) that was defeated in a notable sea battle. The history of these repeated sea-fights against numerically far larger forces and of the stubborn defence of the *A Famosa* fort of Malacca, often by mere handfuls of fever-stricken men in the humid equatorial heat, is full of tales of courage and resource. They must command one's admiration, however much the combination of religious bigotry, cruelty and rapacity of the Portuguese of that era may repel one.

In spite of the precarious position of their main base, the Portuguese succeeded in establishing the virtual monopoly of the spice trade. Each year, between November and January, the spice fleet would set out from Malacca for the Moluccas via Amboyna. The whole of the clove crop would be reserved

25

for them at Ternate. For the nutmeg of Amboyna and the Banda Islands they had to trade in the normal way; but Javanese traders were chronically short of shipping owing to their disastrous defeats in 1513 and 1551, and as a result of ruthless attacks by Portuguese cruisers whenever they met at sea. Those who survived were denied access to the *entrepôt* of Malacca and, though they in time developed outlets for their spices to China at Patani in the Malay Peninsula and at Brunei, they were unable to satisfy the Gujerati and other Indian traders.

The latter tried unsuccessfully to dispose of their cargoes of valued cotton cloth at Sumatran ports; occasionally they flouted Portuguese orders by running large convoys through the straits without stopping at Malacca. But for the most part it was only at Malacca that the spices essential for their lucrative trade with the Near East (and on to Europe) could be obtained and even there it was necessary to pay exorbitant bribes to Portuguese officials to obtain them. Thus the Portuguese were able to gather virtually the whole of the spice supply of Europe into their hands. The decline of Venice as the leading naval power in the Mediterranean dates from this time.

The opponents of this Portuguese trade monopoly were initially natural enemies as followers of the Prophet and therefore committed by the tenets of their faith to the forcible conversion of the infidel; the Portuguese similarly favoured extermination of such unprofitable material for their burning missionary zeal as the Muslims invariably were. Thus on both sides material aims which could vary in degree from honest trading ambitions to sheer rapacity, were given the cloak of piety. Portuguese guns would sink the ships of Muslim rivals with the blessing of the Church; Mohammedan rajahs would take to ruthless piracy in the name of Allah. One consequence of the latter which arose when Mohammedanism spread to the ports of Western Java and southern Borneo, was the denial of these as stopping points for Portuguese ships on the run to and from the Spice Islands. When the seamen of East Borneo and Celebes, the warlike Bugis, took to unabashed piracy, the route became so dangerous that the Portuguese eventually preferred to accept the hazards of the Sulu Islands passage and the North Borneo coast.

In 1521, however, a new factor was introduced by the arrival at Brunei of a patched and battered carrack flying the flag of Spain, Portugal's only serious European naval rival in that period. This was the *Victoria*, sole survivor of Ferdinand Magellan's expedition which was to complete the first circumnavigation of the globe. Magellan, a Portuguese who had been pilot to Sequeira at Malacca in 1509, had offered his services to Spain and had been commissioned to command a squadron sent to find a route to the Spice Islands by sailing westwards. Discovering the straits that bear his name, he had entered and named the Pacific Ocean and had been carried across it in the latitude of the trade winds to make landfall on the Philippine Islands.

There Magellan had been killed in a brush with the natives, but his flagship had continued the voyage westwards to arrive at Brunei. When fighting broke out there also, the ship was turned east again and after sailing through the difficult channels amongst the Sulu Islands, arrived at Tidore, to the west of Halmahera, and rival centre of the spice trade to the neighbouring Ternate. When the *Victoria* arrived home in 1522, Spanish claims to the Spice Islands were put forward.

The rival claimants, Spain and Portugal, were bound by the decision of Pope Alexander VI in 1493 by which the new world being gradually discovered was divided between the two countries. To the west of a line drawn from pole to pole passing 100 leagues to the westward of the Cape Verde Islands all would belong to Spain ; to the eastward all was to be Portuguese. Unfortunately the difficulty of establishing the longitude of a place even approximately with the means available at the time made it impossible to say where the demarcation line ran with regard to the East Indies ; no agreement could be come to at a conference in 1524. Spanish efforts in the next few years were ineffective owing to the difficulties and hazards of the long haul across the Pacific. As a result of the Treaty of Saragossa in 1529 the Spaniards withdrew their claims for some years, selling their rights in the Moluccas to the Portuguese and fixing the dividing line seventeen degrees to the eastward of those islands. The King of Spain, however, reserved the right to annul his agreement, in which case arbitrators would decide the ownership of the Spice Islands. The Portuguese had, therefore, prepared against future trouble by building a fort on Ternate and espousing the cause of the Sultan against his rival on Tidore.

While the Portuguese were thus establishing, amidst unceasing conflict, their control of the East Indian trade, the pioneering genius and the commercial ability (or, as St Francis Xavier was to condemn it, the insatiable rapacity) of their seamen had been taking them ever further afield. In 1517 a squadron of seven ships under Fernando Perez de Andrade, victor of the sea-fight of 1513, arrived off Canton carrying a valuable cargo. Though the gun salute with which the Portuguese announced their arrival violated the code of conduct imposed on visiting foreign ships and Andrade had to make apologies for it, relations were thereafter friendly and permission to build a factory for the housing of goods on an off-shore island was granted.

Accompanying the expedition as ambassador was Tomé Pires who had previously visited China and written an account of it in his *Suma Oriental* in 1515. From Canton, Pires was sent on to the Chinese court at Peking in September 1518, while Andrade, with part of his squadron, returned to Malacca. The remainder, in company with some Liu-chiu Islands junks sailed on northwards to Ningpo where another factory was built and trade was opened with other parts of China, with fortified posts at Amoy and Foochow also.

This satisfactory opening of European trade with China was not to persist for long, however. The old bone of contention, China's claim to the overlordship of all southern Asia, was brought out when Pires arrived at Peking. A letter from the deposed Sultan of Malacca had reached the Emperor, reminding him of Malacca's vassal status and requesting Chinese assistance to eject the invaders. Pires, not authorized to acknowledge Chinese suzerainty in the same way, was put under arrest and conducted back to Canton, where he was to remain a prisoner until his death in 1540.

In 1521 Fernando de Andrade's brother, Simon, arrived off Canton with another expedition. The high-handed arrogance which was the fatal defect of the Portuguese in their heyday was to cause his downfall. Just when negotiations for the opening of Chinese ports to trade were reaching a satisfactory conclusion, he offended the Chinese authorities by erecting a factory and fort on an off-shore island, without permission, ostensibly as protection against pirates ; and there he proceeded to exercise sovereign rights, demonstrated by his trial and execution of one of his sailors. A Chinese fleet of war junks attacked him, destroying all but three of his ships with which he was lucky to escape.

Nevertheless Portuguese trade with China through the former's fortified posts at Amoy, Foochow and Ningpo persisted until 1545 when their aggressive behaviour finally led to their being expelled. The survivors, apparently learning their lesson at last, now adopted a conciliatory and suppliant attitude ; they were eventually permitted in 1557 to build a trading post on the island of Macao (in the approaches to Canton), which has persisted as a Portuguese colony to this day.

For the next fifty years the Portuguese enjoyed a monopoly of direct trade with China using their own ships, while at the same time Chinese junks traded to the Philippines, to Brunei, to Patani and occasionally to Malacca, though the extortionate charges levied there discouraged them. Another country opened up to Portuguese exclusive trade at that time was Japan ; an expedition reaching Kagoshima in 1542 set up a trading post which enjoyed total absence of European competition for fifty years.

Far otherwise was the situation of the Portuguese in the Indonesian Archipelago. Besides the unceasing hostilities between Christian and Muslim in the Malacca Straits, with frequent full-scale naval expeditions by the Sultan of Atjeh against Malacca itself, the Portuguese hold on the Spice Islands was constantly under attack by the inhabitants and their rajahs, resentful of Portuguese arrogance and made desperate by their cruelty and greed.

Much of the Portuguese difficulties in the Spice Islands stemmed from their ruthless and often treacherous treatment of the native rulers and, conversely, from these Muslim rulers' opposition to attempts to make Christian converts amongst their subjects. Indeed, Portuguese cupidity and missionary zeal were always at loggerheads to the frustration of the efforts of such as Francis Xavier, who laboured in the Moluccas from 1546 to 1548. The type of man sent out to govern the Portuguese settlements was more often than not bent on personal enrichment to the exclusion of other aims ; or, if he bestirred himself to restrain the peculations of his subordinates he was liable to have a mutiny on his hands, and more than one governor was murdered for his pains. Throughout the century of Portuguese control of the Spice Islands, only one governor, Antonio Galväo 1536-40, left behind him a reputation for rectitude and fair dealing with the natives. He consequently returned poor to Lisbon, and there died in poverty.

In 1544 the ruler of Ternate, who claimed the overlordship of the Banda Islands as well as the Moluccas, made over Amboyna to the Portuguese who thereupon occupied the island, thus obtaining a more ample and secure base than the tiny islands of Ternate and Tidore, where strife was endemic, with the rival rajahs sometimes at war with each other, perhaps with the support of Portuguese or Spaniards, or in alliance with each other to attack the Portuguese strongholds.

The Spaniards had abrogated the agreement of 1529 in 1542 and had established prior and exclusive rights for themselves on Tidore. But for the next twenty years they were unable to follow this up. Though they could reach the area by sailing westwards across the Pacific from Mexico, until an eastward return route across the Pacific had been discovered, they would have had to return to Spain by completing the circumnavigation of the globe and thus to traverse waters dominated by the fighting galleons of their jealous Portuguese rivals. It was not until 1565 that a Spanish expedition of five ships, having landed the nucleus of a settlement at Cebu in the Philippines under Legaspi, was sailed northwards on the south-west monsoon by Andres de Urdaneta to discover the region of fairly constant westerlies between the parallels of 32 and 38 degrees north and so to reach the shores of California whence they could coast southwards to Mexico. Legaspi's settlement at Cebu was considered an intrusion by the Portuguese, who showed their resentment by sending a squadron of ten ships to besiege it in 1568. They failed to dislodge the Spanish, however.

More of a threat to the Spanish colonizing efforts were the native Moros of the southern islands of the Philippines. Converts to Islam, they made formidable enemies and lived largely by piracy. In 1570, therefore, Legaspi moved his settlement to Luzon where he founded the city of Manila. There, after repulsing an attack in the following year by a Moro fleet, the Spaniards laid the foundations of a centre for both missionary work amongst the pagan inhabitants of Luzon and trade with the Chinese merchants from Fukien who brought their silks to exchange for Mexican silver. Neither of these objectives was possible amongst the belligerent Muslims further south and the Spanish left them discreetly alone.

After the foundation of Manila, Spanish ships again appeared in the Moluccas to dispute the Portuguese monopoly. By this time Portuguese misrule and the cruel cupidity of often mutinous forces had fanned the enmity of the natives and loosened the Portuguese hold on the Spice Islands. Amboyna had narrowly survived an attack by a Javanese force ; the Portuguese fort on Ternate was besieged by forces under the Sultan of Tidore, a siege which was to end with its surrender in 1575. The Spaniards were then able to gain a foothold on Ternate for a time ; the Portuguese shifted their spice trading headquarters to Tidore. An open struggle between the two Iberian powers was, however, avoided through the unification of the two countries under Philip II of Spain in 1580.

Future events were now casting their shadows before them. In 1579 Francis Drake's *Golden Hind*, on her voyage of circumnavigation, had called briefly at Ternate, after refitting in Celebes, and loaded a quantity of spices. In the following year the Netherlands began its revolt against the rule of Spain. Both English and Dutch were soon to challenge the Portuguese/Spanish claims to exclusive trading rights, though it was the Dutch who were to take the leading part in the East Indies.

Dutch procurement of the spices and other commodities of the East had for a long time been by means of their own ships sent to load them at Lisbon, and much of the supply of oriental pepper and spices to northern Europe had been in the hands of Dutch merchants. In 1585, however, Philip II gave orders for the seizure of all Dutch ships found in Spanish waters. For another nine years this regulation was to a great extent flouted so that no particular hardship was thereby suffered by the Netherlands.

The Dutch, whose trading and exploring ventures had been spreading far and wide, had, however, long coveted a direct share in the trade with the East Indies. In 1592, Huyghen van Linschoten returned from a nine-year sojourn in India possessed of all the necessary geographic and navigational information for the voyage to the East Indies which he published in his *Itinerario* in 1595. When Lisbon was finally closed to Dutch trade in 1594, therefore, it was not long before an expedition of four ships was organized which sailed in the spring of 1595 under Cornelis van Houtman, and arrived at the Javanese port of Bantam in June 1596.

Here they were amicably received ; a treaty of friendship with the Sultan was concluded and a cargo of pepper was soon being loaded. Unfortunately van Houtman had neither the wit nor the manners to take advantage of this and strife soon broke out. As a result further supplies of pepper were refused at other Javanese ports and, when his crew refused to venture further to the Spice Islands, Houtman was forced to return with little profit.

Nevertheless the flood-gates of Dutch trade with the East Indies had been opened. Making use of the constant west winds, the 'Roaring Forties' south of the Indian Ocean, for their easting, which made them independent of the seasonal monsoons, they established the fastest route to a trading post set up at Bantam via the Cape of Good Hope and the Sunda Strait between Sumatra and Java. Thirteen ships took this route during 1598, returning with vast profits. Others, usually sailing in squadrons for mutual protection, followed. From Bantam they voyaged on to the Banda Islands and Ternate at both of which places they were welcomed and were able to establish trading posts. Peaceful trade being the expressed aim of the ship owners, invitations to assist the natives against the hated Portuguese were at first declined. But in 1600 the Admiral of one of these squadrons, Steven van der Haghen, made a treaty of alliance with the inhabitants of the island of Amboyna against the Portuguese, receiving in return promises of a monopoly of the spice trade.

The Portuguese were now thoroughly alarmed ; under Admiral Furtado de Mendoza a fleet of eight large and twenty smaller ships set out from Malacca with the initial aim of driving the Dutch from Bantam. A Dutch squadron of three large and two small ships under Wolfert Harmensz, arriving from the west, without hesitation fell upon the Portuguese armada in the roadstead of Bantam on Christmas Day 1601. The odds were by no means as great as they might seem, in fact. The Dutch at that time shared with the English the leadership in the development of the fighting galleons, ships of greatly improved sailing qualities, armed with broadsides of long-range culverins and far superior to the high-charged, clumsy carracks on which the Portuguese still relied both for war and trade.

Mendoza's fleet was driven off with the loss of two ships and Bantam was saved. But when Harmensz's squadron sailed away to the Moluccas and split up amongst the islands to load spices, the Amboynese were left unaided to suffer retribution at Mendoza's hands. A further effort by the Portuguese to discipline Ternate failed, however.

Up to this time the various Dutch expeditions had been equipped and financed by a number of rival companies. In 1602, however, the Dutch East Indies Company, absorbing all the others, with a monopoly of trade between the Cape of Good Hope and the Magellan Strait, empowered to maintain armed forces, fortify trading posts, arm its ships and even to declare war, received its charter from the States-General of the Dutch Republic.

While the Dutch were thus laying the foundations on which a trading empire was to be built, the English, absorbed in their long-drawn naval war with Spain had concentrated rather upon direct action against Spanish ships in the Atlantic and the West Indies.

In 1592, however, James Lancaster, in his ship the *Edward Bonaventure*, had arrived from England in the Straits of Malacca and had followed a career of privateering or piracy (according to the point of view) for some months, during which a number of Portuguese ships and their cargoes had been captured. By 1600 negotiations for a peace with Spain were approaching a tentative conclusion. The English East India Company (which was in process of formation and was to receive its charter on the last day of that year) fitted out its first expedition : a squadron of four ships under Lancaster in the *Dragon*, which left England in April 1600 and arrived at Atjeh on 5 June 1601. A cargo of pepper was loaded there and at Bantam, where a trading post was established, and Lancaster reached England again in September 1602.

A second venture by the East India Company left England in March 1604, commanded by Henry Middleton. Arriving in the midst of the turmoil of the struggle between the Dutch on one side, Portuguese and Spanish on the other, Middleton obtained a full cargo of spices by playing off one side against the other, conduct which was copied by subsequent voyagers during the next few years, although considered self-seeking and irresponsible by the Dutch. It led to increasing hostility between Dutch and English in which the latter, enjoying only a fraction of the capital funds and government support of the former were to be steadily squeezed out of the Indonesian trade.

For the next 180 years, therefore, Dutch sea power was to dominate the seas and islands of the South-West Pacific, spreading for a time northwards into the China Sea.

3

RISE OF THE DUTCH EAST
INDIAN EMPIRE

The first thirty years following the early Dutch expeditions to Indonesia was a period of great confusion in the archipelago.

Although the sea power of the Portuguese and Spaniards was declining, they were still able to muster fleets from Goa and Manila with which to dispute Dutch efforts to establish themselves in Java or on the Spice Islands. The Dutch, in return, launched more than one unsuccessful expedition against the Spanish in the Philippines. Episodes in the conflict between Portuguese and Dutch for control of Bantam, Ternate and Amboyna in 1602 were described in the previous chapter. The situation was to remain fluid for many years, however, with Spanish, Portuguese and Dutch control alternating in the individual Spice Islands. Meanwhile the English, nominally at peace with all three, profited in parasitic fashion by operating trading posts in places dominated by the Dutch, but were not averse to siding with the Spanish or with the natives if it suited their commercial aims.

While this sporadic warfare went on at one end of the island chain, at the other the Muslim state of Atjeh at the northern end of Sumatra had become the leading Muslim sea power, following the capture of Malacca by the Portuguese. With the aid of the Gujeratis, of the descendants of the deposed ruler of Malacca, who had re-established themselves as Sultans of Johore, and of Javanese states, the Sultan of Atjeh had made repeated attempts to oust the Portuguese from Malacca. In 1587, however, he had made peace with the Portuguese and proceeded to extend his rule over the whole of Sumatra and, turning against his chief rival, Johore, of much of Malaya.

At the time of the arrival of the Dutch and English in the East Indies, the Sultan was exercising a large measure of control over the sea traffic through the Straits of Malacca, while in

Atjeh he was concentrating the cloth market of the Gujeratis who were forbidden access to other ports under his rule. Native vessels caught intruding on his preserves were confiscated and the crews enslaved. The first English expedition under Lancaster made its initial call in the islands at Atjeh and a treaty was concluded permitting these foreigners to trade. The Dutch had misread the situation and had ignored Atjeh, even taking the rival, Johore, as an ally in their first attack on Malacca in 1606. In the following year, however, the realities of the pattern of power forced them also to make a treaty with Atjeh. This had been asked for by Sultan Iskander Muda only because he was at the time threatened by a Portuguese fleet coming from Goa. When the danger passed Atjeh ignored the treaty.

With a monopoly of the pepper trade, in which the Sultan played off the Dutch, English and other foreigners against each other to raise the price continually, and another monopoly in the output of tin from the mines of Kedah in Malaya, Atjeh's wealth and power were supreme in the area, particularly after Iskander Muda's forces attacked Johore in 1613 and captured the Sultan. European traders, including the Dutch, were forced to obtain permits at Atjeh to trade in Sumatran ports for pepper.

Between the Sumatra/Malaya power complex dominated by Atjeh and the Spice Islands, stretched the long northern coastline of Java with its numerous ports, including Bantam where Dutch and English had their trading headquarters. Throughout most of the sixteenth century, this coast had been the base for a powerful sea power under the rule of the Sultans of Demak which had defied the Portuguese efforts to control and use the Java Sea, forcing them eventually to take the difficult route north of Borneo to and from the Moluccas. At the time of the Dutch and English incursion, however, the whole area was in process of succumbing to a resurgence of the Central Javanese power of Mataram. This was entirely land-orientated, with the Sultan affecting to scorn the business of commerce and unable to appreciate the meaning of sea power. The Dutch were granted wide privileges in the Javanese ports whose own maritime importance rapidly declined.

This sea power vacuum did not remain, however. Across the Java Sea, at the southern extremity of Celebes, the port and state of Macassar rose to fill it. Its able and determined sultans ignored Dutch claims to a monopoly in the Spice Islands, particularly the Bandas, and established a flourishing trade with them, exporting rice in exchange for spices. Foreign traders – English, Portuguese, Gujeratis, Chinese – were encouraged to come to Macassar for the latter. This was to become the cause of continual disturbances in the Banda Islands where the natives, often encouraged by the English, refused to honour the agreement made in 1602 which gave the Dutch a monopoly of the nutmeg trade. Meanwhile Macassar became the centre of opposition to Dutch hegemony for the next sixty years.

Such, in brief, was the situation in the Indonesian Archipelago in the early years of the seventeenth century. Portuguese, Spanish and Dutch, and to a lesser degree the English, all strove to maintain exclusive trading posts by agreement with local rulers either by diplomacy or force. The Dutch East India Company despatched several powerful fleets with orders to attack the Portuguese wherever met. In 1606 such a fleet of eleven galleons under Admiral Matalieff laid siege to Malacca ; but after four months the fortress was still holding out when news of the approach of a Portuguese fleet of twelve galleons, four galleys and a large number of smaller craft from Goa under the Viceroy Dom Martin Affonso de Castro forced the Dutch to abandon the siege and to put to sea to engage the Portuguese fleet. An indecisive battle spread over nine days ensued. The Dutch then withdrew to make good their battle damage, whereupon the Viceroy unwisely divided his fleet, sending half to meet and escort a Javanese convoy bringing urgently needed provisions to Malacca while the remainder sailed for the Nicobars to meet reinforcements from Goa. The Dutch were able to engage each of these forces separately and destroy them. They were unable, however, to resume the siege of Malacca, which was left alone for the next eight years.

Meanwhile the Dutch concentrated their efforts in the Moluccas where the Spanish from Manila had, in 1606, attacked Ternate, driven out both the Sultan and the Dutch and annexed Tidore. Though the Dutch succeeded in retaking Ternate in 1608 Tidore remained under the Spanish for another fifty-five years. Desultory fighting continued elsewhere in the

Moluccas and when the Spanish commander at Manila appealed in 1615 to the Portuguese Viceroy at Goa for aid, the result was another sea battle in the Straits of Malacca.

News of a Dutch fleet being fitted out for a renewed attack on Malacca had reached Goa and reinforcements of a squadron of eight galleons under Diogo de Mendoza Furtado had been sent. Four more galleons under Admiral Anriques reached Malacca, in reply to the Spanish appeal. When a large war fleet of Atjeh appeared in the Straits, the combined force of galleons put out under Anriques to engage it. In a two-day bloody battle the fleet of Atjeh was driven off. The Dutch squadron of eight ships now arrived and, though their fresh and always superior fighting ships defeated the battle-weary Portuguese, they were left at the end of the day in no condition to undertake an amphibious assault on Malacca, which thus gained another fifteen years' respite before being called upon again to defend itself.

Under such disturbed conditions in all parts of Indonesia, it is not surprising that the early dreams and indications of fat profits from the spice trade were not yet fulfilling themselves for the Dutch. The constant state of guerilla warfare and the outfitting of war fleets constituted crippling overheads. Bad debts accumulated through advances made to native rulers and communities in respect of future crops. The money was often spent on luxuries, pomp and display and the crops not forthcoming, having perhaps been sold again to other customers. Competition in the spice market was fierce and led to rising prices. During the first eight years of the Dutch East India Company's operations no dividends were declared, while from the Netherlands came continual exhortations from the Directors to the Governors General to secure a monopoly by the use of force if necessary. The latter resisted the use of such harsh methods, fearing, with good reason, uprisings against the trading posts scattered throughout the islands.

A young man after the Directors' hearts was about to come to the fore, however. In 1614, Jan Pieterszoon Coen, at that time aged twenty-seven and occupying the post of director of commerce at Bantam, wrote a *Discourse on the State of India* justifying Dutch pretensions. Apart from their justification as a blow at the power of Spain with whom the Netherlands were still at war, Dutch claims, he insisted, had legal foundations in the fact that the Dutch had begun trading at points where the Spanish and Portuguese had no establishments and that the subsequent capture of the port of Amboyna in 1605 (the only territorial possession at that time) had come about as a result of Spanish and Portuguese unjustified attacks on the 'peacefully trading' Dutch. Subsequent formal treaties with the people of Ternate, Amboyna and the Banda Islands had guaranteed a monopoly of trade ; the Dutch had a right, therefore, to punish those who had broken such contracts.

Coen went on to recommend the foundation of Dutch settlements to secure the complete possession of the Moluccas, Amboyna and the Banda Islands, and the establishment of a fortified port at Bantam or at Jacatra some fifty miles to the eastward, where a small Dutch factory had been built. A fleet should be sent to capture Manila and Macao and drive out the Spaniards and Portuguese.

Though such ambitious plans were beyond the capabilities of the Dutch East India Company at that time, Coen was appointed Governor General in 1618 for a first term of five years and soon found ample scope for his energies. At Bantam the competition of English and Chinese in the pepper trade was encouraging the Sultan to raise the price to an uneconomic level. At Japara the forces of the Sultan Agung of Mataram, engaged in the subjugation of central Java, had destroyed the Netherlands trading post, killing three Dutchmen and taking others prisoner. In the Moluccas the Dutch claims to a monopoly were being flouted by the natives.

Coen tackled the problem of Bantam first. By boycotting the pepper market there and giving out that the Dutch head-quarters would be moved to Jacatra, which was independent of Bantam, he succeeded in lowering the price of pepper. But he could not get the co-operation of the English. Hostility between Dutch and English was, indeed, endemic with fighting taking place between them in which men on both sides were killed in the streets of Bantam ; at sea, ships of the two East India Companies fought whenever they met. Coen now prepared to move his headquarters to Jacatra where he gave orders for the Dutch post to be strongly fortified.

Coen had good reason for fearing competition by the

English at this time ; for the English East India Company had recently increased its capital and, with the aim of securing a proper share in the trade with the archipelago, had fitted out a large number of well-armed ships. Five new arrivals on 8 December 1618 brought their number off Bantam up to fifteen. As the majority of the Dutch strength was deployed in the Moluccas, the English felt in a strong enough position to take the offensive, their first step being to capture a richly-laden Dutch ship. The Sultan of Bantam threw in his lot with the apparently stronger English.

Hearing that the fort at Jacatra was besieged by the soldiers of the local rajah in alliance with some English and that eleven of the English ships had gone there, Coen sailed with seven of his own to attack the latter. Repulsed by the superior numbers of the enemy and short of ammunition, the Governor General sailed off to the Moluccas to get help, leaving the garrison of Jacatra with orders to hold out at all costs. They were not in fact called upon for heroism, being left unassailed while the English and the Jacatrans bickered, and had, indeed, made up their minds to surrender when a force from Bantam arrived, annexing the territory and expelling the rajah. The English retired to Bantam to guard their property there. When Coen returned in May 1619 to the fort, to which the garrison had meanwhile given the name of Batavia, the ancient name of Holland, he met little opposition to a sortie which destroyed the native town. A larger fortress and a new Dutch-style town were thereupon constructed and the territory annexed for the East India Company to become eventually the capital of the East Indies.

A blockade of Bantam by the Dutch followed and ended for the time being that port's importance as a trading centre, forcing the English traders also to move to Batavia where they came under Dutch restrictions aimed at squeezing them out. The English ships which had been dispersed for trade were sought out and captured by superior squadrons of Dutch East Indiamen. A treaty of alliance between the English and Dutch East India Companies against the Spaniards had, in fact, been signed in London on 17 July 1619, but news of this did not reach the East Indies until March 1620. For a time, subsequently, relations between the English traders, who by the terms of the treaty were permitted to function in Dutch settlements, and the Dutch authorities became more friendly. Semi-piratical encounters at sea between ships of the two Companies continued, however, and it was not long before the old antagonisms rose again on shore, finally leading to action by the Dutch governor in Amboyna in 1623 which horrified and infuriated the English.

Alleging that the English were plotting to seize the island with the help of the natives, the Governor had the English agent Gabriel Towerson and eight residents arrested and examined under torture. On the evidence so extracted they were convicted by the local court and executed. Whether the Englishmen were guilty or not (and they died protesting their innocence) the proceedings were contrary to the treaty which laid down that international disputes should be referred to a mixed council of the two nations. This 'Massacre of Amboyna' as it was called in England, was to remain a source of bitter enmity between the two nations. It was one of the causes of the first Dutch War and compensation for it was exacted by Cromwell as one of the peace terms on its conclusion.

From this time onwards, the English in the East Indies were restricted to trade at Bantam, where they re-established their headquarters in 1628, at the Javanese port of Japara and at Macassar. Meanwhile the Dutch under Coen's energetic and ruthless leadership consolidated their position in the Spice Islands. Opposition to the Dutch monopoly by the people of the Banda Islands was met by occupation by force of arms during which the population was virtually exterminated. Coen's cruelty earned him a reprimand from the Company Directors in Amsterdam ; but his territorial gains remained and in 1627 he was appointed to a second term as Governor General.

He found himself involved in a desperate defence of the infant colony of Batavia which, standing in the way of Sultan Agung of Mataram in his campaign to subdue Bantam and the western end of Java, was besieged by a huge Javanese army. Dutch sea power alone saved the situation. Agung's troops were dependent for supplies of food by sea ; when the Dutch fleet systematically destroyed the native shipping, the Javanese army was soon so weakened by starvation that it could make no impression on the gallantly defended fort ; after five weeks it was forced to retreat in confusion. Batavia was never again threatened.

Coen did not live to see this triumphant outcome of his strategy; he died of cholera on 20 September 1629. Nor, indeed, was the decisiveness of Mataram's defeat generally apparent. Sultan Agung continued to impose a harsh and bloody rule over all Java except Bantam and Batavia in the west. Balambangan in the east which, together with the neighbouring island of Bali, was the last outpost of Hindu civilization in the archipelago, was assaulted, de-populated and devastated in a 'holy war' in 1639. Bali successfully defied him, however, and its people have remained unconverted to Islam to this day. Nevertheless, Mataram's prestige continued to soar, with ambassadors from Palembang and from Banjermassin in Borneo hailing Agung as the great successor of the kings of mighty Madjapahit.

A state of war with the Dutch continued; but as the Dutch contented themselves with mainly sea-borne power and Mataram was uninterested in such a concept or in commercial empire, such clashes as occurred were sporadic. The former had meanwhile taken the first steps to erase the last Portuguese obstacle to their maritime supremacy by instituting in 1630 a seaward blockade of Malacca. This was to last with few intermissions for eleven years during which trading ships, native or foreign, were forbidden entrance and diverted to Batavia. The great port, which had defied effort after effort by Dutch and Sumatran amphibious forces to capture it, now began to wither on the vine. Though food supplies could be obtained through the native hinterland, the severance of communications with Goa and so with the homeland, whence normally came the replacements for those of the garrison who died from tropical diseases or deserted to seek their fortunes in the service of Malayan rajahs, steadily reduced the strength and morale of the defenders; meanwhile the clatter of the once-busy market was replaced by a gloomy silence and the jungle growth encroached on the streets. By the middle of 1640 the port and fortress seemed to the Dutch Governor-General, Anthony van Diemen, to be ripe for the picking and he ordered a close investment and attack to begin. That the valour of the early conquistadores still sustained the defenders is evident from the five months of hopeless defiance they maintained before surrendering on 14 January 1641.

This eradication of the last vestige of Portuguese rule from Indonesia was only the first step in a wider campaign waged by the Dutch in an effort to gather into their hands the whole trade with the East. Goa, like Malacca, was put under blockade in 1636, a process which was strictly maintained even after Portugal threw off the Spanish yoke in 1641 and entered into anti-Spanish treaties with Britain and the Netherlands. Though Goa was not directly attacked and was to remain Portuguese, it was wholly ruined by the blockade and diversion of trade elsewhere. The large and lushly fertile island of Ceylon, however, was absorbed piecemeal over a period of twenty years, the last Portuguese stronghold being captured in 1658 ; and by 1660 all ports along the Malabar coast, where Vasco da Gama and his successors had founded the Portuguese Empire, had also fallen to Dutch sea power ; only the ruined ports of Goa and Diu and a few minor posts, one of which was the little fishing village of Bombay remained as Portuguese remnants.

The march of events in the Indian Ocean, however, is strictly outside the scope of this book, even though developments in the South-West Pacific, where sea power was being wielded by western powers, were often dependent upon the support coming from an Indian base. Elsewhere in the Pacific, too, in the China Seas and the Sea of Japan events of great maritime importance had been taking place since the end of the sixteenth century which will form the subject of the next chapter. For the time being it is the consolidation of Dutch supremacy in the Indonesian archipelago that must be followed.

While the elimination of Malacca was being encompassed, at the other end of the island chain the Dutch were putting an end to the existing system of spice production which, from their selfish point of view, was so inefficient. Too many cloves were being grown to maintain a profitable price based on scarcity value. This abundance also tempted the islanders to break the Dutch monopoly by selling directly to English, French, Danish, Portuguese and Chinese traders who were encouraged by the Sultan of Macassar to use that port as an *entrepôt*.

This situation was particularly galling to the Dutch in view of the fact that they paid the natives of the Spice Islands in advance for produce which was often not forthcoming so that the natives were becoming hopelessly insolvent. To put an end to this situation the Dutch bought with a yearly subsidy the consent of the Sultan of Ternate, ruler of the majority of the islands, to confiscation of the plantations by the Company and the reduction of his subjects to the status of forced labourers. They then proceeded to destroy all surplus clove trees, forcing the natives to turn their land over to food production. Unable to grow sufficient for themselves on the steep volcanic slopes, they were forced to buy rice from the Dutch East India Company at an inflated price. Poverty and hunger then completed their subjugation.

In 1635 and again in 1650 they rose in revolt only to be ruthlessly subdued by force of arms, the inhabitants of rebellious islands being often eliminated or sold into slavery in Java. Dutch control in the Spice Islands, except for Tidore where the Spaniards for a while still held sway, was thereafter total. Cultivation of spices in the Banda Islands for instance was confined to nutmeg, while in Amboyna only cloves might be grown. At sea, Indonesian ships using the Java Sea were required to carry a Dutch permit stating their cargo and destination. Failure to do so rendered them liable to the enslavement or extermination of their crews as pirates. Although in European waters, Cromwell's Commonwealth navy soundly defeated the Dutch in the war of 1652-4, in South-East Asia, the ships of the latter enjoyed a largely unchallenged supremacy.

In spite of this, however, ships under the control of the Sultan of Macassar regularly defied the regulations to trade with Banda and Ceram. For more than a decade the Dutch held back from trying conclusions with the Sultan, who had grasped the leadership of Islam in the archipelago following the decline of the influence of the Sultans of Ternate. A religious basis for hostility was provided by Dutch support for the Christian Amboynese. Buying arms and ammunition from the Portuguese, British and Danish traders, the Sultan fortified Macassar and armed his own ships.

War was eventually inevitable. The government at Batavia had indeed declared a state of war against Macassar from 1653 to 1655 and again in 1660. The Directors of the Company, however, as well as the Governors-General who had followed van Diemen, were strongly opposed to territorial expansion which they believed had been the chief cause of the over-extension and final collapse of Portuguese power. So far only Batavia had been declared Netherlands territory, the Dutch considering that supremacy could be achieved by sea power alone. Hostilities had thus stopped short of a direct clash.

Johan Maetsuycker who became Governor-General in 1653 held to these views until 1666 against the urgings of his two most prominent subordinates, Rijklof van Goens who had commanded the Company's forces in Ceylon and India, and Cornelis Speelman, a merchant who had amassed great wealth and was now to serve both as an admiral and a general with conspicuous success. An appeal to the Dutch for aid from the ruler of the island of Buton, a vassal of Ternate and therefore now of the Company, who was under siege by Macassar forces, finally became a *casus belli*. Speelman was launched in command of a fleet of twenty-one ships, a force of 600 European soldiers and a large body of Indonesian auxiliaries. The last-named were partly Amboynese under Captain Jonkers – an Amboynese despite his Dutch name – and partly composed of warlike Bugis under their own prince, Aru Palacca of Boni, a district of Celebes from which the prince had been driven into exile by his powerful neighbour of Macassar. Aru Palacca was seeking revenge and reinstatement.

Buton was quickly relieved; Speelman then sailed to the Moluccas where he forced those mortal enemies, the Sultans of Ternate and Tidore, to end their age-old bickering and agree to a durable peace. Since the Spaniards had finally abandoned the latter in 1663, withdrawing to the Philippines, the Dutch had taken over their abandoned forts. Now Tidore as well as Ternate acknowledged the overlordship of the Company, thus putting the last of the Spice Islands under Dutch domination.

The troops of Ternate now joined Speelman's force as it returned to attack Macassar. Aru Palacca landed in Boni where he was welcomed by his people who joined him in the field. Macassar fiercely resisted all attacks for four months but finally surrendered and the Sultan consented to a treaty in November 1668, the terms of which stripped him of all territory outside the city and its immediate surroundings; even there a Dutch fortress called Rotterdam was raised to ensure his submission. His lost provinces of Boni and Buton were nominally restored to their rulers, while the northern and eastern coasts were ceded to Ternate ; but all came under the real control of the Company.

Over the same period during which the downfall of Macassar was being prepared and executed, the powerful sultanate of Atjeh in northern Sumatra was also collapsing, not without intrigues to encourage the process by the Dutch, whose covetous eyes had settled on the growing output of the tin-mines of Perak on the Malay Peninsula, a state subject to Atjeh. The several petty rajahs of Sumatra's west coast were encouraged to revolt with the aid of the Bugi warriors of Aru Palacca and Captain Jonkers' fighting Amboynese. In return for the protection of the Company and its guarantee of independence from Atjeh, the Dutch secured an absolute monopoly of trade. A similar process of dismemberment was encouraged on the other side of Sumatra where the islands of Banka and Billiton threw off the rule of Palembang and put themselves under the protection of the Company. At the same time Palembang and Djambi promised the Company a monopoly of their pepper trade and Dutch agents extra-territorial rights. The monopoly was, in fact, far from complete, and Chinese, English and others could still get cargoes by judicious bribery.

Only Mataram now remained independent of Dutch suzerainty. Since the death of Agung in 1645 it had been ruled by his son Amangkurat, otherwise known as Sunan Tegalwangi, an unbalanced degenerate and monstrously cruel autocrat who would put to death hundreds of innocent followers for a whim and on one occasion had thousands of Muslim priests and their families slaughtered to break the power of the priesthood. Debauchery finally reduced the Sultan to idiocy. Mataram was ripe for destruction, but in the meantime its ineffective rule suited Dutch interests. In 1674, however, Trunajoyo, ruler of Madura, rose in revolt ; all disaffected elements and the numerous exiles from Macassar flocked to his support.

At the same time Sultan Abulfatah of Bantam had been raising that state to new heights of prosperity and strength by encouraging all opponents of the Dutch monopoly, i.e., British,

Danish, French, Indian, Chinese and Arabian traders, to use Bantam as their *entrepôt* instead of Batavia. His success in this direction led him on to ambitious schemes to conquer all Java, where Batavia was threatened, and Sumatra, where Dutch ports were attacked, and to share in the spice trade of the Moluccas and the tin-mining of Perak.

In spite of all this, Governor Maetsuycker, faithful to the Company's policy of avoiding landward intervention, resisted the appeals of Speelman to take energetic action. He did send Speelman with a fleet and troops to occupy Surabaya and part of Madura ; but this did not prevent Trunajoyo from defeating Amangkurat's army and setting himself up at Kediri, East Java, as the legitimate heir of the ancient kings of Majapahit.

The son and heir of Amangkurat, on the advice of his dying father, appealed to the Dutch for help, promising trading monopolies, the cession of the port of Semarang and a large territory inland of Batavia and repayment of any expenses incurred. A treaty to this effect was signed in 1677. Even this, however, did not persuade the reluctant Maetsuycker to positive action ; it was not until his death in 1678 and succession by the forceful Rijklof van Goens, supported in the Council of the Indies by the ardent Speelman, that advantage was taken of the splendid opportunity being offered. A force of Dutch troops, together with the Bugis of Aru Palacca and Jonkers' Amboynese, fought their way to Kediri, drove Trunajoyo out and restored the weakling Amangkurat II to the throne of Mataram : a campaign in the interior of Java having stamped out the last embers of revolt, Mataram was re-established as a protectorate, with a Dutch garrison stationed in the new capital Kartasura. Three years later it was Bantam's turn to suffer the fatal effects of Company intervention when Sultan Abulfatah's son appealed for help against his father. The Sultan's anti-Dutch activities made Cornelis Speelman, Governor-General since Van Goen's death in 1681, very ready to send the redoubtable Jonkers and his Amboynese again into action.

Abulfatah was captured in 1684 and deposed ; his son agreed to hold Bantam as a vassal of the Company and to expel all foreign traders. The British factory was now removed to Bencoolen in Sumatra where it continued as a lonely outpost of the East India Company for the next 150 years.

47

As a result of these events, the Dutch Company became at last supreme and unchallenged in Indonesia ; for the first time it took a share in the administration of the inland districts of Java. Over the next century this was to be converted gradually to full Dutch rule over the whole archipelago.

4

EUROPEAN ADVANCE INTO THE
CHINA SEAS AND JAPAN

If up to this point attention has been concentrated almost entirely upon the sea area embracing the great archipelago today known as Indonesia and Malaysia, it is because elsewhere sea power as such was little exercised. Chinese junks from Fukien carried on an extensive trade with Luzon, principal island of the northern Philippines, and with Brunei, Macassar and Formosa. Only in connection with the Philippines and with Formosa had they attempted to prevent by force the competition of foreigners.

In the former, the establishment of Manila and the gathering of trade into Spanish hands was resented. In 1574 a challenge by a fleet of war junks was defeated, and when the Chinese found that, apart from their long-established barter trade with the natives for such local produce as wax, cotton, pearls, shells and betel nuts, they could obtain silver in the shape of Mexican dollars from the Spaniards in exchange for their wares, a peaceful trading pattern was established. A trading fleet of thirty to forty junks arrived each year in March from Fukien and an ever-growing Chinese community settled down outside the walls of Manila, the latter a potential threat should disagreement arise.

And, indeed, this peaceful scene was violently disrupted from time to time. In 1593 when the Chinese crew of a Spanish galley mutinied and murdered the passengers, amongst whom was the Governor Dasmarinas, retaliatory executions were carried out. In reply a fleet of several hundred war junks attacked Manila but was driven off. Ten years later the Chinese community rose in revolt and again in 1639 and 1662. On each occasion Spanish artillery fire saved the day and the city. All these were local affairs ; the Chinese Imperial government was basically uninterested in their overseas nationals and did little to support them. At the same time, as elsewhere throughout the east, the Chinese played an essential part as business men and shopkeepers so that between these upheavals they were allowed to return and resume their occupations.

It has been related earlier how the Spaniards from Manila at first disputed Portuguese rights to the Moluccas, then shared them during the period that the two crowns were united, and for a time co-operated to oppose the Dutch. From 1606 to 1663 they held the Spice Island of Tidore. During this period, though a nominal Spanish rule was imposed on most of the Philippines, trade was largely concentrated in Manila whence, once a year, the proceeds of it were shipped to Acapulco in one or two large argosies, generally known as the Manila or Acapulco Galleons.

By the middle of the seventeenth century Spanish power was on the decline everywhere, and support for their eastern possessions and enterprises no longer forthcoming. In 1663 they abandoned Tidore and their chief settlement in the southern Philippines, Zamboanga. Their rule over the islands south of the Visayas, always shadowy, was now dissolved, leaving the native Moros and Chinese pirates in lawless control.

Manila remained an important trading centre, however, served as before by the annual 'Galleons'. The westward voyage with a large passenger list and a cargo mainly of silver would take some two to three months in the zone of the brisk north-east trade winds. The return voyage with holds packed with silks of every kind, jewellery, ivory, drugs and all manner of precious goods and victualled and watered for a voyage of seven to nine months, started in June to take advantage of the south-west monsoon which would take them to about 15 degrees north latitude. But not until 32 degrees north could steady westerly winds be expected. In the interval, along the route eastward of the Ryu-kyus (Liu-chius) and southern Japan, they were liable to be plagued by variable winds and calms interspersed with devastating typhoons, and were frequently forced to return to Manila. At the worst they risked shipwreck on the hostile shores of Japan or capture by pirates or privateers such as the Englishman, Cavendish, in 1587; at best long weeks of tedious sailing during which scurvy, hunger and thirst could assail them, if they had a bad journey, even before the westerlies and the long crossing of the Pacific began. It was never less than seven months and could be twelve before Acapulco was reached.

Spanish attempts to spread their trade northwards met with little success, more through the opposition of rival Europeans than that of the Chinese and Japanese. The Portuguese from their base at Macao intrigued to have the Spanish excluded from trade with China even during the period the two crowns were united. A Spanish foothold was obtained in Formosa in 1626 when they took and fortified Chi-Lung (Keelung) on the north coast, but this was destined to be liquidated by the Dutch sixteen years later. Meanwhile in the last years of the sixteenth century the first Spanish and Dutch ships had reached Japan at the moment that the country was emerging from two hundred years of internal chaos and civil war.

The seemingly endless struggle for power between the great territorial nobles or *Daimyos* had been resolved by the victory over his rivals of the *Daimyo* Nobunaga ; when he was assassinated in 1582 the leadership was taken over by Hideyoshi, the most brilliant and determined of his generals who in 1588 had himself appointed *Taiko* or regent for the powerless Mikado. In 1590 the last of the unruly *Daimyos* submitted to his dictatorship, and internal peace and a strong central government were imposed.

Hideyoshi's ambitions did not stop short at the pacification and unification of Japan, however. They moved on to embrace plans aimed at imperial expansion, with Korea as the first objective. Vengeance for the Mongol invasion attempts of 320 years earlier was invoked as justification and when the King of Korea refused to assist in an attack on his suzerain, the Ming Emperor of China, a Japanese armed invasion by some 240,000 men in a fleet of 4,000 small vessels was launched. The Koreans were taken by surprise and an unopposed landing was achieved at Pusan across the Tsu-shima Strait.

The Koreans proved no match for the invaders who quickly overran the peninsula, capturing the capital city of Seoul whence the King had fled. The Japanese now faced the massive counter-invasion by a Chinese army from across the Yalu River. To be able to resist this, they had to maintain their line of supply from the homeland. A vital link in this was the passage across the Tsu-shima Strait ; for its security they must meet the Koreans at sea, the element on which the Koreans had long been supreme in that part of the world. And from the ranks of the generally incompetent Korean leaders there emerged in the moment of desperate crisis a naval commander of genius, Admiral Yi Sun-sin.

Superior Korean seamanship under his inspired leadership was reinforced by Yi Sun-sin's fabulous invention, the Kwi-sün or tortoise boat. This galley, designed for speed under oars, had a curved deck made of iron plates to protect fighters and rowers from the enemy's shot and bristling with iron spikes to prevent him from boarding, thus ante-dating by more than 250 years the 'ironclad' ship. In the bow, above a ram, was a fearsome dragon's head, through whose grinning mouth flaming arrows and other missiles were fired. Other openings for the same purpose were situated along either side and in the stern.

Yi Sun-sin's first success was against a Japanese fleet which had landed reinforcements of 60,000 men and was found lying at anchor. Sweeping down the wind on to them, his flaming arrows set a number of the enemy ablaze ; the remainder cut their cables to flee, but few escaped destruction. A second Japanese fleet bringing reinforcements was met amongst the off-shore islands. Greatly inferior in numbers, Yi Sun-sin simulated flight ; when the Japanese, in chase, became strung out in disorder, the Koreans turned about and, headed by the tortoise boat, annihilated them.

The Korean fleet now commanded the strait, effectively cutting off the Japanese armies from their supplies. Facing starvation they were soon in full retreat before a far from aggressive Sino-Korean army and finally established themselves in a fortified strip of the Korean south coast, where they were able to feed off the country. After three years of negotiation, the Japanese army at last sailed home and a peace was agreed.

It was not to hold good for long, however. The rebuffed and infuriated Hideyoshi, determined to be avenged on the Koreans, planned a new invasion. For this it was necessary somehow to wrest the control of the Tsu-shima Strait from them. Well aware of the festering jealousies which constituted a fatal cancer in the Korean leadership, the Japanese felt confident that the removal of Yi Sun-sin would leave the defences wide open. By a stratagem they brought this about.

A false spy insinuated into the Korean headquarters was briefed to give them intelligence of a Japanese invasion fleet which would be passing a coastal point on a certain day. Yi Sun-sin was ordered to sea to intercept it ; but recognizing the deception for what it was, he refused. He was thereupon arrested and carried to the capital where he was degraded and reduced to the rank of a simple soldier.

The Japanese fleet now felt safe to set sail and at the beginning of 1597 it arrived unopposed and landed the army safely. Yi's successor proved himself so incompetent that when he at last by chance came across an enemy fleet his captains deserted him at the first onset and fled. In the face of this disaster the King had no alternative but to reinstate his country's naval hero. Gathering a handful of ships, Yi cleverly ambushed the Japanese fleet as it filed between two islands. The leaders were destroyed but the remainder escaped by scattering and when he next encountered them Yi was faced by a formidable superiority of numbers. Nevertheless he led into the midst of the enemy fleet where by sheer fighting skill and *élan*, his men sank thirty of the enemy ships, killed the Japanese commander, and put the remainder to flight.

Once again Korean sea power held the key and the fate of the Japanese army of invasion was sealed. After initial successes it was, as before, forced to retreat by a combined Chinese and Korean army. The Japanese now finally accepted defeat (1598) and agreed to evacuate their armies ; but they had still the Strait of Tsu-shima to cross, where the implacable Yi, impervious to appeals and bribes, lay waiting. Certain that, with the end of the war, jealous rivals would have him dragged down to disgrace, he determined to bring about one last overwhelming victory over the Japanese.

And so it came about : introducing new tactics by means of which he encircled the enemy fleet and herded their ships into a helpless mass he set them ablaze with an incendiary device, his 'spraying tube', details of which have not survived. He himself stood prominently exposed in the prow of his flagship, and there was fatally wounded by an enemy shot. As he lay dying he ordered his men to suppress news of his death until decisive victory had been achieved. Interesting similarities with the Korean War of 1951–3 will be apparent ; but in that case sea power was to be in the hands of the allies of the South Koreans, ensuring them supplies and mobility which gave them the victory over the invading North Koreans and Chinese.

Hideyoshi died in the year of his defeat and was succeeded by Iyeyasu, another military dictator, and it was at the beginning of the latter's long rule that foreign trade with Japan entered on a brief flowering season before being frozen by the perennial isolationism of her people.

The Portuguese, it will be remembered, had reached Japan as early as 1542, establishing a trading post at Kagoshima in southern Kyushu, while their missionaries, mainly Jesuits, had such success with their proselytizing that forty years later there were more than two hundred thousand Christians in Japan. Until 1592 they suffered no competition in either of these activities ; but in that year there arrived the first Spanish ship and, though the two countries were united at that time and owed allegiance to the same church, there was immediate rivalry. Spanish trade never achieved great proportions, while the Dominican and Franciscan missionaries who arrived with them were soon at loggerheads with the Jesuits, a state of affairs which had its influence in initiating the persecution of the Christians which began in 1596 when a number of priests were crucified at Nagasaki.

In 1600 there reached the port of Beppu in north-eastern Kyushu what were to become much more serious rivals, when the Dutch ship *Liefde*, one of five which had left Holland in 1598 for China and Japan via the Straits of Magellan, cast anchor after a long and scurvy-ridden passage. Included in her cargo was a quantity of firearms and munitions, but of greater significance was the personality of her English pilot, Will Adams. In spite of Portuguese efforts to persuade the Japanese that the newcomers were thieves and enemies, and should be put summarily to death, Adams was taken to Osaka, where Iyeyasu held his court, and on being interrogated made such a good impression on the ruler that the Portuguese were rebuffed. It is likely that the armament in the *Liefde's* hold had its influence on Iyeyasu's attitude ; for he was at that time facing a new insurrection by the *Daimyos*.

54

The *Liefde* was brought to Osaka – the first European ship to make the entrancing passage through the Inland Sea – where guns were unloaded and, with Dutch crews to operate them, were incorporated in Iyeyasu's army. In the Battle of Sekigahara (21 October 1600) Iyeyasu finally decisively defeated the rebels and three years later became Shogun, the *de facto* ruler of Japan in parallel with the powerless Mikado. Iyeyasu's descendants, as the Tokugawa line of shoguns, were to hold power for the next 256 years.

Another merit of the newcomers in the eyes of Iyeyasu was the quality of construction of the *Liefde*. The exposure of Japanese backwardness in shipbuilding and design in the battles of the Korean war had not been forgotten ; at the Shogun's behest, therefore, Will Adams, no doubt aided by the ship's carpenter, Pieter Janszoon of Rotterdam, had several ships built for which he was highly rewarded and honoured. Taking a Japanese wife, he remained under the Shogun's protection for the rest of his life.

Fully occupied, as they were, with establishing themselves in the Spice Islands at this time, it was not until July 1609, when two ships arrived at Nagasaki, that the next Hollanders reached Japan. With the aid of Will Adams' good offices they were well received, and, at a time when both the Portuguese and Spanish were falling more and more out of favour, largely on account of their missionary activities, they were granted freedom to trade and permission to build a factory at Hirado. From this time onwards the Dutch gradually ousted all foreign competitors, including the English East India Company which made a brief, unprofitable attempt to trade between 1614 and 1623. Both the Spanish and Portuguese were expelled in 1624 leaving the Dutch a clear monopoly. The Hollanders did not permit religious scruples to interfere with commerce ; to keep in the good graces of the Japanese authorities they gave their services as gunners to assist in the suppression of the rebellion of 1637–8 under the Christian Arima when some forty thousand Catholic converts were massacred.

Thus it was that in 1641 when Japanese intercourse with the West was cut off by order of the Shogun, an isolation that was to last for 219 years, the Dutch were permitted throughout that period to maintain a small trading post on the island of Deshima in Nagasaki Bay. Even they, however, lived a life so restricted and confined that they were virtually prisoners and always in fear for their lives should they disobey any of the rules by which they were bound. Not until October 1808, when the British frigate *Phaeton* entered Nagasaki Harbour under Dutch colours to spy out the situation, did the full misery of the Dutch factors' existence become known outside Dutch East India Company circles. Captain Pellew's report described how strictly the ban on their receiving even articles of personal comfort, food, clothes and so on from abroad was enforced, and the terror that they felt at being brought on board the *Phaeton* lest they should be punished for it. That their fears were founded may be gauged from the fact that, following the *Phaeton*'s departure after forcing the Japanese authorities to supply water and fresh victuals, the Governor of Nagasaki and five of his principal military officers committed *hara-kiri*, while the three Japanese who acted as interpreters drowned themselves.

Dutch efforts to establish trade with China were less successful. The Portuguese, from their long-established base of Macao, took steps to protect their monopoly by inflaming the Chinese authorities against any rivals. Several attempts to get a mission through to the capital were frustrated. In 1622, therefore, Governor-General Coen at Batavia despatched a squadron under Cornelis Reyerszoon to attack Macao and drive the Portuguese out. The assault badly miscarried; the Dutch, driven off, sailed away to the Pescadores where they attempted to set up a trading post, only to be ejected by the Chinese. The latter raised no objection, however, to a Dutch settlement on nearby Formosa, which was not Chinese territory, and there they finally established themselves in 1624 building up a flourishing *entrepôt* for trade with both China and Japan. As mentioned earlier, the Spanish also set up a fortified post in Formosa in 1626, but by 1642 they had been expelled by the Dutch who then became masters of the whole island. Four years later the Dutch made a last attempt to drive the Spanish from Manila also; they got a foothold on the peninsula of Bataan but were forced to withdraw.

With traders of all other nations forbidden access to Japan (which at the same time prohibited any Japanese from travelling abroad and thus removed the chief competitors of the Dutch in Formosa), and the Chinese Empire of the Mings disintegrating under the assault of the Manchus, the ships of the Netherlands sailed supreme and unchallenged in eastern waters for the next twenty years. Nevertheless during that time Dutch military power was withering at the root as the burghers of Amsterdam grew rich out of the profits of overseas trade but grudged any expenditure on its defence.

Although, as recounted earlier, the Dutch East India Company's forces were taking advantage of the rebellions and inter-state conflicts in Indonesia during the last half of the seventeenth century to extend Dutch authority throughout Java and Sumatra, the defences of the Formosan trading posts were neglected on land and sea. In the spring of 1661 a Chinese fleet was able to cross over from Amoy and land a force which besieged the principal fortified post of Zeelandia. The attacker was the doughty Chinese corsair Cheng Ch'eng-kung or, Europeanized, Koxinga.

Koxinga's father, a Chinese pirate captain, who had married a Japanese woman, had refused to acknowledge the conquering Manchu who had replaced the last Ming Emperor on the Dragon Throne, and he had continued to fight until captured in 1646, when he made his submission to the new dynasty. His son had fought on and from his base at Amoy had waged a successful amphibious campaign, first against the Manchu governors of the southern coastal provinces; by 1655 he had brought all Fukien under his rule. By 1658 he was raiding Chekiang and Kiangsu provinces from the sea and had captured the key city of Chekiang on the Yangtse River. In 1659 he pressed on up the river to besiege Nanking; there he was heavily repulsed. In 1661, therefore, he determined to capture Formosa and hold it on behalf of the Mings. After a siege lasting ten months, Zeelandia was surrendered. The Dutch, forced to abandon the whole island, were permitted to withdraw to Batavia; but for almost a century afterwards their direct trade with China was at a standstill. Koxinga was planning a fresh maritime expedition in 1662 with the aim of capturing Manila, where the Chinese were in revolt against the Spanish, when he died at the age of thirty-nine. His descendants continued to hold Formosa until 1683, when his grandson finally submitted to the Manchu Emperor and the island became part of the province of Fukien.

While the closure of Japan to foreign intercourse in 1641, the expulsion of the Ming dynasty by the Manchus in China in 1644 and the withdrawal of Dutch power from the China Sea in 1662 were combining to leave a vacuum in foreign trade with the Far East, events in Europe were occurring which, by altering the balance of naval power, were to transform the pattern of European-Chinese trade relations.

5

BRITISH COMMERCE AND SEA POWER REACH THE FAR EAST

The rise of Dutch commercial supremacy during the first half of the seventeenth century, world-wide and not confined to the Far East, was in the long run self-destructive. It raised the mortal enmity of the English who saw clearly that only by means of a general naval war would they be able to obtain a fair share in sea-borne trade. In 1652 the means to wage such a war with a reasonable prospect of success was at hand in the large new fleet built by Cromwell's Commonwealth government after the end of the Civil War. Moreover the fleet was better-manned and more efficiently administered than ever before.

The Dutch, the most experienced and skilful seamen of that time, hardened veterans of their long sea wars with Spain and Portugal, might have seemed clear favourites in any estimate of the prospects of the two belligerents. This would have been overlooking England's geographical advantage, with her south coast lining the long, narrow Channel through which the Dutch were forced to bring the merchant convoys on which their wealth and power depended. It was with attacks on these that hostilities began in May 1652. A series of bloody contests between English fleets commanded by Blake and Monk and the Dutch under Martin Tromp ended in decisive victory for the former. In the treaty of peace signed in 1654, apart from compensation for the 'massacre of Amboyna' the chief term enforced was Dutch acceptance of Cromwell's Navigation Acts which forbade British trade being carried in other than British ships.

It was a poor return for so great a victory and did not go far towards increasing the English share in world trade. Another war was inevitable : it broke out in 1665 and followed a similar pattern to the first with the fighting at sea ending in a

British victory on 25 July 1666 and followed by a massive destruction of Dutch merchant shipping. The other fruits were to elude the British grasp, however. The peace negotiations which followed were prolonged ; impatient to retrench, Charles II's government paid off their warships and laid them up in the Medway ; and there the great Michael de Ruyter fell upon them in a surprise attack in June 1667, destroyed a number of them and captured the fleet flagship *Royal Charles*.

The peace terms, hastily agreed, acknowledged Dutch paramountcy in the East Indies. It seemed that nothing short of a fight to the finish could settle the differences between the two nations. And in 1672, Charles II sent Britain, in alliance this time with Louis XIV of France, once again against the Netherlands. In the naval war which followed, neither side emerged the victor ; but when Charles II was forced in 1674 by public opinion to withdraw from his unnatural alliance and make peace, the Dutch were left to fight on until 1678 in defence of their land frontier. They succeeded, but at a cost which spelt ruin to their economy.

The Netherlands had not recovered from this catastrophe when, in 1688, their Stadtholder, William of Orange, came to the throne of England in succession to the deposed James II. For the next seventy years they were virtually a satellite of Britain and involved in a series of wars against France at Britain's side – wars in which their energies were inevitably concentrated in the campaigns on land. It is not surprising therefore that, as seen in the previous chapter, their power and influence in the Far East declined, becoming confined to consolidation in the East Indies. The British, on the other hand, took the lead in establishing an immensely profitable trade with China, a trade whose maintenance would eventually call for the exercise of sea power.

The English, in fact, had been feeble late-comers in the trade with China. Their first attempt to open such a trade had been in 1637 when the Portuguese had been established at Macao for eighty years, Spanish trade through Manila for sixty-two years and Dutch through Formosa for thirteen. The attempt made by Captain John Weddell with six ships was a failure. Arriving at Macao he was met by Portuguese opposition but in spite of it sailed on to Canton where he seized a small

native fort with the object of setting up a factory. When his
supercargoes were arrested by the Chinese, however, he was
forced to seek the aid of the Portuguese to obtain their release
and to give up his attempt having achieved nothing.

Over the next thirty years several English ships reached
Macao ; but trade was at a standstill in the confusion arising
from the Manchu conquest. In 1662, as a result of Koxinga's
incursions, the Emperor ordered all ports closed to foreign
trade and coastal inhabitants to withdraw inland. Only Macao
was officially exempted, but the closure of Canton was not
strictly enforced. Nevertheless the English East India Company,
with a new charter granted by Cromwell, entered into relations
with Koxinga's son and heir in 1671, selling him arms and
ammunition ; in return they were allowed to establish a factory
at Amoy and trade in Formosa. This enterprise came to an end
with the pacification of Formosa in 1685 ; but at the same
time the Emperor K'ang Hsi lifted the ban on sea trade and
opened customs houses at Canton, Chang-chou (Fukien),
Ningpo and Yün-t'ai-shan (Kiangsu). The first English ship to
conduct a normal peaceful trade at Canton was the *Macclesfield*
in 1699, in which year an English factory was formally established, where trade goods were stored and the Company's
supercargoes were allowed to live during the trading season,
transferring to Macao on its conclusion.

So riddled with corruption was the port authority, however,
and so heavy the dues exacted that the East India Company
tried for a time to make use of the more northerly ports and a
factory was also set up at Ting Hai near Ningpo. Finding
conditions no better there they reverted to Canton where trade
was regularized around 1715 with a council of supercargoes
making up the permanent staff of the factory. When another
attempt to use Ningpo was made forty years later, it was quickly
nipped in the bud, at the request of the Chinese Viceroy of
Canton, by the imposition of unacceptably high duties at the
northern ports which from that time onwards ensured that
Canton became the only port open to foreign trade. In 1759
this was reinforced by an imperial decree to this effect, though
this had its origin rather in the better facilities at Canton for
controlling the 'barbarian' traders and their ships.

As relations between Europe and the Far East for the next

hundred years and more were to be governed almost entirely by disputes over the conduct of the commerce at Canton and lead eventually to war in which sea power was to have the predominating influence, a brief description of the conditions under which it was carried on (unparalleled as they were and astonishing to a western mind) must be given.

First the geography must be understood. Canton lies on the Pearl River some forty miles above the point where it flows past the fortified Bocca Tigris (Tiger's Mouth) or Bogue into the broad estuary ninety miles long and fifty wide at its seaward end where Macao on the western headland looks across towards the group of islands which today comprise the colony of Hong Kong. On arrival from Europe, normally during the early autumn, having taken advantage of the south-west monsoon, the sailing ship called at Macao where a pilot, an interpreter and a comprador who arranged for provisions for the crew were embarked. The ship then sailed on to the Bocca Tigris where measurements to calculate the port dues were taken and fees paid before she went on to the anchorage at Whampoa, some seven miles down stream from the city and where all foreign shipping lay under the guns of more forts during their stay.

The next point (and one which was to be a fundamental cause of eventual war) was the Chinese attitude to the foreigners who came seeking to trade. Apart from the unquestioned belief that all other nations were subordinate to China, the Middle Kingdom, and owed tribute to the 'Son of Heaven', the attitude of the Emperor, as explicitly stated in 1793, was : 'We possess all things. I set no value on objects strange or ingenious, and have no use for your country's manufactures'. Any trade was thus represented to be entirely for the foreigners' benefit. Local government officials from the Viceroy downwards, including the Superintendent of Customs or 'Hoppo' the Emperor's personal appointee, whose post was created in 1702, though responsible for the prosperity of their province and for forwarding to Peking the taxes based on it, had officially to express the same views. Furthermore, as representatives of the Emperor, they could on no account demean themselves by having any direct communication with the suppliant barbarians from distant vassal states of the Middle Kingdom, whose only permitted form of communication, 'humble petitions', must therefore come to them through intermediaries.

Such intermediaries were supplied in the form of the leading members of the Chinese commercial firms known as Hongs, who were made the sole agents of foreign trade. In 1720 they were formed into a guild, known as the Co-Hong, the members of which had a monopoly of trade with foreigners. Disbanded a year later, the Co-Hong was revived between 1760 and 1771 and again in 1782. A further barrier to any normal intercourse between Chinese and foreigners was the prohibition against any Chinese teaching the latter their language. All official communications had to be made through Chinese interpreters with usually a distorted idea of the European language concerned. There grew up, therefore, the grotesque and indeed hilarious language known as pidgin English, a mixture of English, Portuguese and Indian words put together in Chinese syntax, which made it difficult for a foreigner to treat seriously any negotiations carried on in it.

Strict rules of behaviour which emphasized lowly status rather than inflicting any real hardship were laid down for the foreign merchants confined within the limits of the little island of Shameen in the river opposite the city : no white woman was allowed to reside there ; foreigners were forbidden to use sedan chairs ; the number of servants they might employ was limited etc.

According to whence any trading ship came, a particular Hong merchant was fully responsible for all that concerned her during her stay at Canton, European and (later) American ships being supervised for instance by the Wai-yang Hong. British trade was carried on initially by ships of the East India Company or, as its full sonorous title was from 1708 when under a new charter it absorbed the original or 'Old Company', the Honourable East India Company. It soon became shared, however, with 'country' vessels, ships built in India at the expense of private British or British-Indian (usually Parsee) businesses in India, manned by Indian Lascar sailors and officered by British. These ships operated under licence from the East India Company ; the fact that they were not under direct Company control was to have its convenient aspect when opium became a principal, although unsavoury, import into

China. At the same time this licence was to prove an embarrass-ment when the Company's representative was held by the Chinese authorities to be responsible for the conduct of all British traders.

The goods embarked in English ships at Canton were tea (which composed 90 to 95 per cent of the cargo), raw silk, china and lacquer work, rhubarb and cassia. In return they delivered woollens, lead, tin, iron, copper, furs, linen etc. The 'country' ships embarked mainly nankeen cloth, alum, camphor, pepper, vermilion etc., and bought raw cotton, ivory and sandalwood. The balance of this trade was in each case strongly in favour of the Chinese and until about 1773 the difference was made up by payment in silver. A solution to this imbalance was found when the Chinese susceptibility to opium smoking and avid demands for greater supplies of the drug were appreciated.

Although opium had been brought to China much earlier, probably by the Arabs, the smoking of it was introduced between 1624 and 1662 through Formosa and Amoy by the Dutch who had used the drug mixed with tobacco and arsenic and smoked in an ordinary pipe as a cure for the malaria that was the scourge of the East Indies. After the departure of the Dutch the monopoly of importing opium was held by the Portuguese though East India Company ships were import-ing it in a small way from Madras as early as 1730. The total quantities at that time were comparatively small : some 200 chests annually, of 140 to 160 pounds weight each. Nevertheless the demoralizing effect of the habit was already appreciated by the Imperial government and an edict against its import was promulgated in 1729, as a result of which Company ships were officially forbidden to trade in it.

The traffic continued, nevertheless, in the licensed 'country' vessels as well as in foreign ships. These well-armed ships engaged in an aggressive sales promotion, and by 1773, through the connivance of Chinese merchants and officials – the latter freely accepting large bribes – the trade had grown to as much as 1,000 chests a year. To prevent conflicts between traders of various nations, the Company then assumed control of the entire production and sale of Indian opium. When the adverse balance of other trade with China became oppressive to the Company, the idea of substituting for silver the opium so keenly sought by the Chinese, was born; in 1780 the Company made the trade from India its own monopoly. After 1783, however, ships of the newborn United States of America joined the trade with China and were soon the keenest rivals of the British, even in the import of opium which they obtained from Turkey. With the advent of the speedy clipper ships developed in American shipyards, they soon bid fair to eclipse the British trade, particularly during the Napoleonic wars, when they enjoyed the various benefits of being neutrals until 1812. By 1790 the annual amount imported had grown to 4,054 chests.

Further edicts on the evils of opium smoking followed; when the import, as well as Chinese home production of opium, was totally prohibited in 1800, the East India Company and the Co-Hong ceased to traffic directly in it. Its production in India, the principal source, remained a Company monopoly, however, and it was widely cultivated for sale at annual auction to the 'country' firms and foreign traders who shipped it in their vessels throughout the East, though more particularly to Canton. There, official Chinese eyes were sealed with bribes, and Chinese merchants collaborated in the unloading of foreign ships outside the port limits. The quantity of opium imported grew ever greater.

In the meantime a long-suffered cause of discontent by the foreigners – their subjection to what seemed to them the 'strange and barbarous' Chinese system of criminal justice – had been highlighted by an incident concerning the British merchant ship *Lady Hughes* in 1787. The system embodied the law of 'a life for a life' and the handing over by the headmen of foreign communities of alleged criminals for summary trial by courts in which their guilt was assumed unless incontrovertible evidence to the contrary were produced.

A gun salute fired by the *Lady Hughes* accidentally killed two minor mandarins, whereupon it was demanded that the gunner should be surrendered for execution. The gunner was reported as having disappeared; but when substitutes were seized he was produced and handed over and, in spite of all protests by the British community, was executed by strangulation.

The foreign communities had consistently demanded exemption from such a primitive system of criminal law. The British

Government now decided to despatch a mission to Peking to arrange some form of treaty. The first Ambassador chosen, Colonel Cathcart, died from consumption during the voyage in June 1788. The outbreak of war with Revolutionary France delayed further steps ; but in 1792 an impressive mission under Lord Macartney sailed charged with the task of opening the whole of the East to British trade and placing relations with China on a regular treaty basis.

Arriving at the court of Emperor Ch'ien Lung in September 1793, Macartney was given a courteous reception. His mission was doomed from the start, however. He was received as one bringing tribute from a vassal state and was expected to acknowledge this by prostrating himself in the servile kowtow. When he agreed to do this only if a Chinese official of his own rank performed a similar obeisance to a portrait of King George, he was excused and permitted to kneel on one knee. But any idea of entering into diplomatic negotiations never entered the Emperor's head and when the ambassador attempted to do so it was firmly conveyed to him that he would have outstayed his welcome if he did not leave at once. The sublimely arrogant replies of the Emperor in a letter to the King of England made it evident that nothing short of a complete change of attitude by the Chinese government towards the foreigners, on whom they looked as uncivilized and contemptible barbarians, could bring about any improvement in relations. As this was unimaginable to the Manchu Ch'ing dynasty, the seeds of eventual war were already planted and germinating.

The exposition above of conditions existing at Canton up to the time of the Macartney Mission to Peking in 1793 has tacitly included the acquisition of the lion's share of a growing China trade by the British up to 1783 and by the British and Americans fairly equally following the foundation of the United States. The sea power which had brought this about had been wielded mainly elsewhere than the Pacific.

Throughout the eighteenth and during the early part of the nineteenth centuries, the trade with China had a mainly Indian base whence came the majority of the goods the Chinese were prepared to accept in exchange for their tea, silk, rhubarb, etc.

Up to 1763 the British and French had been rivals for political control of India with the fading power of Holland holding Ceylon. French participation in the China trade was minimal, in fact, though the French East India Company maintained a factory at Canton from 1720 to 1770. At the conclusion of the Seven Years' War in 1763, French political influence in India was theoretically eliminated.

Spain also suffered defeat in that war and in 1762 Manila was captured by a British expeditionary force. Manila's commercial weakness without the annual import of silver from Spanish America was exposed during the twenty months of the British occupation, and it was with no more than a show of reluctance that it was restored to Spain by the Treaty of Paris in February 1763 in return for a large indemnity.

When the French and Dutch took advantage of Britain's difficulties with her American colonies to enter the war against her, Dutch commerce in the East suffered disastrously, the Dutch East India Company being ruined through the elimination of its trade with India and the forced abandonment of all Dutch claims to trading monopolies in Indonesia. The British-owned 'country' vessels mentioned earlier, with opium in their holds as an eagerly accepted bargaining counter, were now free to compete throughout Indonesia. The French, on the other hand, by means of a naval squadron in the Indian Ocean under their great Admiral Suffren, posed a serious threat to Madras and Calcutta in 1782–3 and prevented the British from taking Ceylon from the Dutch. A decisive French naval defeat at the Battle of the Saintes on the other side of the world, finally saved Britain from having to make any serious concessions in the peace treaty in 1783 and the French were permitted to return to only five 'purely commercial' posts in India.

Suffren's operations, based on Atjeh and Mergui, had exposed Britain's need for a naval base on the eastern side of the Indian Ocean and covering the approaches to the Malacca Strait. In 1786, therefore, the East India Company obtained a lease of Penang Island from the Malay Sultan of Kedah, followed by a clear treaty of cession in 1791, with the addition of a coastal strip of the mainland opposite the island in 1800.

The renewal of war in 1793 between Britain and France – now under a Republican government – was of no immediate consequence in the Far East until 1795 when French armies overran the Netherlands, expelled the Stadtholder, the Prince of Orange, and set up a puppet Batavian Republic. It was of vital importance to the safety of British trade that those key way stations on the route to China, the Cape of Good Hope, Ceylon and Malacca, should be denied to the French. The Stadtholder placed Dutch overseas possessions under British protective custody on the understanding that they should be restored to the legitimate government when peace was achieved. This was only partially accepted by the Dutch authorities who were divided in their loyalties; so that although the commanders of the British expeditions sent by Commodore Rainier, commanding the East Indies Station, were armed with letters from the Prince, in each case a show of force was necessary. At Malacca this proved to be minimal and, as soon as troops were landed in August 1795, the Dutch capitulated almost without firing a shot.

The safe passage of the seasonal convoys to and from Canton through the Strait was now assured. A threat in the South China Sea from Batavia remained; but sufficient troops to assault and occupy the Dutch colony there were not immediately available, and meanwhile covetous eyes were being directed towards the fabled wealth of the Spice Islands where little resistance was to be expected. Indeed, when Rainier arrived off Amboyna in February 1796 with the ships-of-the-line *Suffolk* (74), *Centurion* (50), the sloop *Swift* (16) and a handful of European and Indian troops in three transports, he was able to take possession of the port and its stocks of cloves with little or no resistance; he then went on to Banda to do the same with its nutmegs and mace. Rainier now found himself involved in settling local disturbances, including a native revolt in Amboyna. He was thus prevented from going on to Ternate where further quantities of spices were stored.

He was still detained at Amboyna at the end of November. It was time for him to take himself to Macao to assume escort for the homeward-bound Indiamen, for the French had now come on the scene with a squadron of six large frigates under Rear Admiral Sercey which, after an unsuccessful attempt to raid Penang, was lying in wait at Batavia.

On 30 December Rainier sailed from Macao with four of the

East Indiamen and two other ships, the convoy taking the route through the Straits of Malacca. For some reason he did not wait for six other Indiamen which were therefore instructed by the Select Committee of Supercargoes, the Company's representatives at Canton, to enter the Indian Ocean through one of the straits to the eastward of Java. News of this plan reached Sercey and on 28 January he intercepted them in the Straits of Bali.

The majority of East Indiamen were armed ; but they were no match for an equal number of heavy frigates, the largest of which, Sercey's flagship *Forte*, was in fact an eighty-gun ship cut down and mounting thirty 24-pounders and twenty-two smaller guns. Captain Charles Lennox, in command of the Indiamen, resorted to bluff. Forming line-of-battle, he hoisted the flag of a Rear-Admiral of the Blue at his masthead while all his ships broke out blue ensigns and the masthead pendants of men-of-war. When the French frigate *Cybele* was detached to reconnoitre, Lennox ordered two of his own ships out to keep her at a distance. The Frenchman signalled that the British ships were two of the line and four frigates, whereupon Sercey bore away leaving the merchantmen unscathed to tell an only slightly exaggerated tale of how they had chased away an enemy squadron.

A fresh threat to the China trade had meanwhile arisen from the entry of Spain into the war at France's side in October, 1796, news of which reached the East Indies in April 1797. The Spanish squadron at Manila was believed to comprise three 74's and four frigates. Though all had been dismasted in a typhoon, repairs were presumably being hastened and a combined operation against Manila was therefore planned, using troops from India. This would probably have had little difficulty in destroying the Spanish ships, but before it could be mounted, there came news from Europe of Napoleon's brilliant campaign in Italy and the collapse of Austria, marked by the Treaty of Campo Formio. Bonaparte was now free to turn his attentions eastwards, and on 1 July 1798 his armies landed in Egypt.

With such a threat looming from the west, no troops could be spared, nor could Rainier afford sufficient ships for the expedition which was therefore cancelled. The China trade would have to rely upon escorted convoy for its safety. That the

Spanish threat was negligible during the early part of 1798 was, in fact, revealed by the impudent penetration of Manila harbour in January of that year by the senior officer of the escort, Captain Edward Cooke, with two of his frigates disguised as French ships. Having entertained various unsuspecting Spanish authorities and obtained confirmation that the Spanish squadron could not be ready for sea for some months, Cooke threw off the disguise, captured three Spanish gunboats unopposed and sailed out of harbour without a shot being fired at him.

The Spanish squadron was ready for sea in time to operate against the homeward China trade at the beginning of 1798 and on 27 January they appeared off Macao with two 74s, two Spanish and two French frigates. They found at anchor and waiting for the season's convoy, the British *Intrepid* (64), *Arrogant* (74) and the frigate *La Virginie* which at once slipped their cables and stood out to sea in pursuit. With the safe and timely arrival of his convoy his primary objective, Captain Hargood of the *Intrepid*, the senior British officer, can have had no wish to force a fight with the superior enemy force. In heavy weather, with the onset of darkness he prudently anchored amidst the Ladrone Islands in the mouth of the Pearl River Estuary for the night; by the morning no enemy were in sight and they were not seen again before Hargood sailed with the convoy on 7 February. The Spanish admiral had in fact returned to Manila. No further attempts were made to interfere with the China trade which of course was regularly convoyed while hostilities continued.

In May 1800 an expedition to capture Java was prepared only to be cancelled, owing to a renewed threat anticipated from Egypt. Batavia was closely blockaded, however, by a small squadron for two and a half months during which the trade of the port was brought to a standstill; but it was at a heavy cost in deaths amongst the crews from the fever for which Batavia was notorious.

The last occurrence before the temporary Peace of Amiens in March 1802 was the surrender of Ternate to the British on 20 June 1801 where the Dutch Governor had withstood a long siege. Both Java and Manila had been saved by the far distant threat of Bonaparte's armies in Egypt. By the terms of the treaty, Malacca, Amboyna, Banda and Ternate were all returned to the Dutch; Ceylon alone of the Dutch colonies remained under the British flag.

News of the renewal of the war reached India in September 1803 where the British fleet was in considerable disarray with all but one of Rear Admiral Rainier's ships-of-the-line undergoing essential refits as a result of weather damage from a cyclone in the Bay of Bengal or from decay brought about by long service in tropical waters. Nor had the Commander-in-Chief any firm intelligence of the strength or whereabouts of the Franco-Dutch forces on the station or at what point of the wide-spread trade network the enemy was planning to attack.

Assessing the Bay of Bengal to be the most vulnerable, Rainier confined himself, so far as the trade from China was concerned, to despatching two frigates to Penang to meet the homeward convoy due to sail from Canton in January. This decision was to have notable consequences. His French opponent, Rear Admiral Charles Durand de Linois, who had replaced Sercey, and was at Mauritius with his flag in the *Marengo* (74), had other views and on 8 October 1803 he sailed with the frigates *Berceau*, *Semillante* and *Belle Poule*. His object was to proceed to Batavia, taking the news of war, and, having persuaded the Dutch naval force there under Rear Admiral Dekker to co-operate, to steer to intercept the fleet of East Indiamen and 'country' ships as they approached the southern entrance to the Straits of Malacca. In a surprise raid on the British trading post of Bencoolen, West Sumatra, two merchant ships were captured, five others burnt by their own crews and the factory devastated. Linois then sailed on to Batavia arriving on 12 December only to find that Dekker had sailed some time earlier with his squadron for Mauritius. The only reinforcement he obtained from the far from enthusiastic Dutch allies was the brig *Aventurier*.

With his five ships, Linois duly took up station; reports from Macao were that the convoy would consist of seventeen East Indiamen, six country ships and a brig. The regular Company ships, though painted in chequerboard style like two-decker men-of-war, were usually armed with up to thirty-six 18-pounder guns on one deck; this did not make them a match for a warship similarly armed. Their complement was too small to man all the guns effectively, the gundecks were cluttered and their scantlings were too light to put up with much battle damage. Rumours had reached Linois, however, that three ships had been armed as double-decker 64s.

It was with some anxiety, therefore, that Linois contemplated the coming encounter. Dawn on 14 February 1804 revealed a cloud of sail to the northward; the *Berceau* and *Aventurier* were the nearest and were soon signalling twenty-eight ships in sight, four more than expected. Linois was at once filled with alarm, fearing that this was confirmation of the rumours or that an escort of frigates had been provided unknown to him; the sight of four ships standing boldly out to reconnoitre while the remainder were forming in line of battle, added strength to his fears. Even when the *Belle Poule* returned from a closer reconnaissance to report that only two of the ships were armed with lower deck guns, he remained doubtful. It was by this time 5.30 pm and he decided to delay action until the next day, meanwhile working his way to windward of the convoy. If there were no escort, he reasoned, the merchantmen would take advantage of this to try to escape and be revealed as the easy prey he had been hoping for.

The fact was that the convoy had no ships armed on two decks and the only escort was the Honourable East India Company's brig *Ganges*. It was otherwise composed of sixteen HEI Co. ships and twelve 'country' ships. The senior officer, Nathaniel Dance of the *Earl Camden*, refused to be stampeded, however. Having formed the East Indiamen into line of battle with the 'country' ships under their lee, he lay to for the night. All ships were darkened except for the flagship and two others, the *Royal George* and *Hope*, which were detailed to play the part of men-of-war. At daylight these three and the *Ganges* hoisted blue ensigns, the remainder red. For three hours the two forces lay some three miles apart before Dance, losing patience, ordered the convoy to resume course for the straits.

This show of calm confidence had convinced Linois that his fears were justified. Nevertheless, he now began to edge down towards the line of East Indiamen, steering to cut off its rear, whereupon Captain John Timmins of the *Royal George*, leading the line, tacked to go in support, being followed in succession by the *Earl Camden*, the *Ganges* and two others. A long-range cannonade between the French and English ships followed, lasting some forty minutes, with only minor damage inflicted on either side. When the *Marengo's* rigging began to suffer, however, Linois would risk no more ; he hauled his wind and stood away to the eastward. The signal for 'general chase' was hoisted amidst cheers in the *Earl Camden* and the strange sight was seen of a French line-of-battle ship and three large frigates being pursued by the East Indiamen. The deep-laden, broad-bellied merchantmen had little hope of overtaking, in fact, and after two hours Dance gave the signal to tack and led away for the Straits. The China fleet worth some eight million pounds had been saved.

Nathaniel Dance was knighted for this exploit and all the other masters of East Indiamen rewarded. Linois' timidity dealt his reputation a brutal blow and earned him the scathing contempt of Napoleon. An unbiassed student of the technique of commerce raiding at sea, the *guerre de course*, by the forces of a weaker sea power may find himself able to grant a measure of sympathy ; particularly one from a generation that has seen such episodes of the Second World War as the destruction of the *Admiral Graf Spee* through an underestimation of an enemy's strength or the repeated refusal of German heavy ships to risk being damaged by weaker opponents defending convoys. Linois, without knowledge of the whereabouts of the several British ships of the line in Eastern waters could not afford to have the *Marengo* dismasted. Ironically the *Marengo*, still flying Linois' flag, and the *Belle Poule* were to be captured two years later in the Atlantic through approaching what they took for merchantmen only to find they were the *London* (98), *Foudroyant* (80) and *Amazon* (38). That Linois possessed courage was shown in the five and a half hours of resistance against odds that his flagship offered before surrendering.

Following Linois' unproductive attempt to waylay the China fleet, British sea power remained supreme in the Pacific for the rest of the Napoleonic War. The French confined themselves to a *guerre de course* with a few frigates in the Indian Ocean until the capture of Mauritius in 1810 brought even this to an end. The Dutch squadron was eliminated by an attack on Batavia by the British East Indies squadron in October 1806 and a combined operation in November 1807 which captured the port of Gresik in eastern Java where the last three Dutch ships-of-the-line were taken and burned. Subsequently Malacca and Amboyna were once again occupied by the British and finally, in 1811, Java itself came under British rule with the occupation of Batavia.

All was to be restored to the Dutch in the years following the general peace, the British agreeing to the relinquishment of any settlements in Sumatra (where Bencoolen was exchanged for Malacca) and the Spice Islands, while the Dutch surrendered all claims to Malaya. Two spheres of influence were thereby tacitly established. More pregnant with consequences for the future was the lease on behalf of the British East India Company, by Stamford Raffles, of the island of Singapore off the southern tip of Malaya and its establishment as a free trade *entrepôt* in 1819, a full British title being negotiated with the Sultans of Johore and Riau in 1824. Two years later, by Act of Parliament, the Straits Settlements were set up uniting Penang, Malacca and Singapore. Not only was the principle of free trade to attract the great majority of the commerce of South-East Asia to Singapore, but the strategic centre of the whole area had fallen into the hands of the supreme maritime power of the day. An era of British hegemony was about to begin.

6

THE OPIUM TRAFFIC — CONFLICT AT CANTON

The rolling thunder of war that shook all Europe from 1797 to 1815 was muted to a distant rumble in the Orient, and British trade with China grew ever larger chiefly as a result of an insatiable demand on the one hand for tea, on the other for opium. However, while threats to the China fleet were confined to the irresolute attempts by Sercey and Linois in 1796 and 1804, respectively, unjustified fears led on two occasions to British occupation of Macao to thwart any such move by the French. The first, in 1802, was very brief and ended with the conclusion of the peace Treaty of Amiens. The second occasion, in 1808, is of interest chiefly as a forewarning of the sort of trouble which would arise if attempts were made to replace the purely commercial relations between Chinese and foreigners at Canton by any political arrangement.

The fact that Macao was not actually Portuguese territory, being held only by permission of the Emperor, was bound to make a landing by British troops, even at the invitation of the Portuguese, into an act calling for reprisals by the Cantonese authorities. These would certainly take the form of a cessation of trade ruinous to the foreign merchants. It is difficult therefore to see why the East India Company's representatives, the Select Committee of Super-cargoes, did not do all in their power to prevent such an act ; unless the fact that the Chinese Hong merchants, the Viceroy of Canton, and even the Emperor's personal representative, the *Hoppo*, would then be equally ruined made them believe that it would be overlooked. This ignored the other fact : that the Viceroy could not risk keeping the news from the Emperor who would expect such an insult by the 'outer barbarians' to be punished.

Be that as it may, when a British squadron comprising one ship-of-the-line (flying the flag of Rear Admiral O'Brien

Drury) and four frigates arrived off Macao in September 1808 with a body of troops on board which were put ashore at Macao at the urging of the President of the Select Committee, a situation arose, with all trade at a standstill, which could only be resolved by force or by an ignominious withdrawal. This came to a head at the end of November when Drury, who had taken two of his frigates up to the Whampoa anchorage past the impotent, antique batteries of the Bocca Tigris forts, accompanied a force of armed ships' boats sent to fetch stores from the English factory at Canton. They were stopped by a line of armed junks drawn across the river and, though this opposition could have been easily overcome, Drury, who had humane objections to shedding blood in so petty a cause, would not permit fire to be opened and the boats retreated. The Chinese, who had palpably gained considerable face, claimed a naval victory.

This situation placed a whole season's trade at risk, so when an ultimatum from the Emperor arrived threatening a permanent closure of Canton, the Select Committee gave in, requesting Drury to re-embark the troops and withdraw, which he gladly did.

The significance of this episode lies chiefly in its exposure of the total lack of appreciation by the government at Peking or the Imperial officers in the provinces, who never made personal acquaintance with any 'outer barbarian', of the realities of world power. The British, since Trafalgar the undisputed supreme naval power in the world, were unlikely to continue to accept the Chinese opposition to free trade or the ignominious status allotted to them at Canton. With the end of the war they would be no longer too pre-occupied to take steps to rectify matters.

Even before that time, in 1814, the Chinese bluff of threatening to cut off trade to settle a dispute was successfully challenged by the Select Committee. The situation arose out of an episode of the War of 1812 between Britain and the United States when the American steamer *Hunter* was seized by the British frigate *Doris* in the Pearl River. The Chinese threatened to cut off trade unless the latter left, whereupon the president of the Select Committee, Sir George Staunton, ordered the withdrawal of the British community. The Viceroy, facing ruin, then agreed to discuss terms and the incident was amicably closed.

A first breach had been made in the irksome Chinese regulations aimed at keeping the barbarians in subjection and at arm's length. Nevertheless the British government decided to send another mission to Peking to put trade and diplomatic relations between China and Britain on a more satisfactory basis. Lord Amherst was selected to lead it and arrived at Tientsin on 13 August 1816. At once the vexed question was raised whether the Ambassador would perform, as befitted a bearer of tribute from one of China's more distant vassal states, the kowtow with its triple prostration and ninefold knocking of the forehead on the ground at the feet of the Son of Heaven. Amherst made it clear that he was prepared only to raise his hat thrice and bow nine times ; to which the Emperor Chia Ch'ing finally agreed, acknowledging that mere 'outer barbarians' were no doubt unfamiliar with proper ceremonial.

The mission was then permitted to proceed, the barges in which it traversed the canal from Tientsin flying flags indicating that it was a tribute-bearing mission. Whether any penetration of the thick wall of mutual incomprehension would have resulted from an audience with the Emperor is doubtful, but it was not put to the test. Arriving at 5 in the morning in Peking, Amherst was bidden by court officials to present himself at once, dusty, tired and unwashed, although an audience for the following day had been fixed. His refusal and request for time to prepare himself properly was taken as an impertinence and an edict was issued expelling the mission from the capital.

With its departure a failure, three alternatives to future relations between the foreign traders (of which the British made up the large majority) and the Manchu government and officials ruling China remained : submission to the irksome and humiliating regulations, the use of force to have them abolished or the abandonment of trade. The last of these, in view of the fact that trade had by this time grown so phenomenally in value to all concerned, was unthinkable. Submission might have remained possible if the old system had persisted of a trade monopoly by the East India Company. A Select Committee of Supercargoes could put up with humiliation to keep trade moving, which a government representative could not.

The independent companies, however, growing ever more prosperous and powerful through their profitable participation in the opium traffic, were bringing pressure to bear on the British government to abolish the Company's monopoly and appoint a representative of the Crown to negotiate a free system of trade as was usual in other parts of the world ; if all else failed they advocated the use of force. Against this, they correctly estimated, the Manchu troops, scattered about the country to hold the Chinese in subjection, could offer negligible resistance being armed with bows and arrows, pikes and shields, and the clumsy Chinese war junks with their antique cannon.

The East India Company monopoly of British China trade was finally abolished in 1834. Before embarking on an account of the events which followed, the state of the trade and its disreputable relation the opium traffic must be noted. Both were making a phenomenal growth, but by 1820 the amount of private trade was greater than that carried in the Company's own ships, while the quantity of opium entering China had outstripped all other articles combined.

As mentioned earlier, the Company had held a monopoly of British trade with China since 1773, private traders operating under licence from the Company. The principal export from China was the annual tea crop, the demand for which had grown continuously. Imports into China were rigidly controlled by the Imperial government whose attitude was that China had no use for the goods of the barbarian West. Payment for the tea crop would have had to be in silver – and, indeed, for a time had been – if Chinese craving for opium had not provided a substitute.

The Company had assumed control of the entire production of Indian opium, the highest grade, and sold it at annual auctions to traders of all nations. In spite of Imperial edicts against the evils of opium smoking, imports grew from a thousand chests annually in 1773 to some five thousand by 1800, including a quantity of lower-grade Turkish opium which was imported by American firms. Apart from the demoralizing effect of the drug, this was reversing the trade balance and causing a drain of Chinese silver resources. In that year, therefore, the Emperor finally issued an edict forbidding both home cultivation and import of the drug. Both the East India Company and the Co-Hong ceased from that time to trade directly in it. The crop was still offered for sale, however, and eagerly bought by independent traders, its sale to them comprising one of the chief sources of revenue of the Indian Government.

The embargo did nothing to reduce the flow. With the connivance of all Chinese officials up to and including the Viceroy himself and the *Hoppo*, responsible for transmitting to Peking the customs receipts of the port, the opium was discharged outside port limits into fast Chinese galleys, known as 'smugboats', 'fast crabs' or 'scrambling dragons'. Armed, and propelled by twenty or more oars on each side, these could easily evade any customs boats even if the latter had not been bribed to leave them alone. By 1831 between a hundred and two hundred of these craft were in operation carrying the opium, payment for which had been made in Canton, to convenient harbours whence it was conveyed inland. The next development was the establishment of receiving ships moored under the lee of Lintin Island in the Pearl River Estuary. There the opium could be discharged and stored, until either the necessary negotiations for bribery or 'squeeze' with the local officials had been completed, or one of the numerous small ships operated by the independent traders for the purpose was ready to load it for carriage to one of the ports up the coast.

This state of affairs was perfectly satisfactory to the majority of those concerned. Chinese officials as well as traders, Chinese and Western alike, were making huge profits. In addition, the *Hoppo* was able to transmit enough to Peking to satisfy the Emperor while himself waxing rich ; the East India Company's government of India was kept solvent ; the tea crop was duly loaded at Whampoa each winter, paid for with a portion of the silver received for opium. Except on a few enlightened men either in Britain or in China, the fact that the opium-smoking habit was demoralizing a large proportion of the Chinese population made little impact.

Rumours of the impending cancellation of the Honourable East India Company's charter reached the Viceroy in 1831.

SEA POWER IN THE PACIFIC

As this would remove the Select Committee with whom the Co-Hong carried on all negotiations with the 'barbarians', the Viceroy made it known that he expected a *Taipan* (or head merchant) to be appointed in their place. The Viceroy himself, of course, never demeaned himself by actually meeting a 'barbarian'. The British government decided to appoint a Chief Superintendent of Trade with two Assistant Superintendents and a Master Attendant to take charge of all British ships and crews inside the Bocca Tigris. Even though this would introduce, for the first time, a representative of the British Crown into relationships at Canton, a fact which was not understood at first, the idea that the long-standing rules which kept the foreigners subservient and at arm's length might have to be modified never crossed the Viceroy's mind.

Thus when, following the abrogation of the charter, Lord William Napier arrived in the frigate *Andromache* in July 1834 as Chief Superintendent and proceeded at once to the English factory at Canton whence he attempted to communicate by letter directly with the Viceroy, he not only committed, in the latter's view, a dreadful solecism, but violated Chinese regulations. These laid down that any foreign official must first go to Macao and there ask permission through the Co-Hong to go on to Canton. The Viceroy therefore refused to receive Napier's letter and ordered him to leave.

The situation, indeed, was one of almost total mutual incomprehension and one which ultimately only arbitration by force would be able to clarify. To the Viceroy it was unthinkable that a representative of merchants from a barbarian vassal country of Celestial China should presume to negotiate directly with him. To Napier, a naval officer by profession and one who had fought at Trafalgar, it was ridiculous that the representative of the world's greatest sea power should be treated with such ignorant contempt. Though his instructions from Lord Palmerston, the Foreign Secretary, were to be conciliatory and moderate and to refrain from asking for the help of the Navy except when 'the most evident necessity shall require . . . that any such appeal should be made', the insult to the Crown implicit in the Viceroy's contemptuous dismissal could not, he felt, be disregarded. Unfortunately, however, he was in no position to achieve his ends by force. Not only was the force at his disposal limited to the *Andromache*, and a second frigate, the *Imogen*, which had arrived to relieve her (neither of which could get higher up the river than Whampoa), but the Viceroy possessed a weapon against which there was no way of retaliating in his ability to order a total stoppage of trade with the British ; and this at the very season when the annual tea crop was about to be loaded.

No doubt the successful calling of the Viceroy's bluff in this respect in 1814, mentioned earlier, had an influence on Napier's proceedings. But this time the bluff was on Napier's part. When the Viceroy ordered all Chinese employees of the British factory to withdraw, cut off the supplies of food and stopped all trade for the British firms, Napier ordered the frigates to force their way past the Bocca Tigris forts. They had no difficulty in doing this, the numerous batteries, unable to inflict more than negligible damage on the ships, being quickly silenced. The Viceroy, however, trumped this trick by blocking the river below and above them with chain booms and sunken lighters loaded with stones, and surrounding the factories with troops and armed boats.

With no further shots in the locker, Napier resisted for ten more days during which each side published fulminating edicts against the other ; but the Superintendent had the support of only half the British trading community. When he was stricken down by a fever his will was sapped and, on 14 September 1834, he capitulated by asking for a permit to return to Macao. This was granted as soon as he had ordered the frigates to return to Lintin ; and on the twenty-first in a Chinese boat and under guard – a vital sop to the Viceroy's face – he set off. The journey, at a snail's pace, took five days during which Napier's fever flared up ; he was mortally ill when he landed at Macao and on 11 October 1834 he died.

The Second Superintendent, Sir John Davis, previously a member of the Select Committee, took over the leadership of the commission. His reversion to the Company policy of 'absolute silence and quiescence' had the support of the British Foreign Secretary. The legitimate trade at Canton had been reopened by the Viceroy and the season's tea was being loaded at Whampoa as usual. The opium traffic had not been affected by the Napier imbroglio and neither Davis nor Sir George

Robinson, who succeeded him, had any instructions to interfere with it.

In December 1836, Robinson resigned, his place being taken
by Captain Charles Elliot, RN, who had been functioning as
Master Attendant. Elliot was a man of greater resolution than
the two East India Company servants who had preceded him.
His training as a naval officer had taught him to use his
initiative when, as in the present circumstances, he was out of
touch with his superior, the Foreign Secretary, whose communications to him were four months in transit. As it was clear
that if he was to achieve anything he must be in residence in
Canton, he decided that he must accept, for the time being at
least, the humiliating Chinese rules. Using the superscription
suitable for an inferior addressing a superior, he sent a petition
to the Viceroy through the Hong merchants. Praising the
Barbarian for his reverence and submission, the Viceroy replied
to the Co-Hong, giving permission. Henceforth the new
Superintendent was looked on by the Chinese authorities
simply as head of the merchants. For this action Elliott was to
receive a sharp reproof from Lord Palmerston, but no suggestions as to how else he was to perform the duties entrusted to
him.

The Superintendent now turned his attention to the question
of the opium trade, which he viewed with repugnance. To
Palmerston, he wrote, 'that such an article should have grown
to be by far the most important part of our import trade, is of
itself a source of painful reflection'. He had neither the means
nor the authority to stop it, however. Indeed, a sudden inter-
ruption of the opium trade would entirely paralyse commerce
as the movement of money at Canton depended on it. He was
therefore relieved to hear rumours, as a result of a memorial
to the Emperor, of the coming legalization of the growth of the
poppy in China, which would cause a steady but more gradual
reduction of imports.

The rumours were wrong, however ; other memorials
advising total prohibition had also reached Peking as a result
of which new and far more categorical Imperial Edicts were
issued to this effect at last forcing the venal Chinese authorities
at Canton to forgo their bribes and take genuine steps to put
an end to the smuggling in the Pearl River. The death penalty

for dealers and owners of opium dens was decreed ; the river police were goaded into energetic chase and capture of smug-boats, whose crews were executed by strangling. That opium was also being brought up river in British-owned boats posed the threat of incidents in which Elliot would be unable to protect British employees from the consequences. Such an incident occurred in December 1838 when a boat was arrested taking a small amount of opium from a ship at Whampoa on behalf of the opium merchant James Innes. A week later, no doubt with the object of impressing the Barbarians with the seriousness of his purpose, the Viceroy ordered an opium-seller to be executed by strangling in the square in front of the factories. A crowd of British and America merchants poured out of the buildings, and aided by a party of British sailors, broke up the apparatus of execution and forced the presiding mandarin and guards to remove themselves and they executed their prisoner elsewhere. A Chinese mob, several thousand strong, then flooded into the square and drove the foreigners back into their factories, which they proceeded to attack. Using battering rams, they must soon have broken in and exterminated the inmates if, in the nick of time, one of the chief Hong merchants had not got a message through to the city's chief magistrate who sent troops to the rescue.

This incident exposed the degree to which the foreign com-munity was being endangered by the smuggling traffic and persuaded Elliot to adopt a firm attitude. All British-owned opium boats were ordered out of the river ; no protection would be afforded for any that remained. As the year 1838 came to an end the opium traffic in the Pearl River had been virtually eliminated.

Nevertheless the coastal route by which opium was carried from the receiving ships at Lintin to other ports continued to flourish. The harassed Elliot was held responsible although, as he pointed out, such authority as he had could only be exercised over British firms and, though these certainly comprised the majority, Americans, French, Dutch, Spanish and Danes were all engaged in the opium trade, each having receiving ships at Lintin. Furthermore, bearing in mind the wide-spread corrupt-ion amongst Chinese officials at that time, it seemed certain that the smuggling at Canton would start up again eventually.

It was at this point, however, that there appeared one of that almost extinct breed, the honest and incorruptible Chinese official. Lin Tse-hsü, governor of the provinces of Hupeh and Honan, had not only been one of those who memorialized the Emperor, urging a programme of merciless punishment of opium dealers and smokers and destruction of all stocks of the drug, but had already succeeded in stamping out the vice in his own provinces by such methods. He was now appointed Imperial Commissioner, with powers equal to those of the Viceroy, entrusted with the suppression of the traffic. On 10 March 1839 he arrived in considerable state in Canton.

Eight days later he struck his first blow with the issue of an edict ordering the surrender of all opium in the possession of the foreign merchants, who were also required to sign a bond that their vessels would never again bring in opium under penalty of death. That Lin really meant business was made apparent when all communications between Canton and Whampoa were cut by Chinese gunboats in the river, backed by troops deployed along the river banks. A meeting of the British merchants thus imprisoned in the factories held on the twenty-first, condemned almost unanimously the continuance of the opium traffic and offered to deliver up 1,037 cases of opium that belonged to them. Lin refused to accept this amount, insisting that all the opium in the receiving ships at Lintin must also be surrendered ; meanwhile he demanded that Mr Lancelot Dent, head of the largest British firm, should appear before him.

Like the penalties included in the bond governing the future conduct of the merchants, this raised the question of submission of British subjects to the criminal jurisdiction of the mandarins, refusal of which since the case of the gunner of the *Lady Hughes* had been an article of faith with the British community. Dent himself said he was willing to go, but his fellow merchants insisted that he should not unless a safe-conduct and a guarantee of safe return was given.

Elliot had gone to Macao on hearing of warlike preparations being made there, and as a result had ordered all British ships to assemble in the anchorage between Hong Kong, a barren and almost uninhabited island, and the mainland. He then started for Canton in his cutter, *Louise*. At Whampoa on the twenty-fourth, hearing of the blockade, he shifted to the gig of the sloop, HMS *Larne* and, in his naval uniform, with pendant and ensign flying from the boat, he set off under oars. His resolute air and the steadiness of the crew overawed the armed boats which approached to stop him and he arrived unmolested at the factory, where he ordered the ensign to be hoisted, finding, as he was to say in his report 'a sense of support in that honoured flag'.

Elliot now took Dent under his personal protection, offering to bring him to Lin if a safe-conduct were supplied. Lin's response was a stiffening of the blockade of the factory area with troops and armed boats, a withdrawal of Chinese employees and a stoppage of supplies of food and water. On the following day, therefore, Elliot demanded passports for all English ships and people to leave Canton ; to which Lin replied that all opium in the receiving ships must first be surrendered.

The Superintendent had reached the limit of his powers of resistance and now, pleading *force majeure*, ordered the British merchants to deliver all their opium to him, guaranteeing government compensation in due course. By the twenty-eighth he was able to inform Lin that 20,283 chests were available for surrender. Similar demands had been made of the American, French and Dutch opium merchants, but Lin eventually accepted that their stocks were included in this figure. Arrangements for the opium to be delivered at the river mouth were made whereupon Lin promised that the blockade would be lifted in progressive stages governed by the amount of opium delivered to his officers.

The merchants had meanwhile signed an undertaking in wide terms to abjure the opium trade. The bond, agreeing to submit themselves to Chinese justice was a different matter : Elliot tore it up and eventually, on 5 May, by which time 15,501 chests had been delivered, the blockade was lifted and passports issued for all but sixteen British subjects. When Elliot refused to leave them, a demand was made that they should sign a bond never to return to China as a condition of their release. As this contained no penal clause, Elliot advised them to sign and on 24 May the British factories were finally abandoned. On 3 June, in the presence of Commissioner Lin, the surrendered opium was publicly destroyed.

Lin Tse-hsü had without doubt displayed his noble qualities of honesty and high-minded resolution. Only the ignorance of the realities of global power, however, the inability of Chinese officialdom common to all from the Emperor downwards to imagine foreign nations as anything other than tributary peoples owing subservience and obedience to the Son of Heaven, could have made him believe that the opium traffic had been scotched for ever or that conditions of legitimate trade with the British would now revert to their old form following the seizure of goods valued at some two and a half million pounds. Reporting what had occurred, Elliot had impressed on the British government that the time had come for the use of force to establish proper and direct diplomatic relations with Peking and a colony under the British flag where merchants and seamen engaged in trade could not only be afforded protection but also disciplined to prevent an anarchical and piratical development of the opium traffic. At the same time Elliot wrote to Lord Auckland, Governor General of India, asking for warships for the protection of British subjects.

Elliot's report would not reach London until 21 September. Meanwhile, in spite of Commissioner Lin's insistence that normal trading should be resumed at Canton, the British merchants refused to put themselves again in jeopardy and conducted their business from Macao through their American *confrères* who had signed Lin's bond and remained at Canton. Elliot forbade British ships arriving for the season's trade to enter the river; instead they assembled in the anchorage of Hong Kong. Lin's next step, therefore, was to erect batteries on the mainland shore at Kowloon to command the anchorage. And it was there that on 12 July 1839 an incident occurred to light the train which was finally to erupt into war.

British and American sailors became involved in the sort of riot always liable to result from drinking the concoction sold in the Chinese drink shops set up for their entertainment – a mixture of alcohol, tobacco juice, sugar and arsenic. At the end of it a Chinese lay dead. Elliot at once had compensation paid to the man's family; six sailors were tried before a court convened on board a merchant ship; one of them, accused of murder, was acquitted for lack of evidence, the remainder were convicted of rioting and sentenced to terms of imprisonment and fines. The Chinese refusal to recognize Elliot's judicial right and their demand for the surrender of the accused men are understandable ; but they brought into the open one of the most irreconcilable differences of opinion between the two races. The case of the *Lady Hughes* and the unjust fate of her gunner delivered up to Chinese justice by his compatriots had never been forgotten.

When Elliot refused to do likewise, Lin brought pressure to bear by assembling troops for an attack on Macao, forbidding supplies and withdrawing all Chinese servants of the British. In mid-August, therefore, the British community was transferred to Hong Kong where they lived aboard the fleet of ships, some fifty in number, which had arrived for the season's trade. Elliot set up his headquarters in the *Fort William*. Lin thereupon made a triumphal entry into Macao and a tour of the city escorted by Portuguese troops ; having thus emphasized Chinese sovereignty and the purely permissive terms on which Macao was held by the foreigners, he withdrew after warning the Governor never to let the English return.

For the moment the Commissioner was thus able to impose his will on the British, at least on land, where they could deploy no defensive force. His next move, however, exposed his total incomprehension of world affairs and of the sea power that he was challenging. A proclamation was issued instructing the Chinese to take up arms and to seize the British whenever they came on shore. Wells at Hong Kong were to be poisoned and supplies of food at Kowloon were to be denied them. When the latter order was ignored, war junks were moved into the anchorage to cut off communication with the shore.

By this time the 28-gun frigate *Volage* (Captain Smith) had arrived from India in response to Elliot's appeal and, when negotiations proved unavailing, he decided that time for a show-down had arrived. But in fact there was no need for the *Volage's* broadsides. The guns of Elliot's cutter *Louise*, a little armed vessel *Pearl*, and the frigate's pinnace were sufficient to drive off the Chinese warships and normal intercourse with the shore was restored. In spite of further fulminations and threats from Commissioner Lin, local officials were conciliatory and in the more friendly atmosphere Elliot began negotiations during October for the merchant fleet to discharge and load below Ch'uan-pi where the most seaward of the Bocca Tigris forts were situated. These arrangements were progressing well ; it had been agreed that the masters of the merchantmen need not execute the bond submitting themselves to capital punishment if any opium were found on board, and some of the merchantmen had arrived at Ch'uan-pi when all was thrown again into confusion by the master of one of them, the *Thomas Coutts*.

Being uninvolved in the opium trade, and so with nothing personally to fear, he signed the bond, was given a pass and sailed his ship up to Whampoa. What Elliot had been trying to avoid at once occurred. With a British ship and crew in his power, Lin broke off negotiations and issued his edict that all British merchantmen should follow the example of the *Thomas Coutts* or depart from Chinese waters within three days on pain of destruction by the fleet of war junks and fireships which had assembled in the mouth of the river.

The point had plainly been reached when one side or the other would have to submit to terms imposed by force. Captain Smith of the *Volage*, which had now been joined by the 18-gun *Hyacinth*, was ordered to assemble the merchant fleet at an anchorage some distance below Ch'uan-pi and to forward a letter to Lin from Elliot demanding a cancellation of the proclamation. This was returned, unopened ; then the Chinese fleet of fifteen men-of-war and fourteen fireships under Admiral Kuan T'ien-p'ei, emerged from the Bocca Tigris and anchored in a line stretching south from Ch'uan-pi. Elliot, on board the *Volage*, torn between his government's injunctions to act with restraint, the need to uphold his country's prestige and his naval officer's feeling for the honour of the flag, made one last effort to avert a battle which, in spite of the disparity in numbers, he knew could only result in a humiliating defeat for the Chinese. A letter demanding Kuan's withdrawal was met by a renewal of the Chinese demand for the surrender of the man responsible for the death of the Chinese villager in the Kowloon riot six months earlier. At last Elliot gave way to the urgings of Captain Smith and gave him permission to attack. The signal to engage was hoisted ; in line ahead in close order the *Volage* and *Hyacinth* sailed slowly down the Chinese line at a range of fifty yards pouring in their starboard broadsides with devastating effect. The Chinese gunners replied as best they could, but as the elevation of their pieces was fixed they could not depress them sufficiently to bear on the frigates' hulls, and minor damage to the rigging was all they could achieve. By the time the frigates had reached the end of the line and turned to repeat the process with their larboard guns, several Chinese ships had gone down, one blowing up, and the remainder, holed and waterlogged, had cut their cables to flee, some being abandoned by their crews. Elliot now persuaded Captain Smith to order the 'Cease Fire', allowing the remnants of the enemy fleet, including the flagship, to work their way to safety up river.

7

THE 'OPIUM WARS' — TREATY
OF NANKING

Oriental preoccupation with face, as well as the need to avoid the dire punishment meted out to unsuccessful officials, required that the Battle of Ch'uan-pi, as it was called, should be represented as a Chinese victory. Admiral Kuan's story was that it had arisen out of his successful attempt to assist the British ship *Royal Saxon* to proceed to Whampoa after her master had signed the opium bond and was being stopped by shots from the *Volage*. The Emperor was sufficiently hood-winked to order the bestowal of a high decoration on the Admiral.

A period of false and uneasy calm now ensued. Commissioner Lin, proud of his initial success in smashing the local traffic in opium and unable to realize what forces he must have set in motion by his threats to the life and property of British subjects, was quietly confident that his edict putting an end to trade with the British 'for ever' would eventually bring Elliot and the British merchants to heel. The fact was, however, that the coastal traffic in opium was resumed as soon as the coast mandarins found safe ways to avoid Lin's repressive measures ; while the loading and discharging of legitimate cargoes was carried on perfectly satisfactorily at Hong Kong or the anchorage at Tongku near Lintin, arrangements being made with the Hongs through the American merchants who, by signing Lin's bond, had been able to continue living at Canton.

Thus when in February 1840 advance information reached Elliot that an expedition to demand redress of the Chinese was being prepared, he was in the happy position of being able to report that thirty million pounds weight of tea had been safely loaded for Europe. The expedition being prepared by the Indian government was to be under the command of Rear Admiral the Hon. George Elliot, a cousin of the

Superintendent of Trade with whom he was accredited as Joint Plenipotentiary for negotiations with the Chinese government. It was to consist of sixteen warships, three of which were 74-gun ships-of-the-line, four armed steamers of the Honourable East India Company, twenty-seven transports and a troopship carrying three regiments of British infantry, a volunteer regiment of Indian troops, two companies of British artillery and two companies of sappers and miners.

Instructions for the two Plenipotentiaries from Lord Palmerston, Foreign Secretary, were that all ports on the China coast were to be blockaded, the island of Chusan in the Yangtse Estuary was to be occupied until an indemnity covering the cost of the expedition had been paid and the reply of the Imperial government to a number of treaty conditions was to be demanded at the mouth of the Pei-ho River, the seaward approach to Peking.

Apart from general satisfaction for the illegal detention of the British trading community at Canton in the previous year, these conditions were that compensation be given for the opium seized by Lin as their 'ransom', that freedom of trade and residence be given to British subjects at Canton, Amoy, Foochow, Shanghai and Ningpo and that one or more islands be ceded where British subjects could do business under protection of the British flag. The last of these conditions could be modified in the face of Chinese unwillingness, the grant of factories and permanent arrangements for carrying on a trade on the mainland subject only to a fixed tariff being acceptable instead. The remainder of the conditions were categorically laid down, leaving the Plenipotentiaries no freedom to modify them. A letter from Lord Palmerston was to be delivered to Chinese officials at either Amoy, Ningpo or the Pei-ho for transmission to the Imperial government. It may be noted that there is no mention in the above of the opium trade as such. No British government, indeed, could have embarked on a war to protect such a disreputable trade. The so-called 'Opium War', about to start, was in fact fought in reprisal for past injuries to British subjects, to defend the right to legitimate trade and to regularize the position of British officials and subjects in China. In the state of mutual incomprehension existing between East and West, however, the Chinese government saw themselves simply as crusaders against the sale and smoking of opium.

The first naval units began assembling in the Pearl River Estuary in June 1840 under Commodore Sir James Bremer with his broad pendant in HMS *Wellesley* (74). Confident that this presaged an attack on Canton, Commissioner Lin took energetic steps to put his defences in order, gathering sixty war junks, replacing the obsolete guns in the Bocca Tigris forts with two hundred new foreign guns and establishing other fortified batteries, while booms of iron chains were placed ready to block the river. The fleet, however, merely blockaded the estuary and, as soon as Admiral Elliot had joined in the *Melville* (74) and taken over command, the expedition sailed north up the coast.

An effort to deliver Palmerston's letter at Amoy under a flag of truce was met by gunfire from the shore in reply to which the frigate *Blonde* bombarded and silenced the batteries. At Ningpo the letter was accepted by officials but they refused to forward the original version to Peking. Meanwhile Chusan Island and its chief city, Ting-hai, had been occupied without opposition. Leaving a garrison there, the fleet sailed on and arrived off the Pei-ho on 8 August. Here they were courteously received by the Governor General of the province, Ch'i-shan, who accepted the letter and forwarded it to the Emperor.

News of the capture of Chusan and of the blockade of the coasts had by this time reached Peking and, for the first time some inkling of the forces unleashed against him by Lin's actions was borne in on the Emperor. Up to now Lin had been encouraged in his aggressiveness; but a powerful threat within a hundred miles of Peking caused a complete change of heart. In a letter couched in bitter and furious terms, the Commissioner was dismissed and recalled to Peking in disgrace where he was fortunate to avoid a death sentence, being exiled instead, to the bleak frontier town of Ili.

Ch'i-shan was now given the perilous task of negotiating for the Emperor from a position of hopeless weakness. With only the Manchu 'bannermen' for troops – soldiers still armed as they had been when they overthrew the Ming armies two hundred years earlier – with cannon of the same date and with no Imperial navy, he had virtually no defence against the British expedition. Yet he could not inflict on the Son of Heaven the humiliation of acceptance of the British terms. His object, he realized, must be initially to get the intrusive barbarians to return to Canton where, at a safe distance from Peking, at the outer fringe of the kingdom, and where apparently strong defences had been organized, negotiations could be carried on under more equal conditions. Though he refused to agree to the justice of the demand for compensation for the confiscated opium, he agreed that punishment for the molestation of British subjects should be meted out to the responsible officers. And if the mission would return to Canton to continue negotiations with a representative of the Emperor on the other conditions they demanded, Ch'i-shan indicated, a sum of money that would satisfy the British would undoubtedly be forthcoming.

To Ch'i-shan's delight, the two Elliots, deceived by his honeyed words and influenced no doubt by the approach of the bitter northern winter, agreed with this proposal. On their way south they stopped to inspect the garrison on Chusan; the ravages of disease which the troops had suffered during the summer months (448 of the European troops alone had died) made a deep impression and persuaded them that, to avoid prolonged hostilities, they should be prepared to accept easier terms than those so categorically laid down by Palmerston. The Rear Admiral now fell sick himself and sailed for home, leaving Captain Elliot once again in sole authority.

By the middle of November the latter was back at Macao, while Ch'i-shan, whose handling of the crisis had impressed the Emperor, was appointed Commissioner in the place of the disgraced Lin. With the immediate threat to Peking removed, the Emperor's confidence returned. Ch'i-shan was instructed to be apparently conciliatory and to drag out negotiations while Chinese forces were mobilized. That negotiations had been nothing but an elaborate charade became clear to Elliot at the beginning of January when Ch'i-shan finally informed him that Imperial approval for the cession of the island of Hong Kong or even for the opening of trade at other ports than Canton would never be obtained. For four months Elliot, accepting the responsibility of the 'man on the spot', had modified his demands to a level far below those laid down in his instructions. Now he had no choice but to press hostilities to obtain satisfaction. On 7 January 1841 he ordered the fleet to attack the forts of Ch'uan-pi and Tyocktow which faced each other at the mouth of the Pearl River.

In the bombardments which followed, the newly arrived iron paddle steamer *Nemesis* (captained by Lieutenant William Hall, one of the first British naval officers to make a study of steam), armed with a large cannon at bow and stern, played a conspicuously successful role, as she was destined to do on numerous occasions in the future. New and revolutionary features had been introduced into sea warfare by steam power and iron ship construction. By the end of the day both forts had been captured at the cost of thirty-eight men wounded ; and on the eighth the *Blenheim* (74) led the fleet into the Bocca Tigris to attack the inner forts. They were met by a Chinese emissary ; Elliot, anxious above all for as speedy and bloodless a settlement as possible, in face of such ineffective resistance called off the attack and released the prisoners captured on the seventh. Ch'i-shan now agreed to sign the 'Ch'uan-pi Convention' which provided for the cession of Hong Kong, an indemnity of $6 million, direct, equal intercourse between the officials of the two countries and the reopening of Canton to trade. In return, Elliot agreed to the evacuation of Chusan. These terms were far below those laid down as imperative by Palmerston and news of them was in due course to earn Elliot a stern rebuke followed by dismissal from his post.

At the same time even these terms were more than Ch'i-shan could himself ratify by affixing his seal. All he could do was to memorialize the throne for approval. The Emperor, far removed from the demonstrations of Chinese helplessness in the face of British sea power, was merely enraged at his luckless Commissioner who, in his turn, was recalled to Peking in chains, stripped of his rank and, like Lin before him, banished to exile on the bleak northern frontier of the Empire. In his place the Emperor's nephew, I-shan was despatched as Imperial Commissioner and as 'barbarian-suppressing general' in command of a large force of troops.

Elliot had meanwhile taken official possession of Hong Kong on 26 January 1841, while Chusan had been evacuated. When efforts to obtain ratification of the Ch'uan-pi Convention failed and evidence accumulated of Chinese efforts to repair and re-arm the forts and to obstruct the river with chains and floating booms, hostilities were resumed. Commodore Bremer took the fleet up the Bocca Tigris and once again on 25 February the forts were smashed and captured, Admiral Kuan being one of a large number of Chinese killed. Two days later an advanced division, with the aid of the *Nemesis* and another steamer, pushed on up to the second bar at Whampoa. In a spirited action, much of it conducted from armed boats of the squadron, the boom was cut, the entrenched camp covering it was assaul-ted and a Chinese force of some 2,000 driven off with heavy loss. The squadron then anchored at Whampoa.

Once again Elliot sought to reach agreement with the Commissioner. An armistice was called on 3 March ; but it was quickly apparent that the Chinese were simply playing for time ; on the seventh the advance up river was resumed and by the eighteenth all defensive works below the city of Canton had been neutralized. Another armistice, lasting until the middle of May, during which many of the British merchants moved back into the factories, ensued. The promulgation of Imperial edicts breathing defiance and threats, and news of preparations for war being made in the north soon made it clear that no settlement was intended. On 19 May, Elliot ordered his entire force up river and prepared to besiege the city. British subjects were embarked in the cutter *Louise* and a schooner, the *Aurora*, and narrowly escaped with their lives when an attack by fire-rafts was launched and batteries on shore opened fire on them. In the confused action which followed, during which the fire-rafts were grappled and towed clear by boats of the British warships, the *Nemesis* was here, there and everywhere and, in spite of being for a time disabled, succeeded in silencing the shore batteries and destroying a large number of war junks and boats.

On 24 May the expeditionary troops were landed in two divisions. Four forts on the heights overlooking the city were assaulted and captured. Meanwhile the artillery was deployed and, by the twenty-seventh was ready to open a cannonade. Then, once again, the Chinese asked for terms. Elliot, ever ready to reach an agreement with a minimum of fighting and anxious to free the troops ready for the second expedition to the north which he by now realized would be necessary if a genuine treaty was to be extracted, once more called a halt and agreed to evacuate. Chinese troops were similarly to be withdrawn sixty miles from Canton and a ransom of $6 million paid for the city. The question of a full ratification of the cession of Hong Kong would be postponed. A final proof that a solution of the Chinese problem would never be found through confrontation at the periphery of the Empire came when the armistice was broken by a treacherous attack by some 10,000 Cantonese on the British troops withdrawing to the west of the city, a catastrophe being narrowly averted by the timely intervention of a party of Royal Marines. The subsequent retirement of the whole expeditionary force to Hong Kong was represented by the Chinese as a victory over the barbarians.

By this time the official appointed by the British government to supersede Elliot, Sir Henry Pottinger, had left England in company with Rear Admiral Sir William Parker, the new Commander-in-Chief East Indies and China Station. Their instructions were to bypass Canton, reoccupy Ting-hai, seize strategic places in the Yangtse Estuary and, if necessary, push on to the Pei-ho to open negotiations for an extension of trading to ports other than Canton, for guarantees of security for British subjects in China and for an outright cession of Hong Kong. They reached Macao on 2 August 1841 in the HEI Co. steam frigate *Sesostris*, and on the twentieth, together with Major General Sir Hugh Gough in command of the troops, they sailed north with an expeditionary force composed of two 74-gun ships-of-the-line, eight smaller warships, four steamers and twenty-one transports with 2,700 troops. Arriving off Amoy on the twenty-sixth they occupied the port, dismantled the defences and, leaving troops to garrison the island of Kulangsu overlooking the town and harbour, sailed on to Tinghai.

Not until nearly the end of September did the cumbersome fleet of sailing ships reach the Yangtse Estuary; but then Ting-hai and Ningpo were soon recaptured before the troops went into winter quarters at the latter. None of this led to any progress towards negotiations with the Chinese government. During the winter each side gathered reinforcements, Pottinger's force increasing to twenty-five sailing warships, fourteen steamers and an army of some ten thousand besides artillery. It was the Chinese, however, who re-opened hostilities in the spring with a heavy attack on Ningpo. In the fighting that followed, when the attackers were repulsed with considerable slaughter, the naval squadron played an important part, particularly the steamships with their unprecedented mobility in the riverine waterways.

Similar attacks on Chinhai and Chusan were anticipated and dealt with before the expedition sailed into the Yangtse Estuary, anchoring off Woosung on 13 June 1842 and, having forced the entrance of the Woosung river, ascended it to occupy Shanghai on the eighteenth. The fleet, which included ten paddle steamers, with transports carrying nine thousand soldiers and Royal Marines, now entered the Yangtse-kiang proper and, making slow and laborious progress against the strong current, anchored on 19 July off the inland port of Chinkiang, strategically vital at the junction of China's largest river and the Grand Canal linking North China with the grain-producing provinces. Two days later the army was landed and, though they met a stubborn defence by the Tartar troops of the garrison, who having first killed their wives and children finally committed suicide rather than surrender, were soon in possession of the city.

Preparations were now made for an advance up river to the southern capital, Nanking. By this time, however, the hopelessness of any attempt at defence against the modern weapons of the barbarians, the loss of face suffered by the governing Manchus and the consequent danger of overthrow of their rule by the Chinese were at last realized by the provincial officials who persuaded the Emperor to open peace negotiations. The Tartar Generals of Canton, Ch'i-ying and I-li-pu, were nominated Imperial Commissioners, and were authorized to treat with the barbarians.

Profiting from his predecessor's frustrations, Pottinger completed his preparations for an attack on Nanking and refused to negotiate until Ch'i-ying could produce 'full powers' from the Emperor ; but as soon as this was done negotiations were quickly completed and on 29 August 1842, on board HMS *Cornwallis*, the formal Treaty of Nanking was signed. The principal terms, besides payment of an indemnity to cover military expenses, compensation for the destroyed opium and repayment of the Hong merchants' debts to British traders, permitted the opening of Canton, Amoy, Foochow, Ningpo and Shanghai to trade and residence of British consuls and merchants with their families ; the outright cession of Hong Kong ; the acceptance of equality in official correspondence ; and a fixed tariff to replace the arbitrary and unpredictable tariffs previously imposed. The actual figure of this tariff was fixed by a Supplementary Treaty of the Bogue in October 1843 which also established the right of extra-territoriality by allowing British consuls to try their own subjects for criminal acts, and gave British warships the right to anchor at any of the 'treaty ports' to protect commerce and control their sailors.

The Americans and the French were soon demanding equal rights ; the Chinese were in no position to deny them, nor were they averse from playing off the different breeds of barbarian against one another. In July 1844, therefore, the Treaty of Wanghsia with the United States of America was signed and in October of the same year the Treaty of Whampoa with France.

In the meantime relations between the Chinese, represented by Ch'i-ying (who had become sole Imperial Commissioner on the death of I-li-pu in April 1843), and the British, represented by Pottinger, had been conducted on terms of unprecedented, mutual equality and informal friendliness. Ch'i-ying's attitude, which demonstrated itself in the exchange of lavish entertainment, gifts and expressions of affection, arose out of deliberate efforts to 'soothe and tame' the barbarians, as was made clear eventually when he was constrained to explain his conduct to the Emperor on being accused by anti-foreign officials of excessive obsequiousness. Pottinger, on the other hand, responded from a genuine admiration for Chinese civilization and an understanding, though not an acceptance, of the Imperial assumption of suzerainty over all barbarian nations.

Pottinger was replaced, however, in May 1844 as Superintendent of Trade and Governor of Hong Kong by Sir John Davis, an 'old China hand' and servant of the East India Company, and the happy atmosphere cooled considerably. When the Cantonese refused to allow foreigners to stray beyond

the bounds of the factory area, Ch'i-ying, as head of the governing Manchu officialdom, had insufficient power to discipline
the mob which on various occasions stoned British excursionists
in the city. Davis considered that freedom of movement within
a reasonable distance of the treaty ports was implicit in the
terms of the Treaty of Nanking and the Supplementary Treaty.
Ch'i-ying thus found himself caught between British pressure
to permit entry into Canton and the stubborn resistance of the
inhabitants.

The situation was eased for a time when Davis agreed to
postpone the exercise of the right to enter Canton so long as
Ch'i-ying, on the Emperor's authority, admitted it in principle.
But rioting and clashes between foreigners and Cantonese
continued to occur with deaths occurring on either side. When
Ch'i-ying made an unsatisfactory reply to British demands in
April 1847 for culprits to be punished, Davis called up a naval
and military force of three steamers, a brig and 900 soldiers
which proceeded up river to Canton capturing all the forts and
spiking the 827 guns mounted in them without the loss of a
man. Davis presented an ultimatum to Ch'i-ying as a result of
which he agreed that British subjects would be protected from
molestation, the aggressors in previous riots punished and steps
taken to minimize the threat by the Cantonese mob to the
factories.

The controversy was still festering however, when Davis and
Ch'i-ying were both replaced in the spring of 1848, the former
by Sir George Bonham, the latter by the fiercely anti-foreign
Hsü Kuang-chin. Bonham's efforts to re-open the question and
obtain permission for British entry into Canton met with
stubborn obstruction. Lord Palmerston instructed him not to
force the issue and when Bonham informed Hsü that the matter
would 'remain in abeyance', it was heralded as a triumph both
by the Emperor and his Manchu officials and by the Cantonese
Chinese populace. At Palmerston's orders Bonham issued
stern warnings that British forbearance should not be mistaken
for weakness and reminding Peking of the consequences of such
a mistake in 1839.

The warning was contemptuously dismissed without a reply
being sent. In spite of this a conciliatory attitude was maintained by Bonham and his successor, John Bowring, who

became Governor of Hong Kong in 1852 and met the same blank resistance to all demands for an interview with Hsü's successor Yeh Ming-ch'en. Meanwhile, however, the patience of the French and American governments as well as that of the British was wearing thin and there was a common desire to install resident ministers in Peking to evade the screen of obstruction raised at Canton and to negotiate an extension of trade beyond the five treaty ports. By the terms of the French and American treaties of 1844, a revision might take place in 1856; British rights to 'most favoured nation treatment' would consequently entitle them to any similar revision of the Treaty of Nanking.

When the representatives of the three countries sought to discuss the matter with Yeh in 1854 they were sharply rebuffed; they thereupon decided to travel north and present their demands for treaty revision at the Pei-ho. Two important factors had by this time developed which were to affect negotiations. Much of China was under the control of the Taiping rebels who had reached the vicinity of Tientsin during the previous winter before being repulsed; while Britain and France, involved in the Crimean War, were in no position to press their claims to the point of hostilities.

The envoys anchored in the Pei-ho on 15 October 1854 and, after some preliminary exchanges, were met on shore near the Taku forts guarding the entrance by an Imperial Commissioner to whom Bowring presented eighteen heads of a proposed new treaty. These included the establishment of a resident minister at Peking or at least regular visits to the capital, the right of access by envoys and consuls to the *yamens* of Viceroys, including Canton, and the right of British subjects to enter Canton as had been promised in the agreement of 1847. Of numerous clauses regulating trade, one called for the legalizing of the opium trade to replace the existing chaotic system of bribery and connivance by local mandarins. Another clause provided for co-operation in the suppression of piracy.

To almost all of these demands the Imperial Commissioner returned a blank refusal even to forward them to Peking. The envoys retired, having achieved nothing beyond demonstrating once and for all that only war or the threat of it could bring the Chinese to see reason. For the time being, however, the British government could only order Bowring to exercise moderation. Nevertheless during 1855 the three treaty powers reached agreement to co-operate in a forward policy though any actual demonstration of force was ruled out by the inadequate naval power available.

News of the conclusion of the Crimean War reached China in May 1856. During that year the treaty powers were finally convinced that force must be used : the French owing to the persecution of their missionaries (contrary to a provision of the Treaty of Whampoa), which had culminated in the murder of one of them in February : the Americans by the insulting return of a Presidential letter addressed to the Emperor : the British by Commissioner Yeh's flat refusal to discuss any revision of the Treaty of Nanking. When Bowring recommended the deployment of a force at Tientsin the following summer, the British government requested the Admiralty to supply the necessary strength to the Commander-in-Chief, China Station, Rear Admiral Sir Michael Seymour, who was instructed to co-operate with Bowring. All seemed set for an amphibious expedition in the spring of 1857. But on 8 October 1856 an incident occurred at Canton concerning a small vessel, the *Arrow*, to set hostilities prematurely in motion, to give them the misleading name of the 'Arrow War' and thus somewhat disguise their true origins as specifically British and concerning only a minor dispute ; whereas the basic conflict really arose, as it always had done, from China's refusal to acknowledge the great nations of the West as her equals.

The *Arrow* was a small vessel engaged in carrying goods and passengers around the Pearl River Estuary between Canton, Macao and Hong Kong. She was owned by a Chinese resident of the British colony where she was registered and, consequently, was entitled to fly British colours. Under the Supplementary Treaty of 1843, should the Chinese authorities wish to arrest a Chinese serving in such a ship, even in Chinese territorial waters, they had to apply to the British Consul, who would examine the man and hand him over.

When, therefore, the *Arrow*, lying in the river at Canton, was boarded by a Chinese police 'posse', the Red Ensign hauled down and twelve of her Chinese crew carried off bound, an illegality had clearly been committed. The Consul, Harry

Parkes, young and forceful but already imbued with the importance of maintaining face as well as the details of protocol in dealing with the Chinese, at once addressed a firm protest to Commissioner Yeh Ming-chen, demanding the public release of the twelve crewmen and a written apology. During the next fortnight negotiations between Parkes and Yeh progressed from the latter's initial flat refusal, through a stage when an offer to release nine of the arrested men was rejected by the Consul to finally, on 22 October, the return of all twelve, but not in the public manner demanded ; nor were they accompanied by an apology. On the following day the first shots of the Arrow War were fired when British naval units captured and dismantled the four Barrier Forts between Whampoa and Canton.

Even now, the *Arrow* incident might have taken its place as just another of the repetitive episodes in the uneasy relations between the Cantonese and foreigners if Parkes' superior, Sir John Bowring, had not decided to make use of it to reopen the question of entrance into the city of Canton. While awaiting Yeh's inevitable rejection, a slow but continuous bombardment on the city wall of Canton and on Yeh's *yamen* was opened on 27 October by a single gun from HMS *Encounter* firing one shell every five or ten minutes. The wall having been breached, a force of British seamen and marines was marched through the *yamen* on the twenty-ninth, succumbing to the temptation to loot and pillage – in which they were accompanied by Americans from the factories and by their intoxicated Consul triumphantly waving the Stars and Stripes.

But though the guns of Admiral Seymour's ships dominated the sea approaches to Canton and the river, the British lacked the military force necessary to occupy the city, from which they withdrew. And, as Yeh adamantly refused even to negotiate, a stalemate set in over the next two months with local British forces mounting attacks such as that on 4 December which captured the fort on French Folly, an island in the river below Canton. The Cantonese mob burned down the foreign factories on 15 December, while Commissioner Yeh invoked wholesale murder in Hong Kong by placing a price on the head of every Englishman and encouraging the poisoning of the break supply with arsenic.

Both the French and American ministers were in agreement with the British attitude : the former, however, had not the means available to give active aid, while Dr Peter Parker, the American, could not overtly make common cause without definite instructions from Washington. Nevertheless, when the American flag was fired on by the barrier forts which had been re-occupied by the Chinese, the latter ordered two US men-of-war to silence the offending batteries.

Meanwhile the British and French governments had decided to mount a joint expedition with the French contingent under the orders of Baron Gros as Plenipotentiary while Lord Elgin was similarly appointed in April 1857 as British Plenipotentiary and leader of the whole expedition. Delays were caused by the outbreak of the Indian Mutiny which absorbed most of the British troops detailed and it was not until December 1857 that the Anglo-French force assembled at Hong Kong. Commissioner Yeh, summoned to open direct negotiations with the two Ambassadors on the question of the right of entry into Canton, remained defiant ; on 28 December bombardment was opened and on the following day the city was stormed. On 5 January Yeh was captured, placed on board HMS *Inflexible*, and soon after shipped to Calcutta where he was to die a year later.

Lacking the man-power or organization to control the teeming and turbulent population of Canton, the Allies soon decided to set up a puppet regime under Po-kuei, the Manchu Governor, with law enforcement entrusted to a mixed English-French-Chinese police force. These arrangements worked well and were to remain in force until the end of the war three years later.

The expedition was now free to go north. The American and Russian governments had agreed to send representatives to participate in a peaceful demonstration and the four Ambassadors arrived off the mouth of the Pei-ho on 15 April 1858. As usual, the Chinese representative who met them lacked plenipotentiary powers. Futile negotiations ensued until 20 May when the Governor General of the province was notified that the British and French envoys intended to force their way to Tientsin. The sizeable Anglo-French force which had by this time assembled thereupon captured the Taku forts at the river mouth with little difficulty and few casualties and, on the thirtieth, Elgin and his colleagues arrived at Tientsin to find that, at last, two Imperial Commissioners with power to negotiate had been sent from Peking to meet them.

Even now, however, the first and principal of the Allied demands, the establishment of Embassies in Peking, was the subject of endless prevarication. Deadlock had been reached when there arrived in Tientsin ex-Commissioner Ch'i-ying, the old friend of Pottinger. He had been brought out of banishment by the Emperor to exercise once again his famous charm in 'soothing' and 'restraining' the tiresome barbarians. The Imperial plan was all too apparent, however, and when Ch'i-ying's Memorial of 1844, in which he boasted of his success in hoodwinking the barbarians, and which had been captured amongst Yeh's papers at Canton, was read out to him, the old and ailing man broke down and wept with shame. Ch'i-ying withdrew from Tientsin without Imperial permission ; arrested and sent in chains to Peking, he was condemned to death by suicide.

Negotiations dragged on until the patience of the Allied envoys ran out and, on 26 June 1858, the Hon. Frederick Bruce, Lord Elgin's brother and secretary, informed the Imperial Commissioners that the proposed treaty must either be signed before nightfall or the Allies would march to Peking to enforce signature. The ultimatum was accepted and the Treaty of Tientsin concluded that day between China and Britain. Russia and the United States, having only demanded the right of occasional visits to Peking by their Ambassadors, had been able to conclude Treaties on 13 and 18 June, respectively. The French Treaty, which also dispensed with the right to permanent residence at the capital, was concluded on the twenty-seventh. Under the rule of 'most-favoured-nation' treatment, however, each of the powers acquired the same rights as the British. The senior Imperial Commissioner, Kuei-liang, fearful of the consequences to himself of acceptance of the terms, hastily explained to the Emperor that this was only a ruse whereby the foreign warships could be removed from Tientsin where they threatened the capital and lay athwart its grain supply route : thus persuaded, the Emperor gave his approval on 3 July.

In addition to the vexed question of residence in the capital, the Treaty provided for the opening of ten new ports, including Nanking, Hankow, Kiukiang and Chekiang on the Yangtse River ; foreign travel in all parts of China under passport issued by the appropriate consul and countersigned by Chinese authorities ; a limitation of inland transit dues for foreign imports ; an indemnity to Britain and France to defray the cost of their expedition ; and freedom of movement in all China for Christian missionaries. The exchange of ratifications was to take place in Peking a year later.

It seemed that, at last, the Chinese Empire had acknowledged the political equality of the barbarian nations of the west. Lord Elgin departed for Japan where he was to conclude a similar treaty. He returned to Shanghai in October 1858 for a further conference to fix the customs tariffs. This was successfully staged in an atmosphere of notable goodwill, marked by the conclusion of a 'gentleman's agreement' between Elgin and Kuei-liang that if the British envoy bearing the ratification were properly received at Peking, the Ambassador would visit the capital only occasionally. When Elgin finally left for England after a trip up the Yangtse to Hankow, disturbed only by an exchange of gunfire with Taiping rebels at Nanking, he was confident that the Emperor intended to abide by the terms of the Treaty of Tientsin.

Elgin's brother, Frederick Bruce, had meanwhile been appointed Ambassador with instructions to exchange the ratifications at Peking and subsequently reside at Shanghai. He arrived in China in May 1859 only to find Kuei-liang and his fellow Commissioner Hua Sha-na at Shanghai and pressing for ratification to be exchanged there. Bruce and his French colleague, M. de Bourboulon, refused to be thus deflected from their purpose or even to meet the Commissioners ; they sailed on to the Pei-ho where they anchored outside the shallow tide-waters of the Taku Bar, beyond which lay an Anglo-French force of sixteen British warships (thirteen of them steam gunboats) under Admiral Sir James Hope, and two French warships. Also in company was the new American envoy, Mr J. E. Ward in a ship of the US Navy. Although he was in agreement with the aim of his colleagues and bent on being formally received in Peking, he was not empowered to use force to achieve his object.

The mouth of the Pei-ho was obstructed by booms of heavy logs lashed and chained together. When requests to the Chinese authorities to open these to permit passage of the envoys to Tientsin were ignored, the Admiral gave three days' warning of his intention to destroy them. The interval was unfortunately not utilized to reconnoitre the defences thoroughly. Hope rashly presumed that they would be no more effective than Chinese forts so easily dealt with in the past. He was thus rudely awakened to his mistake when at 2.30 pm on 25 June a storm of accurate cannon-fire from the forts on either bank of the river fell upon the gunboats struggling to destroy the second boom, including the *Plover* in which he had hoisted his flag.

In the three-and-a-half-hour artillery duel which ensued, the ships suffered heavily ; four gunboats had to be run aground within range of the forts and others retired damaged. The Admiral himself had been wounded and knocked out. His second-in-command, Shadwell, seeing that the cannon fire from the forts had slackened, took the disastrous decision to attempt to storm them using a landing party from the ships. The tide had ebbed, leaving hundreds of yards of mud to be crossed by the attacking troops under heavy rifle fire. All but a handful who managed to reach cover close in under the walls of the southern forts were killed or wounded. The fall of darkness, enabling a retreat to be organized, saved them from total annihilation.

Distressed spectators of the *débâcle* had been the American flotilla whose orders prevented them from taking part. Their senior officer, Commodore Tatnall, however, seeing the desperate plight of some British launches laden with wounded, sent one of the small steamers of his command to tow them to safety. 'Blood is thicker than water' was the Commodore's famous comment justifying his technical breach of neutrality.

When it was all over the British casualties were eighty-nine killed and 345 wounded ; three of the gunboats were total losses, others were patched up for passage to Hong Kong for repair. There could be no question of a renewal of the attempt to force a way up river. British prestige had taken a painful knock. Bruce and Bourboulon retired to Shanghai.

Bruce had received, on the morning of Admiral Hope's

attack, too late to countermand it, a proposal from the regional Viceroy that he and his mission should abandon their intention of proceeding up the Pei-ho to Tientsin. Instead they were invited to take a back way to the capital, landing at Pei-t'ang some dozen miles further up the coast from Taku. Apart from the lateness of the invitation, Bruce looked on it as a move to cause the Ambassadors to lose face and even to reduce their status to that of tribute-bearing vassals as in the past.

How right he was (though he was to be reprimanded by the Foreign Secretary for his use of force) was demonstrated when the US envoy, Ward, accepted the alternative route and was subjected to treatment which bordered on the insulting during his journey to the capital ; he failed to obtain an audience to present the President's letter because he refused to make the kneeling and head-knocking kowtow, or even to kneel at all. Finally the ratifications of the US Treaty of Tientsin took place at Pei-t'ang with the Governor General of Chihli.

The Ch'ing dynasty seemed suicidally bent on refusing to acknowledge the equality of the governments of the western barbarians. Britain and France remained determined to establish theirs by exchange of ratifications in Peking using force, if necessary, to obtain a free passage. In the following year Lord Elgin and Baron Gros were once again appointed Plenipotentiaries and supported by an expeditionary force of forty-one warships and 143 transports carrying 11,000 British troops with a further 6,700 French troops.

The Taku forts were on this occasion to be properly out-flanked and attacked from their landward side. During the first week of August 1860 the Allied army was landed at Pei-t'ang whence it advanced to capture the town of Tangku, upstream of the forts on the north bank on the fourteenth. From this position under cover of artillery support, British and French troops assaulted, in the face of stiff opposition, and captured the inner fort, at the cost of some 400 casualties. The remainder then surrendered and the expedition steamed up river to find Tientsin undefended. An Allied army some 4,000 strong slowly advanced thence to Peking. Unfortunately a party which had been detached to reconnoitre was arrested by the Chinese. The captives were subjected to torture, some being barbarously executed. In retaliation Elgin gave orders for the Emperor's

Summer Palace, outside Peking, to be burned, an operation accompanied by disgraceful looting by the troops. The Allied army of 4,000 defeated 20,000 Chinese troops that barred the way ; but Chinese resistance persisted until the Allied artillery was deployed to bombard the city, when at last the Emperor's brother, Prince Kung, left in Peking to take charge of the peace settlement, gave way. On 24 October, Elgin was carried in state in a large, impressively decorated sedan chair with an escort of 500 troops to a ceremony in the Hall of Audience in which the Treaty of Tientsin was finally ratified and a Convention of Peking signed. Under its terms, the indemnity was increased, Tientsin was opened to foreign trade and residence and the Kowloon Peninsula, opposite Hong Kong, was annexed by Britain. A similar ceremony was performed by Baron Gros on the following day.

The Allies were by this time anxious to get away, urged by the Russian Ambassador, Ignatiev, who had been playing a somewhat equivocal role in the proceedings and now wished for a clear field to negotiate territorial concessions for Russia in the Amur region in the north. The Anglo-French force left Peking on 8 November 1860 ; on 14 November, Ignatiev secured the Supplementary Treaty of Peking by which Russia not only obtained confirmation of previous territorial gains north of the Amur, which the Ch'ing Emperors had hitherto refused to recognize, but also the possession of the land east of the Ussuri River which was to become the Maritime Province of Russia.

8

OPENING OF JAPAN —
SINO-JAPANESE WAR

The appearance in our narrative of a Russian Ambassador at the court of the Ch'ing Emperor reminds us that the opening up of intercourse between China and the West had been following a landward as well as a maritime route. The landward advance by the Russians had reached the River Amur in the early years of the Ch'ing dynasty, the city of Nerchinsk being founded in 1658; but there it had been halted. Over the next two hundred years, repeated efforts to establish diplomatic relations, with envoys accepting the performance of the kotow, led to an exchange of missions between 1725 and 1732, the Chinese mission being the first ever to be sent abroad; and though no permanent Russian Embassy had evolved, a religious mission to Peking had been permitted and trade concessions obtained.

In the early nineteenth century the Russians took advantage of Chinese preoccupation with the Opium War to penetrate the Amur Region and in 1858 intimidated the Manchu governor into signing the Treaty of Aigun by which Russia obtained the territory on the northern banks of the Amur and Sungari Rivers and joint possession with China of the land east of the Ussuri River to the sea. It was the confirmation of this treaty that Ignatiev secured as a reward for his mediation between the Anglo-French envoys and the Ch'ing court, as soon as the former withdrew from Peking.

It was at this stage, marked by the foundation of the port and city of Vladivostok, that Russia began to take a notable part in the development of sea power in the Pacific, a process which was to rise to a climax in the Russo-Japanese War forty-four years later.

Russia had, indeed, attempted on previous occasions to establish herself as a Pacific power. In 1725 Peter the Great had commissioned the Danish navigator Vitus Behring to explore the coasts of Siberia. During 1728 Behring had sailed through the straits which bear his name to prove that Siberia was not, as had been thought, connected to America. In a further expedition in 1740 he discovered the Kurile and Aleutian Islands and, crossing to Alaska, explored its coast.

A Russian expedition under Commander Krinizin and Lieutenant Levaschev renewed this eastward move in 1768-9, visiting the Aleutian islands and Alaska where fur factories and fisheries were established. Inspiration for further Russian expansion came from Baranov, a man of immense drive and iron will who had dreams of a great Russian empire in the Pacific region, and in 1796 became Managing Director of the Russo-American Company. In his post he established himself as a virtually unchallenged ruler of the whole Russo-American coasts for the next twenty-three years. North of the Spanish possessions the American Pacific coasts were uninhabited by Europeans at that time ; further south, sea power had been little exercised since the decline of Spanish power in the eighteenth century. Pirates or buccaneers, claiming as a rule to be privateers on the strength of dubious 'letters of marque and reprisal', had roamed the seas seizing Spanish merchantmen and raiding the Spanish-American ports.

The long struggle by the colonists for independence from Spain had begun in 1811. Spanish rule was ineffectual ; Baranov perhaps saw Russia as Spain's successor. In 1812, on his advice, Captain Kuskov set up a factory on the shores of Spanish California not far from San Francisco and a fortified base at Port Ross.

Three years later Baranov encouraged the Russian adventurer, Sheffer, to attempt the establishment of a Russian colony as a fortified base in the Hawaiian Islands. These schemes were brought to nought by the firm attitude of the Hawaiian King Kamehameha at the instigation of his English adviser.

When Baranov died in 1819 on his way to St Petersburg to put his schemes to the Tsar, the inspiration for a Russian Pacific empire died also and though several Russian expeditions of exploration were launched during the next ten years which discovered numerous Pacific islands, they led to no concrete expansion. The Tsar Alexander I stated a Russian claim to the Oregon region in 1821 which gave rise to the announcement in 1823 by President Monroe, on the initiative of the British Foreign Minister, Canning, of the Monroe Doctrine against any further colonization of the American continent or the introduction of European 'systems'.

Russian expansion overseas thus checked, the Russo-American Company was dissolved and Alaska sold to the United States in 1867. This did not put an end, however, to Russian desires to wield sea power in the Pacific. Ambitions to absorb Korea and Manchuria into her sphere of influence called for a Russian squadron to be stationed in the Far East and thus for an ice-free naval base. How this was to lead eventually to a decisive naval war for maritime supremacy in the area will be studied later. First, however, one must examine the emergence of the modern state of Japan, which was to be Russia's antagonist in that struggle.

While the insufferably disdainful Chinese (or more strictly, perhaps, their Manchu rulers) were being slowly and painfully forced to open their gates to the despised barbarian traders, across the Yellow Sea repeated efforts by the same barbarians even to communicate with the almost totally secluded Japanese had met with blank rebuffs. Since 1637, when the Tokugawa Shogun Iyemitsu issued his famous edict, Europeans had been forbidden to land in Japan under penalty of death ; the same penalty faced any Japanese who went abroad. The only exception had been the Dutch who, as a reward for their assistance to the authorities during the extermination of the Christian rebels, had been permitted to maintain the trading post on Deshima Island under the humiliating conditions described by Captain Pellew after his illicit visit to Nagasaki in 1808.

Although the Dutch post had supplied a narrow chink through which a dim conception of western civilization had percolated, Japan had remained in almost total ignorance of the great advances made outside her borders in industry, military and economic science and philosophical thought. In all respects she had remained at the stage of development reached at the beginning of the seventeenth century.

The United States government had in 1837 sent a ship, the

Morrison, with a trade mission to Uraga at the entrance to Tokyo Bay, but the Shogun's officers had ordered her to leave. When she appeared off Kagoshima in Kyushu she was driven off by the cannons of the Satsuma *Daimyo*. In 1845, HMS *Samarang* similarly failed to gain admission. Commodore Biddle, USN, arriving with two ships at Uraga in 1846, unsuccessfully tried to forward to the Shogun copies of the Treaty of Nanking. Two years later HMS *Mariner* met with another firm rebuff.

Then in 1853 came the famous mission by Commodore Perry, USN, and his 'Black Ships', the USS *Sausquehanna*, *Saratoga*, *Plymouth* and *Mississippi*, which arrived at Yokohama in July with a letter from the President of the United States for 'The August Sovereign of Japan'. Whether this was intended for the *de facto* sovereign, the Shogun, or the *de jure* Emperor who was still immured in his palace in Kyoto, it was the Shogun's representative who finally accepted it and was informed that Perry would be back in the spring for an answer. And it was the Shogun's ministers who signed a Japanese-American Treaty of Amity and Friendship with Perry when he returned with an imposing fleet of seven ships in February 1854. By this treaty the ports of Shimoda in southern Honshu and Hakodate in Hokkaido were to be opened for trade. In the same year Rear Admiral Sir James Stirling, at Nagasaki with four British warships, signed a similar Anglo-Japanese treaty. Russia and the Netherlands secured the same trading rights in 1855 and 1856, respectively.

More exacting treaties were negotiated in 1858 by the first American envoy, Townsend Harris and by Lord Elgin, fresh from his successful conclusion of the Treaty of Tientsin, whereby the ports of Yokohama, Nagasaki, Niigata, Kobe and Yedo (Tokyo) were opened to trade and foreign residence, customs tariffs were fixed and consular jurisdiction over their own nationals (extra-territoriality) accepted. Similar treaties with the Netherlands, France and Russia followed.

By concluding these treaties the Shogun infringed the rights of the Emperor. He also antagonized the conservative elements amongst the dominating warrior class (Samurai). The resultant anti-foreign movement with its slogan 'Honour the Emperor and expel the barbarians' was taken over by the four principal western *Daimyos* – leaders of the Satsuma, Choshu, Hizen and Tosa clans – who were bent on restoring the Emperor. The Shogun's hold on the country was weakened ; several of his ministers were assassinated. In September 1862 an Englishman who was deemed not to have shown sufficient respect to the Satsuma *Daimyo* was set upon and killed by the Samurai escort of the *Daimyo*. When reparation was refused, a British fleet bombarded the Satsuma capital, Kagoshima, inflicting great damage and destroying Japanese shipping in the harbour. During 1863 batteries in the Shimonoseki Straits, in the Choshu fief, repeatedly fired at foreign ships ; when the Shogunate admitted it was powerless to discipline the *Daimyo*, a combined fleet of British, French, American and Dutch warships attacked, silenced the batteries and exacted a promise of good behaviour from the chieftain and the payment of an indemnity.

Brutal as these reprisals were, they served to bring home to the Emperor and his foreigner-hating supporters the need for Japan not only to enter into intercourse with Europeans who could no longer be contemptuously thought of and referred to as 'red haired barbarians', but also to modernize herself militarily and industrially and to accept international relations on terms of equality to protect herself from such acts in the future. The Imperial consent was, therefore, given to the Shogun's treaties in October 1865. Meanwhile the Satsuma and Choshu feudatories carried on a civil war against the Shogun and in November 1867 the latter, without waiting for his inevitable final defeat, surrendered his authority to the Emperor.

The Tokugawa era had ended. The Meiji era, named after the young Emperor who had come to the throne in the same year, was about to begin. One of the Emperor's first acts, on 6 April 1868, was, in the presence of the *Daimyos* and the aristocracy, to take the solemn Charter Oath before the Shrine of his Ancestors which promised a popular assembly in which all measures of national policy should be decided, the opening of public offices, civil and military, to all, the abolition of outdated methods of government and justice, and the seeking of knowledge from wherever it existed for building up the foundations of the Empire.

From this moment the transformation of Japan from a medieval into a modern state proceeded at a breath-taking speed. In 1869 the 273 *Daimyos* surrendered their feudatories to the Emperor and became government officials administering their former lands. Within two years the whole feudal clan system had been dismantled with the *Daimyos* deprived of all governing powers but, with the court nobles, graded as peers (later divided into ranks as in the monarchies of the West), while their two million Samurai retainers, though graded as gentry, were dismissed with token pensions which forced them into trade or the civil professions to earn a living. The rest of the population, the commoners, for the first time found themselves not merely privileged to bear arms but, indeed, compelled to do so under a system of compulsory military service designed to establish a modern navy and army on European lines.

Turning to Germany for training and equipment of their army and to Great Britain for ships and naval instructors, the Japanese soon knew themselves to be the leading oriental military power and began to stretch their muscles. The first to feel their strength were the Chinese. Although the humiliating defeats leading up to the enforced treaties with the western powers had opened their eyes to the need to acquire western military and commercial skills and a 'self-strengthening movement' was set on foot under the guiding hand of the all-powerful minister Li Hung-chang, the Chinese people and their Manchu rulers lacked the martial ardour and the sense of purpose that raised the Japanese so rapidly to modern military and industrial power. Arsenals were founded at Shanghai, at Foochow and Nanking where small ships were built and guns manufactured. Chinese students were sent abroad, a naval academy founded at Tientsin and a steam navy, built abroad, was commissioned, or rather four separate navies – at Canton, at Foochow, in the Yangtse River and (in the north) the Peiyang fleet. Only the last of these was under the direct control of the Peking government.

Such an arrangement was an inadequate basis for sea power and when, in 1874, a Japanese expedition was sent to Formosa to exact retribution for the murder of some Ryu-kyu sailors by Formosan aborigines, the Chinese were unable to take any effective steps to protect this overseas outpost of their Empire. Actually the whole basis for the Japanese action was in Chinese eyes false. For the Ryu-kyu Islands had been a regular tributary of China since 1372. But the Japanese Lord of Satsuma had, unknown to the Chinese, subjugated them in 1609, since when the island king had been also a tribute-paying vassal of Satsuma.

Negotiations, in which the British minister to China, Thomas Wade, acted as mediator, led to a settlement by which China paid an indemnity of half a million dollars and agreed not to condemn the Japanese action. This latter concession tacitly implied Chinese acceptance of Japanese sovereignty over the Ryu-kyus and five years later this was confirmed by Japanese formal annexation.

In 1875 it was the Koreans' turn to clash with the newly-awakened aggressive power. Though Christian missionaries had, in spite of periodic persecution, spread their faith widely in the kingdom since the second half of the eighteenth century, the Koreans had successfully resisted all Western efforts to promote trade or establish diplomatic relations. In 1866, following a sweeping massacre of Christian priests, the French had sent a punitive expedition of seven ships and six hundred men which captured Kangwha near Seoul, but after suffering more than thirty casualties in a skirmish outside the city, withdrew. An American merchant ship seeking trade was destroyed and the crew killed in the same year. An American squadron sent to investigate the matter in 1871 steamed into the Han River, on which Seoul lies ; on being fired on by shore batteries, the ships bombarded the city of Kangwha on two successive days but then withdrew, their mission unfulfilled.

To the Japanese, Korea represented either a natural stepping stone to their penetration of the mainland or a pistol pointing at the heart of their country. They soon determined it should be the former. An expedition to force diplomatic and trade relations was planned ; a surveying team with gunboat escort began charting the approaches to the Korean capital in 1875, and when this was fired on, the gunboats retaliated, destroying the Korean forts. A squadron of six Japanese warships appeared. The Chinese government was at that time in no state to interfere on behalf of its tributary state. The Korean Regent was instructed to negotiate and the Treaty of Kangwha, 24 February 1876, was the result. Not only was Korea thereby opened to diplomatic and commercial relations with Japan, but she was recognized as an independent state on an equal footing with Japan and, in the absence of any protest by China, was thus freed of her ancient vassalage.

When the United States concluded a similar treaty in 1882, the Koreans took the opportunity, in a separate statement, voluntarily to acknowledge Chinese suzerainty ; and it was under the auspices of the Chinese government that the treaty and those with Britain, France and Germany which followed it were concluded. Nevertheless Japan soon became influential in Seoul, operating in support of Queen Min, to reform the government and modernize the army, and against the reactionary Regent, Taewongon. In 1882 the latter provoked a rising during which the Japanese legation was burned, seven Japanese officers were killed and the minister forced to flee to Japan.

Both Chinese and Japanese warships arrived to enforce a pacification. The Chinese envoy arrested the Regent and deported him to China. A settlement with Japan was patched up, the most significant feature of which was the establishment of the Japanese right to station troops for the protection of the legation. The Chinese government, however, now took steps to re-assert suzerainty. Extra-territoriality for their nationals was one of the terms of a commercial treaty ; six Chinese battalions were stationed in Korea and a young Chinese officer, Yüan Shih-k'ai, who was in the years ahead to play a leading role in the history of China, was appointed to train the Korean army.

Pro-Chinese and pro-Japanese factions now grew up and in December 1884 the latter, encouraged by the Japanese minister and aided by the Japanese legation troops, staged a revolt in which the royal palace was broken into and the king captured. Yüan Shih-k'ai's troops gained the upper hand, however ; the Japanese, facing annihilation, set fire to their legation and, formed into a square with their wounded and womenfolk in the centre, fought their way through the winter night to the coast.

With a technique that was to become only too familiar, the Japanese made the incident an excuse for sending an expedition to enforce payment of compensation while at the same time a Sino-Japanese Convention was concluded at Tientsin. By its terms both Chinese and Japanese troops were to be withdrawn ; but, deeply significant for the future was the mutual agreement that either China or Japan might send troops into Korea for the restoration of order provided they gave each other prior notice. For the time being, however, Chinese influence was supreme with Yüan Shih-k'ai virtually Governor of Korea.

But the Japanese, growing ever stronger on land and sea, were biding their time, while China, for lack of adequate sea power suffered a humiliating defeat when she attempted to oppose French aggression in Vietnam. Annam, as Vietnam was then called, was an ancient tributary state of China. Tribute missions had been sent to Peking even after the French had annexed the three southern provinces (Cochin-China) following the despatch of a punitive expedition to Saigon in 1859 on account of attacks on missionaries. She established a virtual protectorate over the remainder by another treaty in 1874. French troops were stationed in North Vietnam and fortresses built along the Red River. They were opposed by an irregular Chinese 'Black Flag' army, a remnant of the rebel Taiping army which from 1850–64 had controlled much of China and came near to unseating the Ch'ing dynasty. Regular Chinese troops were also surreptitiously sent to Tonking.

The fighting on land that followed was sporadic and indecisive. But when on 23 August 1884 the French Rear Admiral Courbet, with a squadron consisting of three powerful armoured cruisers and nine smaller ships attacked the Chinese Foochow squadron of one iron vessel, six wooden sloops, two armed transports, two gunboats and a number of war junks, the huge French superiority of force made the encounter into little more than a military execution. It took a mere forty-five minutes, following which the French guns were turned destructively on the arsenal and the defensive forts. The French fleet went on to occupy Keelung in Formosa and the Pescadores.

Meanwhile a blockade of the Yangtse River estuary and stoppage of the tribute grain from South China to the capital had been undermining the warlike resolution of the Empress Dowager ; when a serious defeat of the French army in Tonking offered a face-saving opportunity, a peace treaty was negotiated in June 1885, which recognized France's position in Annam.

Yet another ancient tributary was lost to China in the following year when Burma became a British protectorate. Japanese hunger for a share in the apparent break-up of China strengthened their determination to possess themselves of Korea when the moment was ripe.

In 1894 an uprising by a Korean religious sect known as the Tongkaks, assisted by agents of the Japanese secret society, Genyōsha, caused the Korean government to appeal to Yüan Shih-k'ai for help. A force of about 2,500 Chinese infantry was landed at Asan on the Korean west coast. This was the moment the Japanese had been waiting for : a balanced army eight thousand strong was immediately transported to Chemulpo.

Li Hung-chang turned to the western powers for mediation. Proposals by the British and Americans were rejected by the Japanese and, with war imminent, the Chinese chartered three British steamers to carry reinforcements to Asan. Two of these, escorted by the small protected cruiser, *Tsi-Yuen*, and the sloop, *Kwang-Yi*, reached Asan safely ; but as the two warships put to sea again on 25 July 1894 to return to Taku, they were intercepted by the Japanese Flying Squadron of three fast light cruisers, *Yoshino*, *Naniwa* and *Akitsushima*, under the command of Rear Admiral Tsuboi who had orders to stop the transport of troops to Korea, if necessary by force, and to deal with any Chinese warships met, though war had not yet been declared.

In the unequal fight that developed the Chinese were overwhelmed, the *Tsi-Yuen* being heavily damaged, though she was unaccountably allowed to limp away to the Chinese naval base of Wei-hai-wei ; the little sloop was forced to beach herself, where she was quickly destroyed. While the *Yoshino* was chasing the *Tsi-Yuen* off the scene, there came in sight two more ships. These were the chartered Jardine and Matheson steamer, *Kowshing*, carrying 1,200 Chinese troops, twelve guns and two Chinese generals, and her escort the 572-ton sloop *Tsao-kiang*. The sloop was quickly induced to surrender to the *Akitsushima*.

The *Naniwa*, commanded by Captain Heihachiro Togo (who eleven years later was to be the hero-admiral, victor at the Battle of Tsu-shima), meanwhile signalled the *Kowshing* to stop and, having ascertained that she was carrying troops, ordered her to follow the cruiser. When the British master signalled that the Chinese would not allow him to comply and requested

Togo to take off the Europeans on board, the Japanese captain declined on the grounds that his boat might be attacked. Four hours of unproductive signalling was brought to an end when the *Naniwa* opened fire at point blank range and sank the *Kowshing*. The British officers were picked up by the *Naniwa's* boats; some 512 Chinese managed to swim ashore or cling to wreckage, but loss of life was heavy.

War between China and Japan was formally declared on 1 August. As with all wars, this one would inevitably be concluded by the victory of one of the opposing armies; but the decision would have already been secured at sea, on the local control of which depended the support and supply of both. For although Korea was connected to China at its landward frontier, road communications were so primitive as to be of little use for the despatch of reinforcements or supplies.

That only by battle with the opposing fleet could such an essential control be secured was not understood by Li Hung-chang, who forbade Admiral Ting Ju-ch'ang, commanding the Peiyang fleet, to proceed to the east of a line drawn from his base at Wei-hai-wei to the mouth of the Yalu River. The Japanese fleet arrived off Wei-hai-wei on 10 August and bombarded its forts, but the challenge was not accepted; the Chinese ships remained in harbour. Thus Admiral Ito, the Japanese Commander-in-Chief, was left undisturbed to convoy his land forces to Korea where such a Japanese superiority was quickly built up that the Chinese army was defeated and driven north.

Admiral Ting was now ordered to escort a troop convoy to the Yalu from Port Arthur. This was successfully achieved; but it was off the mouth of the Yalu that Admiral Ito arrived on 17 September 1894, placing himself between Ting and his bases and forcing the Chinese admiral to accept the battle he had professed to desire. Ting at once put to sea and cleared for action.

The two fleets were, on paper, evenly matched. Indeed, to the school that believed that the heavily armoured battleship mounting four 12-inch guns was the arbiter of naval battles, the Chinese was the more powerful. For Ting had two of these, the *Ting Yuen*, his flagship, and the *Chen Yuen* as well as eight cruisers mounting guns varying in calibre from 10.2-inch to

5.9-inch. None of these guns was of the quick-firing type which had been invented seven years earlier.

The Japanese fleet under Admiral Ito was divided into a Main Squadron under his personal command and a fast Flying Squadron under Rear Admiral Tsuboi. The biggest ships of the Japanese Main Squadron were three unarmoured cruisers, *Matsushima* (Ito's flagship), *Itsukushima* and *Hashidate*, which mounted but one 12.6-inch gun each. The remainder of the squadron consisted of two cruisers *Fuso* and *Hiyei*, ancient veterans built seventeen years before, carrying a few antiquated guns, and one, the *Choyoda*, armed with nothing bigger than 4.7-inch guns, but of the quick-firing type.

Rear Admiral Tsuboi's flag flew in the cruiser *Yoshino*, a fine modern ship of 4,150 tons with 6-inch and 4.7-inch quick firers. With him were three other fast cruisers ; *Takachiho* and *Naniwa*, mounting two 10.2-inch guns and six 6-inch each, and the *Akitsushima* which, like the *Yoshino*, carried only quick-firing guns of 6-inch and 4.7-inch calibre. None of these ships was armoured, but even the slowest could make nearly nineteen knots, a good speed at that time.

So far it might seem that the Japanese fleet was much too weak to think of facing the heavy guns of the Chinese. On the other hand all the Japanese ships except *Takachiho*, *Naniwa*, *Fuso* and *Hiyei* carried between ten and twelve quick-firing guns, either 6-inch or 4.7-inch. A meeting between the two fleets might show which of the rival theories was right – that of the believers in the massive blow of a few big guns, or the contrary theory that many quick-firers would smother the slow-firing, big-gun ships before they could score many hits.

When the time came, however, the test was not to be so clear-cut. There were several reasons for this. The Japanese fleet was a highly trained and skilful force, whereas the Chinese, who a few years previously had achieved a high state of efficiency under the guidance of Captain W. M. Lang of the British Navy, had reverted on his departure to the condition of glossed-over incompetence usual in the armed forces of the Empire. The ships were kept outwardly smart and well-painted, but behind this facade there were half-empty magazines and unpractised gunners. Troubles in the shell factories had led to indifferent bursting charges, or even cement and coal dust inserted in their place.

Furthermore, Admiral Ting had a faulty conception of naval fighting tactics based on the outcome of the Battle of Lissa, fought twenty-eight years earlier, in which the Austrian victory had been won by a frontal, line abreast attack on the Italian line, and an eventual recourse to the ram. The fact that the big guns of his two battleships could all fire ahead increased Ting's faith in such a method. He had completely overlooked the fact that guns had greatly increased in range and effectiveness since Lissa, so that a fleet which awaited such an onslaught in line ahead would have a considerable gun advantage for a long period during the approach. The ram had consequently ceased to be a practical proposition.

Such were the two fleets that now steered for an encounter ; the Japanese at about ten knots, which was the best that *Fuso* and *Hiyei* could achieve, the Chinese at a knot or two faster. Ito's fleet was in line ahead with the Flying Squadron in the van. Besides the major units there were present two ships of little or no fighting value, the gunboat *Akagi* and an armed merchant steamer *Saikio Maru*, which were to prove an embarrassment to Ito. It is not clear why the Japanese admiral did not send such vulnerable ships away to the southward, where they would have been clear of the battle. Instead he stationed them on the port side of his Main Squadron, the side away from the enemy.

Meanwhile Ting's squadron was approaching on a south-westerly course in a formation somewhat similar to Tegetthoff's at Lissa, with the two big ships in the centre. But owing to tardiness in getting under way, the two starboard wing ships were lagging, while on the other wing one of the Chinese cruisers, the *Tsi-Yuen*, was well behind and unable to get up into station. In fact, viewed from the Japanese ships, the Chinese squadron seemed to be in considerable disorder.

The tactics of the two admirals were soon evident. At the long range for those days of six thousand yards, the Chinese opened fire with their big guns. With calm confidence the Japanese held their fire, and indeed they could well afford to do so ; for with the rapidly changing range making shooting difficult, the unpractised Chinese gunners failed to score a single hit during the approach.

The Japanese line drew steadily across the Chinese front until the Flying Squadron was able to pass round the starboard wing, and at a range of three thousand yards open a withering fire from their quick-firers on the wing ships of the Chinese formation. Their Main Squadron now came into action, passing close ahead of Ting's flagship and the *Chen Yuen*, which bore down as though to ram, both battleships being heavily shot up in the process. The whole of Ito's squadron except the *Hiyei*, the rear ship, passed safely round the northern flank of Ting's line, and Ito then led round to starboard, circling the now completely disorganized Chinese fleet and keeping up a punishing fire to which only a feeble reply was made.

Indeed the Chinese had more than the enemy's fire with which to reckon. Dense funnel smoke, increased by that from a hundred guns, enveloped the whole scene. The laggard *Tsi-Yuen*, coming up at last, plunged into the smother and ran amok, colliding with two ships of her own side, sinking one and so damaging another that it steamed away blazing to be beached. The *Tsi-Yuen* herself then withdrew to Port Arthur, where her captain subsequently paid for his actions with his head.

Meanwhile the *Hiyei*, unable to follow the Japanese Main Squadron round the Chinese flank, boldly turned to pass through the Chinese. Avoiding two torpedoes fired at her and which strangely enough hit nothing in spite of the milling throng of ships, the *Hiyei* won through, though suffering considerably in the process.

The two weak Japanese ships, *Akagi* and *Saikio Maru*, also cut off, kept on across the Chinese front, the former being badly battered. Seeing this, Rear Admiral Tsuboi led the Flying Squadron round to port to come back and cover them. This brought a temporary relief to the Chinese ships, but by the time Tsuboi had completed his turn the Chinese found themselves between two fires, Ito to the eastward and the Flying Squadron to the north-westward.

By now Ting's squadron was in desperate straits. Apart from the victims of the *Tsi-Yuen's* wild career, two other cruisers, smothered by the rapid fire of Tsuboi's 6-inch and 4.7-inch guns, had gone down. Yet another had struggled away burning furiously, ultimately to be run aground near Port Arthur. Ting was thus left with only four of his original ten ships, all of which had suffered severely and had shot away nearly all their ammunition.

Complete annihilation of the Chinese squadron was in Ito's grasp. The Japanese had not achieved this without damage to themselves, however ; in particular Ito's flagship *Matsushima* had been hit twice by 12-inch shells, once by a 10.2-inch, suffering more than a hundred casualties, and had been set on fire. By the time Ito had transferred his flag to the *Hashidate* and despatched the *Matsushima*, *Hiyei*, *Akagi* and *Saikio* to base for repairs, the sun was sinking low ; and as dusk fell, the two fleets disengaged and formed up on parallel courses in line ahead.

A renewal of the fight might now have wiped out the Chinese force, but a new element had entered the situation. The two torpedo-boats of Ting's squadron had joined him from the Yalu. This caused Ito to decide to await the dawn before completing the enemy's annihilation, and in the night Ting slipped away with his surviving ships, which included his two battleships. Nevertheless the Japanese had won a considerable victory, and had secured control of the disputed sea area, making certain of victory on land. There the Japanese were able to occupy Dairen and to capture the fortified base of Port Arthur by attacking the forts from the rear. They went on to capture Wei-hai-wei in February 1895, turning the guns of the forts on the damaged remnants of the Peiyang fleet. Admiral Ting committed suicide ; the fleet surrendered.

Li Hung-chang, the inspirer of the Self-strengthening Movement by which China had hoped to withstand further foreign aggression, but which had failed primarily because the Chinese public service was so riddled with corruption and incompetence, was disgraced and dismissed. He was reinstated, however, at Japanese insistence upon an envoy of sufficient stature being sent to negotiate a peace settlement. The Treaty of Shimonoseki which was finally signed on 17 April 1895 provided for recognition of Korean independence and termination of tribute to China ; a large indemnity ; the opening of four more Chinese ports ; Japanese right to open factories and engage in industry in China ; finally, and most ominously, the cession to Japan of Formosa, the Pescadores and the Liaotung Peninsula on which Port Arthur and Dairen were situated.

For the moment Japan had in spectacular fashion burst out of her backwardness and obscurity to claim an equal status with the western powers. Great Britain had already offered a treaty revision to abolish her extra-territorial rights and during the next few years her example was followed by other powers. But Japan was now to suffer a humiliating set-back on her road to great power status, one which was to colour her attitude ever afterwards.

9

CAUSES AND OPENING MOVES OF
THE RUSSO-JAPANESE WAR

Hardly was the ink dry on the Treaty of Shimonoseki when the brilliant triumph of the Japanese was shattered by the receipt of a diplomatic note from Germany and Russia, backed by France, 'advising' the Emperor that possession of so large an area of China as the Liaotung Peninsula by a foreign power would be detrimental to peace in the Orient. Thinly disguised verbal threats, particularly by Germany, made it clear to the Japanese, whose resources had been depleted by the China war and whose navy was by no means that of a first-class power, that a dignified compliance was the only course open to them.

On 30 November 1895, therefore, having destroyed the defences of Port Arthur, they returned the territory to China. The wound to Japanese pride was deep and painful. It called for vengeance as soon as the time was ripe ; and the call was soon to be intensified. In 1896, Russia, having come to China's aid with a loan to help her pay her war indemnity, induced her to conclude a treaty permitting the Russians to complete their railway to the Far East by constructing a line through Manchuria to the Pacific port of Vladivostok. The strip of territory on which this Chinese Eastern Railway ran was leased to Russia, who had the right to station her own defensive police along it. A secret clause of the treaty bound the two countries in a mutual defensive alliance against any Japanese attack on China, Korea or the Russian Far East.

Any idea that Russia had altruistic motives in apparently ranging herself alongside China was soon exploded. When in 1897, to enforce reparation for the murder of two missionaries in the interior of Shantung, the Germans occupied the port of Kiaochow and then extracted a ninety-nine-year lease of it as a naval base, the Russians sent a squadron of warships to Port

Arthur on the pretext of defending China against Germany. By March 1898 they had secured a twenty-five-year lease of the Liaotung Peninsula and the right to build a railway joining Port Arthur to the Chinese Eastern Railway with a branch line to the Korean border. Port Arthur itself was garrisoned and steps taken to turn it into a naval base and fortress of immense strength.

This humiliation of Japan was not lessened by Great Britain's compensating lease of Wei-hai-wei for twenty-five years and of the New Territories behind Kowloon for ninety-nine, and a French ninety-nine-year lease of Kwangchow Bay as a naval base. But the Japanese government had already taken the first steps towards revenge by the expansion of her fleet to make it the equal of any in the Orient. The first two of a squadron of modern battleships, the *Fuji* and the *Yashima*, had been launched from British yards in 1896 and were to be followed by four more.

That the eventual opponent for this rapidly expanding navy would be the Russian Far East Fleet was made more certain by events in Korea. There the ineptitude of the Japanese represent-atives had led to the adamant opposition of the King and Court dominated by the Queen, to the widespread reforms forced on them. In October 1896 a Japanese-inspired and -assisted rising in Seoul, the capital, resulted in the capture of the palace, the savagely cruel slaughter of the Queen and her entourage and the flight of the King and the young Crown Prince who took refuge in the Russian Legation where they remained for the next two years.

The Russians took advantage of the situation to obtain from the Japanese an agreement for an equal division of influence and rights, including that of stationing troops in Seoul, while at the same time concessions were secured from the King. One of the latter was the right to cut timber in a huge stretch of country covering the whole length of the Korean side of the border from sea to sea, which was to be of great significance later. When Russia's naval experts pointed out that Port Arthur was of little value as a base owing to its separation from Vladivostok by a long sea passage through the narrow Korean Straits dominated by the Japanese Navy, a Russian naval squadron arrived at Masanpo on the south coast of

Korea in May 1899 to establish a base there in the first-class, land-locked fleet anchorage. The Russian plans were temporarily halted by the purchase by a Japanese subject of the land dominating it. But diplomatic pressure, backed by the threatening presence of Russian cruisers at Chemulpo, the port of Seoul, was renewed in the following year. In reply, Japan made open preparations for war, and at last it became clear to the Russians that a base on the Straits of Korea could be obtained only by fighting for it. Russia was not prepared to fight and so was forced to accept the unsound strategic position which she had brought upon herself by her acquisition of Port Arthur.

The Boxer Rebellion in China, essentially an anti-foreign rising fostered by 'nationalist' elements in protest against the annexations of Chinese territory by foreigners, meant that all countries with a stake in China combined to restore order. These countries naturally included Japan. With her expeditionary force which fought alongside those of European countries and America, Japan demonstrated the high state of training and efficiency her army had achieved under German guidance. Her troops made a great impression upon all who saw them.

Russia, blindly pursuing her course of aggrandisement at the expense of China, used the Boxer Rebellion as a pretext to station as many as a hundred thousand troops in Manchuria, and on conclusion of the troubles it became clear that the Russians intended to make such an arrangement permanent. Furthermore, by means of a Russo-Chinese Bank, they planned to gain control of the whole of the finances of the Empire.

By now Russia's ambitions were antagonizing and alarming all the powers. America came down firmly against the proposed financial agreement. Then, on 30 January 1902, as a result of negotiations which had been held in strict secrecy, England and Japan announced the conclusion of an alliance whose object was the preservation of the independence and integrity of China and Korea and equal opportunities in those countries for the commerce and industry of all nations. The terms of the alliance laid down that if either party had to go to war with a third power in defence of its interests in the Far East, the other would maintain strict neutrality and use its efforts to prevent other powers from intervening against its ally ; and if any such power did intervene, then the neutral party would come to the assistance of its ally, and give actual military assistance.

At last it was borne in on Russia that she would be completly isolated in any dispute with Japan, and that the sympathies of Europe and America were ranged against her. She bowed to the storm. On 8 April 1902 she signed a treaty with China, by the terms of which Russia would evacuate Manchuria in three stages of six months each, leaving China to take responsibility for the safety of the railway and the protection of Russian subjects and establishments in the province.

It was a complete and a startling change of front on the part of Russia. Though she retained her hold on the Liaotung Peninsula, it was quickly apparent that the men in power in Russia had genuinely abandoned all plans for adventurous military expansion.

Japan met the new Russian attitude half-way with proposals for a formal understanding about Korea. Both powers would undertake not to use any port of Korea for military or strategic purposes ; both would mutually guarantee the integrity of China and Korea. In return for a recognition by Russia that Japan had exclusive interests in Korea, Japan would acquiesce in the Russian possession of the Liaotung Peninsula, and recognize her right to take any action necessary to protect her railway.

It began to look as though a solution to Far Eastern tensions might be in sight. While negotiations were in progress, the first six-month period in the promised evacuation of Manchuria expired, and in October 1902 Russia faithfully honoured her obligations to withdraw her troops from the southern part of the province. There was further evidence of Russia's good faith in the fact that no efforts were made to improve the defences or facilities of the naval base at Port Arthur, whereas vast sums were expended on the purely commercial harbour of Dairen. Indeed, Port Arthur necessarily ceased to be of great value if the occupying power did not have control of the hinterland or any good landward communications.

But for all the honeymoon atmosphere, neither side altogether trusted the other. Japan had been devoting a great proportion of her limited resources to building up her armed forces, the naval share of the increase being represented by a building programme which would bring the fleet by 1903 up to six new battleships, six armoured cruisers as good as any of their class anywhere, and eight light cruisers. However, there were no further additions to be expected, so that if war had to come, it would suit Japan for it to come not later than 1904.

During 1903 the Russians, appreciating this, despatched sufficient ships to match those of the Japanese fleet, in numbers, at any rate. These comprised three battleships, one armoured cruiser, seven cruisers, two light cruisers and seven destroyers. Two further battleships, two cruisers, one old armoured cruiser and seven destroyers from the Mediterranean were also under orders for the Far East at the end of 1903.

Meanwhile, the Russo-Japanese negotiations in St Petersburg were not going too smoothly. Though the three chief Ministers of the Russian State, Count Lamsdorf (Foreign Minister), Witte (Minister of Finance) and General Kuropatkin (War Minister), were at one in a desire for peaceful development in the Far East, each for good reasons of his own, a combination of political force was rising which was to overwhelm them. It was a strange alliance of the semi-religious devotion to 'Holy Russia' of the Tsar and his entourage, and the self-interest of a group of ambitious financiers.

The former, observing Japan's increasing influence with the Chinese government, became obsessed with the idea of the Yellow Peril, which was having a vogue in certain European circles at that time.

The latter was under the leadership of a M. Bezobrazov who had acquired the timber-cutting concession on the Korean frontier. The promised evacuation of Manchuria would leave this immensely valuable concession void of any Russian protection, and in the unsettled condition of the country it could not be exploited. Representing this to be a great blow to Russian national aspirations, Bezobrazov obtained the support of the grand dukes and the court. He then went further, and obtained from the local Chinese governor a similar concession on the Manchurian side of the border.

In spite of this, the power of the three ministers was for a little while unshaken, and preparations for the second stage of the evacuation of Manchuria went ahead. Kuropatkin, visiting Tokyo in July to get the feel of the situation for himself, was vastly impressed by the progress of Japanese armed strength. He reported that Japan was no light adversary to provoke, and that Russian intrigues on the Korean border were being taken very seriously.

But Kuropatkin's absence from the capital was fatal to the peace party. By the time he got back to St Petersburg he found that the Court had fallen under the sway of the 'patriotic' clique headed by M. Pleve, the rival of M. Witte for power. From this time onward matters drifted inexorably towards war, though Japan offered concessions. Behind the backs of Lamsdorf, Witte and Kuropatkin, still officially the chief ministers, it was suddenly announced that the whole Far East had been constituted into one province with Admiral Alexeieff, a leader of the 'patriotic' clique and Governor of Port Arthur, as Viceroy.

Kuropatkin at once asked to be relieved of his duties, and Witte was replaced by Pleve. It became clear that Russia was bent on defying Japan and proceeding with her policy of expansion in Manchuria. Only blind ignorance of the realities of the naval situation can have led her to such a course. Her Far Eastern squadron was not only still weaker in numbers than the Japanese, but also its ships were a mixed force, unaccustomed to working together; its crews were ill-trained, and morale was low under the uninspiring leadership of its commander, Vice Admiral Stark. On the other hand Japan's fleet, with its six battleships and six armoured cruisers of homogeneous design and its greatly superior torpedo-boat force, was in all respects ready for war; under its able and energetic leader Admiral Togo, it was only too ready for a fight.

Moreover, the whole strategic position was in Japan's favour. So far as Russia was concerned, the two bones of contention, the Liaotung Peninsula and Korea, were isolated at the end of interminable, primitive lines of communication. The two Russian naval bases, Port Arthur and Vladivostok, were similarly cut off from each other by land, and their sea communications blocked by the Japanese-dominated Straits of Korea. Furthermore, to defeat Japan the Russians would have to invade the island empire, whereas the occupation of Korea and the Liaotung Peninsula would gain the Japanese their objective.

Thus success for either side would depend absolutely upon

command of the Yellow Sea in the early stages, when Japan could be expected to be landing her armies in Korea and on the Liaotung Peninsula. In the long run command of the Sea of Japan would also be necessary if Russia wished to send her armies across to Japan. But unless the Russians divided their fleet between Port Arthur and Vladivostok, the Japanese would be left a free hand to attack one or the other. In any case, Port Arthur lacked facilities to base more than a portion of the Russian Far Eastern squadron.

The Russians were therefore forced back on the conception of keeping a 'fleet in being' at Port Arthur, which though it could not hope to wrest command of the Yellow Sea from the Japanese, could hold it in dispute sufficiently to limit Japanese landings to the southern half of Korea, so delaying their advance on Manchuria long enough to allow Russia to gather her armies for the defence of Port Arthur. Meanwhile the presence of a diversionary force of three armoured cruisers and one protected cruiser at Vladivostok would prevent any Japanese military threat in that area. Finally, Russia's Baltic fleet would be despatched to the Far East, its combination with the Port Arthur squadron making a fleet far superior to anything which the Japanese could muster.

Yet in spite of the difficulties from which Russian plans suffered owing to her lack of sufficient naval force in the Far East, the despatch of reinforcements was put in train with a lack of energy and administrative efficiency only too typical of the Tsarist Russian navy. A battleship, two cruisers and seven destroyers were still in the Mediterranean area when war finally broke out.

By the beginning of January 1904, it was clear to the Japanese that the Russians were simply dragging out negotiations in order to gain time to improve their military situation. The Japanese therefore went ahead with final preparations for a landing in Korea. But they too wished to delay the final outbreak of war, for in the Mediterranean a strange comedy was being played out.

At Genoa were lying two armoured cruisers recently completed for the Argentine Navy and which Japan had bought, renaming them the *Nisshin* and *Kasuga*. At the same time a Russian squadron consisting of the battleship *Oslyabya* (flagship of Rear Admiral Virenius), the armoured cruiser *Dmitri Donskoi*, the protected cruiser *Aurora* and seven destroyers, was passing through the Mediterranean. So when the *Nisshin* and *Kasuga*, flying the Japanese naval ensign though commanded for the passage by British Naval Reserve officers – arrived at Port Said, they found the whole Russian squadron in harbour there, except for the *Dmitri Donskoi*, which had already entered the Suez Canal.

The situation was not without piquancy. Had the Russian admiral possessed a spark of initiative, he could have taken the rest of his squadron through the Canal in time to shadow the Japanese cruisers and hold himself ready to attack them if war should break out. But it was not until six days later that the last of Virenius's squadron mustered at Suez, and then they loitered for the next few months in the Red Sea, not daring to face the risk of being intercepted on passage to Port Arthur or Vladivostok.

By 2 February *Nisshin* and *Kasuga* were at Singapore under orders to sail not later than the sixth. The last obstacle to the opening of hostilities had been cleared from the Japanese path. The troops for the landing on the west coast of Korea at Chemulpo were already embarked in their troopships. The fleet was concentrated at Sasebo under Admiral Togo. Sealed orders were held by general and admiral and on the afternoon of 5 February 1904 the two commanders received instructions to open the orders.

So the die was cast. As the squadrons filed out of Sasebo harbour in line ahead the following morning, to the 'banzais' of an enthusiastic population ashore, a war had begun which was to take Japan, a brief fifty years after her awakening from medieval slumber, into the front rank of world powers. In St Petersburg, however, negotiations still went on in desultory fashion and an absence of good faith on either side, so that it was not until 8 February that the Japanese ambassador finally asked for his passports and announced that his mission would leave on the tenth. Before that time had come, guns and torpedoes had proclaimed the outbreak of war without benefit of formal declaration.

The Japanese naval staff plan for the opening moves of the war had originally visualized a bold attack, using the whole

Japanese fleet, on the Russian squadron in Port Arthur. They expected the Russian ships to come out and offer battle in an attempt to gain control of the Yellow Sea, which was of such vital importance to both sides. The movement of the expeditionary force would await the outcome of this battle. Togo, however, saw clearly that by using his main fleet as a covering force for the troop convoy, the landing could be proceeded with at once without risk, particularly as he correctly judged that the Russian squadron would not, in fact, seek a decisive battle while their paper strength was no greater than that of the Japanese.

Having seen the convoy safely on its way with an escort of cruisers and torpedo boats, Togo pressed on to Port Arthur, where the war was to open with a surprise torpedo attack by his flotillas, under cover of darkness, on the Russian fleet which he expected to find lying in the Roads.

With the first shots of the war about to be fired, it is a convenient moment to examine the relative strength of the opposing fleets. The Japanese were divided into three squadrons, of which the first two, under the supreme command of Admiral Togo, sailed north to cover the troop convoy and subsequently to challenge the Russian fleet in Port Arthur.

They consisted of the following ships :

1ST SQUADRON

1st Division : battleships *Mikasa* (flag of Vice Admiral Togo, Commander-in-Chief), *Asahi*, *Fuji*, *Yashima*, *Shikishima* and *Hatsuse* (flag of Rear Admiral Nashiba) ; main armament of each, four 12-inch ; secondary armament ten or fourteen 6-inch

3rd Division: cruisers *Chitose* (flag of Rear Admiral Dewa), *Takasago*, *Kasagi* (each two 8-inch and ten 4.7-inch) ; *Yoshino* (four 6-inch and eight 4.7-inch)

Three divisions of four destroyers each mounting two 18-inch torpedo-tubes, two 12-pounders and four 6-pounders

Two divisions of four torpedo-boats each mounting three 18-inch torpedo-tubes

133

2ND SQUADRON

> *2nd Division:* armoured cruisers *Idzumo* (flag of Vice Admiral Kamimura), *Adzumo, Asama, Yakumo, Tokiwa* and *Iwate* (flag of Rear Admiral Misu) ; each mounting four 8-inch and twelve or fourteen 6-inch guns
>
> *4th Division:* cruisers *Naniwa* (flag of Rear Admiral Uriu), *Takachiho* and *Niitaka* mounting six or eight 6-inch and *Akashi*, two 6-inch and six 4.7-inch guns
>
> Two destroyer divisions of four boats each, with two 18-inch torpedo tubes, two 12-pounders and four 6-pounders
>
> Two divisions of torpedo-boats as in first squadron

A third squadron of old, obsolescent ships under Vice Admiral Kataoka was charged with holding the Straits of Korea against any sortie by the Russian Vladivostok squadron.

The Russian fleet was divided into two sections also. At Port Arthur under Vice Admiral Stark there were the following:

> *Battleship Division:* Petropavlovsk (flag of Vice Admiral Stark), *Tzesarevitch, Retvizan, Sevastopol, Peresviet* (flag of Rear Admiral Prince Ukhtomsky), *Pobieda* and *Poltava* ; main armament four 12- or 10-inch ; secondary eleven or twelve 6-inch
>
> *Cruiser Division:* Askold (flag of Rear Admiral Reitzenstein), twelve 6-inch ; *Bayan* two 8-inch, eight 6-inch ; *Diana* eight 6-inch ; *Pallada* eight 6-inch ; *Boyarin* six 4.7-inch ; *Novik* six 4.7-inch
>
> Two torpedo-gunboats and twenty-five destroyers mounting two or three 18-inch torpedo-tubes, one 12-pounder and three or five 3-pounders
>
> At Vladivostok there were the three armoured cruisers *Gromoboi* (flag of Rear Admiral Stakelberg), *Rossya* and *Rurik*, mounting four 8-inch and sixteen 6-inch guns, the protected cruiser *Bogatyr*, twelve 6-inch, and seventeen torpedo-boats

At first sight the two fleets were well matched. Though the Japanese had a superiority in cruisers, they were unlikely to be found concentrated at the moment of battle owing to their escorting and patrolling commitments. The Russians had a superiority of one in the main battle line.

The Russian fleet was strong enough on paper to make Togo anxious to reduce its strength before meeting it in battle. He could not even afford to lose ships in a drawn fight, for at the other end of the world Russia's other fleet was being prepared for the Far East. Its arrival and junction with the Port Arthur squadron could decisively alter the balance in Russia's favour.

Quantity alone in ships and guns is no sure guide to relative strength. To the Japanese homogeneous squadron of fast battleships, each capable of eighteen knots, each mounting four 12-inch guns, the Russians opposed a squadron limited by the speed of two of them to a maximum of sixteen knots, their armament varying between 10- and 12-inch guns. The Japanese crews were well trained and enthusiastic; the Russians were demoralized, unpractised and badly led. There were already signs of the revolution which was to break out the next year.

It is of interest therefore to speculate as to what might have happened if Togo, in his encounters with the Port Arthur squadron, had had sufficient confidence in the moral and technical superiority of his fleet to attack with less caution, aiming at annihilation. Had he achieved this, it is unlikely that the Baltic squadron would have been sent on its mission of reinforcement, and the naval side of the war might have been concluded much sooner.

As we have seen, it was inevitable that the Russians should divide their fleet in some way; but whether they ought to have done so in the proportion which they actually did, is open to question. So knowledgeable a student of naval war as the late Sir Julian Corbett has criticized them for a false interpretation of the strategy of the maintenance of a 'fleet in being'. If they had no intention of challenging the Japanese fleet in pitched battle, Corbett considered, they should not have allowed such a strong force to be pinned down in a harbour so easily blockaded, so devoid of facilities for a fleet and of adequate defences, and so liable to be cut off from the hinterland by a land expedition. A smaller force employed would still have been able to threaten the Japanese control of the Yellow Sea sufficiently to require them to keep the modern portion of their fleet there. At the same time the Vladivostok squadron, strengthened by the addition of some battleships, would have posed a serious threat to the Japanese homeland. Instead, Togo was able largely to ignore Rear Admiral Stakelberg's division unless he should come south to join the main body, in which case the Japanese fleet was itself well placed to concentrate.

Indeed the naval strategy of Admiral Alexeieff, supreme commander in the Far East and Viceroy, advised by Rear Admiral Vitgeft, his Chief of Staff, was as inept as the tactics and administration of the fleet commander, Vice Admiral Stark. Though the Russian naval attaché in Tokyo had given clear warning that Japanese operations were to be expected immediately, the Port Arthur squadron lay at anchor in the Roads on 8 February in three lines running east and west, some engaged in coaling. Admittedly Stark had proposed to Alexeieff that precautions should be taken against a sudden attack ; but on being discouraged by the supreme commander, who was at Port Arthur, Stark contented himself by signalling, 'Prepare to repel torpedo attacks', an order which was taken by his un-enlightened and inert captains to be 'for exercise' only. As warning pickets, two destroyers were sent to patrol twenty miles to seaward with instructions to return and report to the flagship if they saw anything suspicious.

Alexeieff had, indeed, been ordered by the Tsar to ensure that if war were to come it should be the Japanese not the Russians, who fired the first shot. But it was a careless neglect of elementary precautions which left the fleet that night with all its normal lights burning, its guns unloaded, the crews turned in on the mess-decks and no arrangements for challenging any vessel seen approaching. Furthermore, the Liao-ti-shan lighthouse was left working, to send out its beam to guide an enemy's approach.

Ashore, the guns of the defensive batteries were left with their winter coating of heavy grease and the recoil cylinders of the 10-inch guns drained. While the Russian fleet lay heedlessly in such a defenceless posture, Japanese destroyer flotillas were slipping through the night, torpedoes and guns at the ready.

At 6 o'clock on that evening, 8 February 1904, the Japanese destroyers had parted company with the fleet to the sound of the rousing 'banzais' of their comrades in the battleships and cruisers. From the Commander-in-Chief had come the order : 'Proceed and attack as arranged. I pray for your complete success.' As the fleet turned back to stand to seaward until daylight, the destroyers – little craft of some 350 tons in those days – went on alone ; ten boats of the 1st, 2nd and 3rd Divisions for Port Arthur, and the eight of the 4th and 5th Divisions for Dairen, where it was believed that some of the Russian ships had gone. The first mass torpedo attack, of the type which was later to become a regular feature of naval tactics, was about to be made.

First, however, there was to be an encounter between the opposing forces which was to have a strong element of farce. From the darkened flotilla making for Port Arthur, the lights of the Russian destroyer patrol were sighted heading straight for them. The Japanese altered course to try to avoid detection. Nevertheless the Russians steamed blindly through the gap between the 1st and 2nd Divisions, so close ahead of the latter that its leader, the *Ikadsuchi*, had to stop engines ; whereupon the next boat, the *Oboro*, came charging up to collide with her stern. Neither was too damaged to continue after making repairs, but the Japanese force was confused and split into several separate units. Meanwhile the Russians had steamed off into the darkness blissfully unaware of anything untoward, although one of the Japanese, the *Sazanami*, actually joined up astern of them for a time before realizing her mistake and continuing alone for the objective.

By midnight Russian searchlight beams sweeping to and fro were plainly in view from the leading Japanese destroyers. Two ships of the Russian fleet, the *Retvizan* and the *Pallada*, had been detailed as searchlight guards. Two duty cruisers, the *Askold* and the *Diana*, lay with steam on their main engines. In the rest of the fleet there was steam only for auxiliary machinery. In the *Petropavlovsk* Admiral Stark was entertaining the Chief of Staff and the Port Commandant who had come on board the flagship for a conference.

It was half an hour after midnight when the first alarm was sounded as the officer of the watch of the *Retvizan* saw two destroyers lit up by the *Pallada's* searchlight. He at once ordered 'Repel Torpedo Attack', but the sleeping gun-crews had to be roused from their hammocks and sent stumbling dazedly to their action stations. Long before they were ready to open fire, a torpedo had exploded against the port side, plunging the ship into darkness and causing her to list heavily.

From the *Pallada* nothing was seen until 12.41 when the alarm was sounded. Even when the guns were made ready her captain feared to give the order to open fire, uncertain whether the destroyers were friend or foe. Only when the track of a torpedo was seen approaching was he sure, and then it was too late. In quick succession three torpedoes exploded, that on the *Retvizan*, one against the *Pallada* and one on the *Tzesarevitch*.

At last the guns came uncertainly into action, but the Japanese 1st Division which had fired at a range of seven hundred yards, was already retiring at high speed. Though some ships of the division were hit, the damage was not serious. Following close behind the 1st Division had come the *Ikadsuchi*, which, meeting the ever-growing storm of shells, turned and fired her torpedoes at somewhat longer range. Though she got away unhit, her torpedoes failed to find a target.

Next came the three destroyers under the leader of the 3rd Division. By the time they arrived the situation was not nearly so favourable for them. The Roads were a blaze of searchlights; guns from every ship were firing furiously, if wildly. When the range had fallen to an estimated 1,600 yards just inside the extreme range of the torpedoes of those days, the destroyers turned and fired. They escaped almost untouched, but once again no hits were scored on the Russian ships. Lastly the *Sazanami*, delayed by her temporary attachment to the Russian destroyers, came gallantly in for her solitary attack. Though continuously in the searchlight-beams, she closed to within 800 yards before firing two torpedoes, yet even so both missed.

As the *Sazanami* slipped away into the darkness, the gunfire died away, only to break out again an hour later with redoubled fury from the now thoroughly-aroused Russian ships. The little *Oboro*, her damaged bow patched up, had got under way again; and now, taking advantage of the lull, she crept into 1,300 yards to fire both her tubes. But though the concentrated fire of the whole fleet failed to damage her, her boldness went unrewarded, for neither of her torpedoes hit.

So the first operation of its kind came to an end, for the flotilla allocated to Dairen found that harbour empty. Great hopes had been pinned on the attack. The Japanese torpedo-men were looked on as something of a *corps d'élite*, highly trained and well practised. Yet in fact the results were paltry considering the favourable conditions under which the attack was made. An unalerted, anchored fleet, its lights burning, its guns unready, full navigational facilities available to the attackers, no boom or net defences; yet out of nineteen torpedoes fired, only three took effect and not one of the ships hit was sunk.

Not for the last time by any means, the effectiveness of the torpedo mounted in surface ships had been greatly exaggerated. Theoretically every torpedo fired which ran correctly should have been a certain hit, but theory did not take in account the blinding effect of the searchlights stabbing through a particularly black night; the bitter cold, accentuated for the destroyer officers and control personnel by the icy wind sweeping across the exposed bridges, blurring vision and numbing thought; the intimidating leap of a forest of shell splashes, and the shock of an occasional hit.

The first division to attack achieved almost complete surprise, pressed into close range and scored three hits out of seven torpedoes fired. The remainder, coming against an alerted defence, were forced to fire at longer range, their target hidden in the dazzle of the searchlights. It is possible they did not even close to the maximum range of their torpedoes. Of the twelve torpedoes fired under these conditions, not one hit.

Meanwhile in the Russian fleet all was bustle and flurry at long last. Smoke belched from funnels as steam was hastily raised, though only one ship, the cruiser *Novik*, sailed in chase, returning some hours later empty-handed. The *Retvizan* and the *Tzesarevitch* were got under way, but were so deep in the water through extensive flooding that they both grounded: the *Tzesarevitch* in the inner harbour and the *Retvizan* in the narrow entrance. The *Pallada* steamed to shallow water close in shore and again anchored.

Disappointing as the results of the attack were to the Japanese, a serious blow had been struck at the Russians, psychologically as well as physically. Two of their best battle-ships were out of action, and there was no dry dock in Port Arthur which could take them in their deep-draught, damaged condition. To a squadron already in low spirits and poor heart under the inept leadership of Admiral Stark, it was a disaster. The dismay was heightened by the news which now reached them of the destruction of the light-cruiser *Variag* and a gunboat which had been foolishly left at Chemulpo to be overwhelmed by Rear Admiral Uriu's squadron escorting the Japanese troopships to that port.

So the first naval war of the ironclad age between fleets roughly equal in initial strength began with a limited though important success to one of them even before war had been formally declared. It set the pattern for the rest of the war, but fortune was not always to smile on the Japanese, who also would have to face calamity in due course.

10

BLOCKADE OF PORT ARTHUR

Had Admiral Togo been prepared to risk a full-scale attack at dawn to take advantage of the confusion caused by the night torpedo attack, there can be little doubt that a decisive Japanese naval victory could have been secured in the first day of the war. But it was not until Rear Admiral Dewa, who had taken his cruisers to within seven thousand yards of the Russian fleet and reconnoitred them without a shot being fired at him, was able to report this evident lack of Russian preparedness that Togo shaped course for the roadstead and, shortly before noon, was in position to engage.

By this time the Russians in the shore batteries as well as in the ships had pulled themselves together and in the resultant exchange of gunfire damage and casualties on each side were roughly equal; when the shore batteries in particular became effective and, after scoring a number of damaging hits on Togo's battleships, shifted their fire to his cruisers, the Japanese admiral retired. The Russians withdrew their fleet into the inner harbour.

This first fleet action, indecisive as it was, had achieved for the Japanese their principal objective, the temporary local control of the Yellow Sea and the safe passage of their armies to Korea. The Russians had withdrawn their ships into the inner harbour (with the exception of the *Retvizan*, still aground at the entrance), and it was clear that for the time being their squadron would not venture to sea. Yet so long as the Russian fleet was 'in being' and able to come out, it was necessary for the Japanese to retain the whole of their modern fleet in the area, which left the Russian Vladivostok squadron unwatched and free to threaten the northern coasts of Japan.

On the other hand the state of unpreparedness of the Port Arthur garrison was such that, as the Russians themselves admitted, had the Japanese taken immediate advantage of their temporary naval supremacy to land an army and take the defences in the rear, the base must have quickly fallen. But this was beyond the limited resources of the Japanese, who were still in process of mobilizing their main armies, and it would have called for a skilful improvization of plan of which the Japanese Imperial General Staff was not capable.

Instead, the carefully prepared war plan with its cautious time-table was adhered to. The Japanese Army was thus condemned to the long siege and bloody assaults which would eventually be necessary to reduce Port Arthur. For the next six months both fleets were committed to a course of skirmishing, during which serious losses were suffered by both sides, chiefly from mines. On several occasions the Japanese attempted to block the harbour exit by sinking merchant ships in the channel, and they sent in their destroyers to make night torpedo attacks. None of these operations succeeded.

The Russians laid extensive minefields in an attempt to embarrass the blockade and to prevent Japanese landings in Talien Bay and elsewhere. The first victims of these, however, were the ship which had laid the mines and the cruiser *Boyarin* which went out to her assistance : both of which were sunk, the former with heavy loss of life. Russian blundering also cost them a destroyer cut off and sunk, two more badly damaged through grounding in a snowstorm, and damage to the cruisers *Bayan*, *Askold* and *Novik*, which were caught outside the harbour and engaged as they ran for shelter.

Russian morale was at its lowest ebb when on 8 March, a new spirit was infused into the fleet by the arrival of Vice Admiral Makaroff to assume the command. He at once roused the squadron from its lethargy. The *Retvizan* was refloated and towed into the harbour, where repairs were pressed ahead with her and the *Tzesarevitch*. Unable to enter the dry dock in their damaged condition, they were fitted with cofferdams, large close-fitting box-like structures sunk against the side of the ship, and then pumped out to enable work to be done on damage below the water-line.

Makaroff instituted strong destroyer patrols to seaward by night, which brought on a brisk destroyer action on his second night in command. Four Japanese and six Russian boats clashed in a wild, scrambling mêlée in the darkness, during which collisions were narrowly avoided, guns sent shells repeatedly into enemy hulls at ranges so close that grenades could be hurled from one ship to another, and a Russian destroyer was disabled by a torpedo from one of her comrades. Both sides were so damaged that they were barely able to retire to seek support.

The action was a tonic to the drooping morale of the Russians; but at daybreak, two other Russian destroyers allowed themselves to be cut off by the enemy and one was quickly disabled. The admiral himself put to sea in the *Novik* to rescue them and though he was driven off and failed to save the disabled boat, his example, in marked contrast to his predecessor's inactivity, dispelled the disheartening sense of inferiority which had permeated the Russian crews.

The Japanese followed up the night's activities by an ineffective long-range bombardment of the harbour, which failed to prevent Makaroff from leading the squadron to sea on the following morning to give them much-needed practice in steam tactics. The sad lack of skill on the part of the Russians was demonstrated when the *Sevastopol* collided with the *Poltava*, fortunately without causing serious damage.

The distressing incompetence of the officers of the Port Arthur squadron was not the least of the new Commander-in-Chief's worries. When on the next occasion of going to sea the *Sevastopol* was again in collision, this time with the *Peresviet*, the captain was relieved of his command; but at all levels the same lack of seaman-like skill was evident. Allied to his harassing strategic problems, it made a burden almost too heavy for even such an outstanding personality as Makaroff.

To counter any further attempts at blocking operations or night torpedo attacks, he had two merchant ships sunk and a timber boom fixed between them. Backing it was a line of gun-boats, while the cruisers *Askold* and *Bayan* were stationed in the harbour entrance where their guns and searchlights could dominate the channel.

Thus when eight Japanese destroyers attempted an attack on the night of 21 March, they received a hot reception and were driven off. When Togo appeared off the port the next morning and detached the battleships *Fuji* and *Yashima* to bombard the harbour, Makaroff led his battleships out and, ranging them within supporting distance of the shore batteries, challenged the

Japanese to action, a challenge which they refused even though they had twelve armoured ships to Makaroff's six.

The new spirit in the Russian squadron was apparent to the Japanese and drove them to a fresh attempt to block the harbour during the night of 26 March. Though four blockships were duly sunk near the entrance, they failed to obstruct the channel, and at daylight the mortified Japanese saw the Russians steaming out of harbour.

Yet the operation had very nearly succeeded, and Makaroff appreciated that fresh attempts were bound to be made. With all haste he had further booms stretched and two triple rows of mines, so laid that a direct approach to the harbour was not possible without fouling one or the other.

For all their early successes, to some extent the fruit of treachery, the Japanese were finding that their failure to follow them up promptly was costing them dearly. Togo was forced to employ his fleet in blockade, a form of warfare which was becoming daily more hazardous as the Russians extended their minefields.

The Japanese Commander-in-Chief's anxieties were greatly increased by the Imperial General Staff's somewhat belated decision to land an army on the Liaotung Peninsula. The area for the landing, Yentoa Bay, was a bare fifty-three miles from Port Arthur. A brief sortie by the Port Arthur squadron during one of the necessary absences of the Japanese battleship division for coaling or maintenance might spell disaster. The need to block the harbour was more vital than ever, and Togo asked for twelve merchant ships to be allocated for the purpose. The General Staff, already desperately short of shipping for troop movements and supply, was unwilling to grant the admiral's request.

While Togo pressed his demand and planned the fresh blocking operation for May, he also decided to take a leaf out of the Russian book by planting two minefields athwart the usual routes taken by the Russian ships on coming to sea, one at the south-western and one at the south-eastern limits of the road-stead in which the Russians usually manoeuvred under the protection of the shore batteries. He hoped then to lure the Russians into an incautious sortie.

During 11 April, Makaroff had taken the squadron for a training cruise along the coast to the eastward. On his return he had sent a force of destroyers to reconnoitre the off-shore islands, with order to return to harbour at daybreak. He had then led the remainder back into Port Arthur.

That evening two Japanese destroyer divisions and a mine-layer set out in pitch darkness and a drizzling rain to lay the planned minefields. As they drew near Port Arthur, searchlight activity showed them that the Russians were fully alert. The tireless, indefatigable Makaroff was indeed fully expecting some form of attack that night, the first calm night after a period of heavy gales, and he had himself gone aboard the *Diana*, the guard cruiser, in the narrows of the entrance.

Around midnight his premonitions had taken him restlessly touring the *Diana's* gun quarters and control positions to see that all was ready and everyone on the alert. As he stood by the captain, a sweeping searchlight steadied and, through the obscuring rain dimly illuminated some objects to the south-eastward of the harbour entrance. The captain asked permission to open fire, but the ill-served admiral could not be sure that the objects were not his own destroyers returning prematurely to the Roads owing to some all-too-probable calamity. He contented himself with arranging for the position to be carefully noted with the object of searching the area at daylight.

The rest of the night was apparently uneventful, and at 4 am Makaroff returned to his flagship *Petropavlovsk*. But in the dark, dripping night the Japanese minelayers had fulfilled their task to the letter and slipped away unhindered.

Meanwhile Makaroff's incompetent destroyer captains had indeed got themselves into the sort of trouble he had feared. Three of the eight boats sent on the mission of reconnaissance lost touch with the remainder. Two of them thereupon made for home, slipping unsighted in the darkness past a Japanese patrol-ing destroyer division, and at first light were nearing harbour. The third, however, the *Strashni*, sighting the Japanese division, took them for her consorts and followed them unsuspectingly while darkness held. Then as the light began to make, the Russian captain realized his terrible mistake. At his utmost speed he turned to escape ; but the four Japanese were after him at once. In spite of a gallant resistance, during which she got off a torpedo which closely missed one of the enemy, the *Strashni* was overwhelmed. The end came when a shell hit her other torpedo still in its tube and exploded it. Brought to a standstill, on fire and settling by the stern, all resistance was at an end, and the Japanese tried to take her in tow.

But now the *Bayan* was seen to be tearing out of harbour to the rescue, and the Japanese were forced to make off though they saw the *Strashni* sink before they left the scene. Togo had anticipated something of this sort. Now his plan to lure the Russian fleet out, either to fight or on to the new minefield, went smoothly into action. As the *Bayan* chased the destroyers to seaward, the masts of Rear Admiral Dewa's light-cruisers were seen coming up over the horizon. The Russian ship was forced to fall back on the support of her consorts, *Novik*, *Askold* and *Diana*, which were now coming out in their turn. Following them were the flagship *Petropavlovsk* and the *Poltava*.

Following his instructions, Dewa turned away to the south-west to lure the Russians in the direction of the westerly of the two minefields; but so far Makaroff was concerned solely with trying to save as many survivors as possible from the *Strashni* and to cover the return of the remainder of his destroyers. He therefore continued in an easterly direction, by pure good fortune clearing the other Japanese minefield as he did so.

The Russian Commander-in-Chief, who had been up all night, apparently unable to delegate any responsibility to his untrustworthy subordinates, had flown into a frenzy of anger when he heard of the latest escapade of his destroyer captains and the loss of the *Strashni*. All thought of the mysterious incident during the night had gone out of his head. Fuming with rage, he had led his battleships out of harbour without taking his usual precaution of having the channel swept before them.

Fog and smoke were by now obscuring the scene; and Dewa, finding the Russians had not followed him, turned back to try again. As he reapproached the eastern end of the roadstead, Makaroff's ships suddenly loomed out of the murk at short range. The guns on both sides roared out. But it was no part of the Japanese plan for Dewa's light-cruisers to be opposed to the Russian armoured ships. Turning hastily away, Dewa signalled to Togo to tell him that his plan of enticement was working and that action with the Russian fleet awaited him if he would come on. Togo was ready, and within fifteen minutes was in sight of the Russian ships, his battle flags hoisted.

However, Makaroff had still only two battleships and four armoured cruisers with him. The remainder of the battleships were still filing out of the harbour, and so he declined to be drawn. Falling back under the protection of the shore batteries, he picked up his other battleships and formed line on a north-easterly course, ready at last to engage.

Now it was Togo's turn to stand off, for Makaroff was leading his whole squadron unsuspectingly across the freshly laid mines. In breathless suspense the Japanese watched and waited as the Russian ships moved majestically forward into the danger zone.

The *Petropavlovsk* reached the eastern end of the roadstead. Surprisingly the Russian ships were still unscathed as the signal for a 180-degree turn back in succession was hoisted. The flagship began to lead round. Suddenly there came a muffled explosion under her, followed by two more, far more terrible, enveloping the flagship in flame, steam and smoke as her magazine exploded. Hurtling upwards could be seen her mizzenmast and funnel, a complete turret and her bridge. In less than a minute her stern had risen high out of the water and the flames were suddenly quenched as she slid to the sea bottom. Even the watching enemy recorded that 'the sight was a most appalling one'.

How much more so must it have been for the Russians. Yet something of their dead commander's personality – he was never seen again – must have continued to hover over the scene; for admirably calm discipline prevailed in the fleet. Boats were smartly lowered for rescue work. The ships held to their ordered formation, and Rear Admiral Prince Ukhtomski had only to signal 'Follow me' and lead off on the south-westerly course that Makaroff had ordered. But now the line was heading for the more westerly of the two Japanese minefields. Once again as they entered it, it became time to turn back, and the *Peresviet* flagship of Prince Ukhtomski led round. She had just steadied on the new course when an explosion shook the *Pobieda* astern of her. The mine had exploded abreast a coal-bunker which absorbed much of the shock, but a group of boilers was put out of action, and the flooded compartments gave the *Pobieda* a considerable list.

This second catastrophe was too much for the already shaken

Russian nerves. A wild panic broke out. Submarines were reported; as the ships turned this way and that and all order vanished, guns were fired at random into the water, the shore batteries adding their quota to that of the ships; there were narrow escapes from collision; shell splinters were flying everywhere. Even when the officers pulled themselves together and ordered the 'Cease Fire', it was only by pulling the crazed sailors bodily away from their guns that they could get the order obeyed.

Fortunately for the Russians all this was hidden from the enemy in the murk. By the time they came in sight again, Ukhtomski had succeeded in reducing them to some order, and behind the crippled *Pobieda* was leading them into harbour.

It had been a calamitous day for the Russians. The one man who might have brought them to fighting pitch had gone, and the new spirit that had been growing died with the *Petropavlovsk*. In addition their battle squadron was reduced to three ships, *Peresviet*, *Sevastopol* and *Poltava*, though repairs to the *Tzesarevitch* and *Retvizan* were well advanced and the *Pobieda* was at once taken in hand.

The Russian Port Arthur squadron was temporarily eliminated; the control of the Yellow Sea was in Japanese hands, allowing them to disembark their troops unhindered. To make this control permanent, either the entrance to Port Arthur had to be sealed off or the Russian squadron brought to decisive action. The Japanese made a valiant attempt to achieve the former with blockships but wild weather and an effective defence by the shore batteries defeated it with heavy casualties. A close blockade of the port had therefore to be established, Togo's cruisers alternating with the Japanese battleship squadron to patrol off the entrance by day, destroyers taking over by night.

While such a policy of keeping the seas in all weather maintained Japanese efficiency at a high level compared to the harbour-bound Russians, it exacted also a price. During a dense fog in the early hours of 15 May, two of the blockading squadron, the light cruiser *Yoshino* and the armoured cruiser *Kasuga* came into violent collision. The former was fatally holed below the water line; the order to abandon ship was given but first the ceremonious disembarkation of the Emperor's portrait into a boat had to be accomplished. While this was going on, the cruiser suddenly heeled over and plunged to the bottom. Thirty officers and 287 men went down with her. The *Kasuga* with serious damage and flooding had to withdraw to Japan for repairs.

The same day was to see an even greater catastrophe occur in the Japanese fleet. The division composed of the battleships *Hatsuse*, *Shikishima* and *Yashima*, accompanied by the cruiser, *Kasagi*, had made the routine take-over from the blockading squadron of cruisers off Port Arthur at dawn and had settled down to the customary off-shore patrol. This, as the captain of the Russian minelayer *Amur* had observed, took them repeatedly through the same stretch of water some ten miles south of Liao-ti-shan Light. The Russian's pleas to be allowed to make a secret sortie to lay his mines there had been repeatedly rejected on the humane grounds that such a lay, outside territorial waters, would expose innocent neutral shipping to danger and was therefore outside the bounds of civilized warfare. But the rapidly deteriorating situation had finally persuaded Admiral Vitgeft, who had succeeded Makaroff in command, to give his permission ; and, on the fourteenth, under cover of the same fog that was to cause the *Yoshino's* collision, the *Amur* had slipped out and spread a line of forty mines 50 to 100 feet apart.

Shortly before 1100 on the fifteenth, first the flagship *Hatsuse* and then the rear battleship *Yashima* were shaken in quick succession by heavy explosions and brought to a standstill listing heavily. Cruisers were ordered up to take the crippled ships in tow, but before they could do so the *Hatsuse* disintegrated in another shattering explosion as a second mine detonated her magazines. Thirty-eight officers and 458 men went down with her. The *Yashima* was kept afloat for some hours but eventually efforts to save her had to be given up and during the night she sank.

In one day the balance of naval power had been reversed, the Japanese slender excess of battleships being converted into a deficiency of two. No replacement of the Japanese ships could be looked for ; as soon as their own ships were repaired, the Russians would be in a position to challenge Togo with six to four. Furthermore, on the other side of the world, Russian reinforcements were assembling in the Baltic under Rear Admiral Rozhestvenski.

The local Russian superiority was, however, largely illusory. Since the loss of the *Petropavlovsk* and the death of Admiral Makaroff, the offensive spirit necessary to make even the defensive role of a 'fleet in being' credible had gone out of the Russian fleet. Its effective units lay idle in Port Arthur under the uninspiring Vitgeft who, with devastating candour, had told his assembled captains, 'I am no leader of a fleet'. When the general commanding the garrison, now closely invested by the Japanese armies, insisted that it was the fleet's function to assist the defence by operations against the enemy's communications, Vitgeft pleaded that the fleet was unready to fight, lacking gunnery practice or general training.

Nevertheless, when, during June, repairs to the *Tzesarevitch*, *Retvizan* and *Pobieda* were completed, the Viceroy Alexeieff sent Vitgeft orders that the squadron should put to sea, though with no clear indication of the purpose of the sortie. And, indeed, when, after sweeping a channel through the minefields outside, the Russians emerged only to find Togo waiting for them, they refused action and fled precipitately back to harbour, harried by Japanese destroyer attacks. Taking the direct route, which took them out of the swept channel. They were fortunate in that only the battleship *Sevastopol* was mined and damaged but was able to make the inner harbour.

The disappointment of the Japanese was intense when they approached the following morning ready to make further attacks on the disabled ships they expected to find, only to discover the roadstead empty. The dreary round of the interminable blockade had to be resumed. Little or nothing had been achieved out of the long-awaited opportunity. Indeed, the whole incident assumed the shape of a serious strategical setback to the Japanese. The parlous condition of the Russian ships, their lack of training and low morale, were not realized. All the Japanese knew was that the damaged battleships had been repaired while the two Japanese ships which had been mined were at the bottom, and that the repeated blocking operations had been entirely unsuccessful. They at once feared for the safety of the troop and supply convoys upon which the whole of their military strategy depended.

The great troop movements which had been ordered in an attempt to initiate an advance into Manchuria were postponed indefinitely. Knowing the state of the Russian fleet, it can be seen that the Japanese were unduly nervous, but the General Staff was no doubt influenced by events which had taken place in the Korean Straits at about the time that the Port Arthur squadron was making its sortie. The Russian Vladivostok division under its new commander, Rear Admiral Bezobrazov, had suddenly appeared on the shipping route between Japan and Korea. There they found and sank two transports carrying troops and stores as well as eighteen 11-inch howitzers destined for the siege of Port Arthur; a third ship was torpedoed, but got back to port. Then after a cruise up the Japanese coast, during which he captured or sank further merchant ships, Bezobrazov, aided by thick weather, had escaped unharmed back into Vladivostok.

However exaggerated may have been the respect with which the revitalized Port Arthur squadron was regarded, the fact that it was once more mobile and at nearly full strength forced Togo to keep his fleet concentrated and ready to engage it should the Russians again attempt a sortie. And indeed such an event was impending. All through July the Viceroy urged Vitgeft to go out and fight, while Vitgeft continued to protest the unpreparedness of his ships and his own unfitness to lead them into battle. Only the imminent fall of Port Arthur could justify him in taking them out on a forlorn hope, he believed.

So the deadlock continued, until the matter was resolved at the end of July by a personal order from the Tsar that the squadron should go out. Reluctantly the Russians set about preparing for sea. By 9 August they were as ready as they could be in the absence of tactical training or target practice. As black smoke pouring from the funnels told of steam being raised, the unhappy Vitgeft was bidding his friends farewell with the discouraging prophetic phrase: 'We shall meet in another world'.

At first light on 10 August 1904 the fleet weighed anchor and, led by the minesweepers, put to sea. Japanese scouts signalled the news to Togo, patrolling some fifty miles to the south-eastward with his division of four battleships. When the Russian squadron, after an initial feint in a westward direction, settled down on a south-easterly course, Togo was well placed to bring off the advantageous tactical manoeuvre of crossing the enemy's 'T' and bringing a concentration of fir eupon his van. While his outlying squadrons sped to join him, therefore, he steered back and forth across the Russian line of advance.

In the battle line with the Russian battleships were the three cruisers under the command of Rear Admiral Reitzenstein, with his flag in the *Askold*. Thus the Russian force as seen from Togo's bridge was a formidable array. Vitgeft's flagship *Tzesarevitch* led the way, followed by *Retvizan*, *Pobieda*, *Peresviet* (flag of Rear Admiral Prince Ukhtomski), *Sevastopol*, *Poltava*, *Askold*, *Pallada* and *Diana*. With the eight Russian destroyers stationed on the landward side of the line were the *Novik* and a hospital ship, *Mongolia*.

Togo's 1st Division, reduced by the loss of the *Hatsuse* and *Yashima* to four ships (*Mikasa*, *Asahi*, *Fuji* and *Shikishima*), had been made up to six by the inclusion of the armoured cruisers *Kasuga* and *Nisshin*, in the latter of which was the flag of Rear Admiral Kataoka. His total force, which included Rear Admiral Dewa's 3rd Division comprising two armoured cruisers and three light cruisers, the 6th Division of five elderly cruisers under Rear Admiral Togo and a (reserve) 5th Division of even older ships under Rear Admiral Yamada, was numerically greatly superior to the Russians'.

But an old lesson from the days of sail navies was shown still to apply in the course of the battle to follow, in that it was soon apparent that once battle was joined it was the capital ships, the ships 'fit to stand in the line', which decided the issue. The unarmoured cruisers on either side played little part.

Nevertheless, it was no doubt in order to await the concentration of his scattered forces that Togo showed himself in no hurry to engage. Keeping out of range, he weaved to and fro across the path of the Russians to head them off from their desired escape route to the south-east, while Vitgeft turned this way and that trying to get away round Togo's stern.

By 1300 these manoeuvres had brought the two heavy squadrons within extreme gun range of each other and both sides opened fire. First blood was, for all their lack of practice, drawn by the Russians. As Togo's ships were swinging under helm to reverse course, his flagship *Mikasa* was twice hit by

12-inch shells, one of which plunged through her deck at the foot of the mainmast and caused numerous casualties.

With his constant preoccupation with the need to preserve his country's battleships against the eventual arrival on the scene of the Russian reinforcements from the Baltic Fleet, it must have given Togo much food for thought. For all its misfortunes, lack of inspired leadership and long inactivity, the Port Arthur squadron had by no means had its fangs drawn. Togo's intention to fight at long range, relying upon his superior gunnery to decide the issue, was not working out well.

On the other hand, time seemed to be on Togo's side from the point of view of the attainment of his strategical object. His far-sighted mind told him that the destruction of the enemy fleet was not the aim if it entailed heavy losses on his own part. The Russians had a fresh battle squadron in reserve assembling in the Baltic; the Japanese had none. Therefore the enemy either must be driven back to Port Arthur or else destroyed piece-meal during the long voyage to Vladivostok. Mutual destruction at point-blank range might bring Togo a tactical victory, but could lose him the strategical object.

The day was more than half gone. With the night Togo's greatly superior torpedo forces would go into action. By the next day the scene of battle would perhaps have shifted to the Korean Straits, where Rear Admiral Kamimura's squadron of armoured ships could come to swell the Japanese strength. There was no immediate hurry.

Meanwhile Togo's line had completed its turn and was once more heading to cross Vitgeft's 'T'. Yet again the Russian admiral turned to the eastward to circle the Japanese rear. A turn, all ships together, such as the Japanese had twice performed, was too difficult a manoeuvre for the unpractised Russians. The long process of a turn in succession was necessary; while it was taking place the Japanese concentrated their fire on the turning-point and now at last they drew blood. The *Tzesarevitch* and *Retvizan* were seen to be hit and on fire.

But this success led Togo into a tactical mistake. Instead of turning back in good time once more to head off the Russians from their escape route, a temporary confusion in the Russian line as they turned in their customary unhandy fashion tempted him to make the most of the advantage. The range was now down to less than 8,000 yards. As he circled the enemy's rear, every gun from 6-inch upwards came into action. The Russian ships were hidden in amid the shell splashes and seemed to be veritably overwhelmed.

Yet with the completion of their turn the Russian line was seen unbelievably to be steaming away in good order, little damaged and returning the fire in great style. As in the previous action of 9 October, it was shown that with indiscriminate fire from guns of many different calibres making spotting impossible it became a matter of luck to score hits.

Togo had now sacrificed his commanding position across Vitgeft's escape route, and all for nothing. Realizing this, he led round to the south-east. By the time he was steering a parallel course to the enemy, his flagship, leading the line, was only just abreast of the enemy's last ship, the rear ships of the Japanese line being so far astern that they were out of range and forced to cease fire. Furthermore at his battle speed of 14 knots, Togo was surprised to find that he was not gaining on the Russians, who were doing much better than he had expected considering they had one ship, the *Poltava*, which had made only 16.2 knots at her original full-speed trials.

The Russian cruisers were now bearing the brunt of the Japanese fire. Vitgeft therefore ordered them to turn away to port out of range, while to shelter them he turned his battleship division 45 degrees to starboard together, for a short while, and so once more came within range of Togo's battleships. However, the gunnery advantage by no means lay with the Japanese. Togo's van was exposed to a concentration of fire, the reverse of the position which the Japanese admiral had always hoped to achieve with superior speed.

At 1450 the *Asahi*, second in the line, was heavily hit. Ten minutes later the *Mikasa* was hit on the water-line, and again below the quarter-deck at 1505. The only apparent effect on the Russians of the exchange of fire was that the *Poltava* was seen to be dropping astern. Actually, this was due to the high speed which she had been forced to maintain; her racing reciprocating engines were unable to take the strain of the prolonged run at full power and were beginning to fail.

Two alternatives now faced Togo. He could either close on the last two ships of the enemy line, the slow *Poltava* and the

Sevastopol, and let the remainder escape for the time being, or else he could disengage and, by using his maximum speed, circle out of gun range until he could come in again from such an angle that he could concentrate on the enemy's van and head him off from his escape route. The briefest consideration showed the first to be unthinkable. The two rear ships were the least valuable. The remainder, if they got away to Vladivostok and joined the armoured cruisers there, would constitute a force capable of engaging the whole Japanese fleet. The arrival of the reinforcements from Europe would give them an overwhelming superiority.

So at 1500 Togo led his ships on a south-easterly course diverging from that of the Russians, and increased to his maximum sustained speed of fifteen knots. As the range opened, the firing died away, but not before the *Mikasa* had received two further hits.

Thus, with the afternoon well advanced Togo was left committed to a long chase. Only with agonizing slowness was he gaining on the enemy. The sun was sinking low. It seemed that contrary to all expectations, even on the part of the Russians, they were going to get away at least for that day; but at 1630 the bearing of the enemy began to drop fast. The *Poltava's* desperate efforts to keep up had come to an end as one set of her engines broke down, leaving her to struggle along on the other. The remainder had for a time reduced speed to stay with her.

At last Togo could turn to close the range again. At 1735 the lagging *Poltava* at a range of less than nine thousand yards, was set upon by the whole Japanese line; but she replied with splendid spirit, giving back at least as good as she got and perhaps better. The tornado of fire and the impenetrable wall of splashes made the Japanese fire control a matter of guesswork, as had been the case earlier in the action. Moreover, Togo's flagship came once again under concentrated fire from the Russian battleships. Vitgeft had been forced to leave the *Poltava* to her fate, and pressing on again at fourteen knots he had prevented Togo from getting as far ahead as the Japanese admiral had hoped. For the next hour a furious cannonade continued, during which misfortune piled on misfortune in the Japanese battleships.

The *Mikasa* was repeatedly hit, her after turret being put out of action and almost destroyed. In the *Shikishima* one of her forward 12-inch guns was disabled for a time. The *Asahi* had bursts in both her after turret guns due to overheating of the barrels. Out of sixteen turret guns in the Japanese battleships, five were thus out of action, and still the Russians sailed on apparently unaffected by the Japanese fire.

At 1830 the situation must have seemed calamitous to the Japanese Commander-in-Chief. Sunset was only half an hour away. His flagship was shuddering under blow after blow from 6-inch and 12-inch shells. Her casualties were severe. On her starboard side a huge hole gaped a bare two feet above the water-line. Except for a disarrangement of the Russian line, there was little sign that the Japanese gunners were achieving comparable results.

Then suddenly, at 1840, the whole picture was changed. The *Tzesarevitch* was seen to swerve out of the line to port, with a heavy list. Pouring smoke, she continued in a wide circle until she charged through her own line ahead of the *Sevastopol*, the rear ship (except for the *Poltava*, now far astern and disabled). Her engines were then stopped.

The two 12-inch shells which were the cause lost the day for the Russians. The first, bursting near the foot of the mainmast, had at one stroke killed the Commander-in-Chief and sixteen others, and wounded and knocked senseless the Chief of Staff and the Flag Captain; the second hit the conning tower and killed or stunned every man in it. The flagship was bereft of all control, its wheel jammed hard a-port. The fleet was without a leader.

In the best regulated fleet such a calamity would have led to some confusion. To the Russians it spelt an end of all order, but not of the gallantry with which their ships had been so far handled. The captain of the *Retvizan* who had followed the *Tzesarevitch* round, not at first realizing she was out of control, steered boldly for the enemy to draw the fire away from the disabled flagship. He was followed by the *Pobieda*.

When Togo saw the Russian line dissolve into a milling throng, he had begun to circle and close for the kill; but this movement of the *Retvizan* and *Pobieda* was so threatening that he was forced to give ground. Onwards the *Retvizan* came, her captain bent on trying to ram the *Mikasa*. Every Japanese gun was concentrated on her until she was completely hidden by smoke and spray, so that the *Mikasa's* gunlayers were forced to cease fire for want of a point of aim. It seemed that nothing could stop the great ship in her desperate ride, but when she had got to within a mile and a half of the *Mikasa*, a 12-inch shell at last got home. A splinter struck the *Retvizan's* captain. Suffering excruciating pain, he was only able to gasp out instructions to take the ship back to join the squadron before he collapsed.

Yet his audacity, coupled with Togo's unwillingness to close to point-blank range for a fight to the finish, probably saved the Russian squadron from annihilation. After remaining motionless for twenty minutes the *Tzesarevitch* got under way again. Steering on her engines she staggered away with the remainder to the north-west. Though Prince Ukhtomski had tried to take over the command and make the signal 'Follow Me', both topmasts of his flagship, the *Peresviet*, had been shot away and his signal was not readable. In complete confusion the Russian ships fled, firing wildly all the while at the circling Japanese battle squadron.

All that Togo needed to annihilate his defeated enemy was a period of daylight, but this was denied him. Darkness was now closing quickly. The waste of time, first in fruitless manoeuvring ahead of the Russians at midday and secondly in the long chase which had been imposed by his tactical error later, was now to exact its toll. As night fell he held back, allowing the Russians to draw away. In spite of the repeated failure of torpedo attack in the past, he feared to expose himself to it, and at the same time he unleashed his own destroyers.

Through the night, as the main body of the Russians made their straggling way back to Port Arthur, the Japanese destroyers and torpedo-boats made attack after attack; but not a single torpedo found a billet. By daybreak the five battleships, *Retvizan, Peresviet, Pobieda, Sevastopol* and *Poltava*, the cruiser *Pallada* and three destroyers, were in the roadstead and passing into the inner harbour.

Of the remainder the *Tzesarevitch*, unable to keep up with the main body, the *Novik* and three destroyers escaped to the German port of Kiaochow where the *Novik* was able to refill her coal bunkers and emerge again to make a desperate attempt to reach Vladivostok after circling the Japanese islands. She was cornered, however, at Korsakovsk in Sakhalin where she was coaling, by the cruiser *Tsu-shima*, and though she succeeded in driving off her powerful opponent her crew had finally to scuttle her in the harbour. The *Tzesarevitch* and the destroyers were interned at Kiaochow, while the cruiser *Askold* and another destroyer suffered the same fate at Shanghai and the cruiser *Diana* at Saigon.

So ended the battle of 10 August 1904. It was tactically indecisive with battleships on both sides seriously damaged. But the Russian squadron would never emerge again and would five months later come to an ignominious end as it lay at its moorings, at the hands of howitzer gunners of the besieging Japanese Army. On 14 August, too, the Vladivostok squadron was brought to action by Kamimura, the *Rurik* being sunk and the other two cruisers heavily damaged. Then the *Gromoboi* ran aground and was wrecked just after her repairs had been completed, leaving only the *Rossya*.

Thus, the Japanese, left in unopposed control of the eastern seas, were granted a breathing space in which to repair their battle squadron before the Russian Baltic Fleet, being slowly gathered and prepared for its long circuit of the globe, would have to be faced.

11

THE BATTLE OF TSU-SHIMA

The battle of 10 August 1904 is little remembered as compared to the more spectacular but pre-ordained massacre in the Tsu-shima Straits which brought the war to an end. But it was the former which in reality placed in Japanese hands the maritime control of the Yellow Sea and the Sea of Japan and made the eventual Russian defeat in the war certain.

Nine days after it, a council of war called by Prince Ukhtomski unanimously decided that there could be no possibility of a further break-out by the Port Arthur squadron, and that every gun and every man not required to fight a defensive action at anchor should be landed to assist the garrison in defending the fortress. This was not known by the Japanese who resumed the close blockade and in consequence suffered casualties from mines (as well as much wear and tear of ships and machinery) in the next five months before Port Arthur finally surrendered to assault from the land on 2 January 1905.

This brought sea warfare virtually to an end for the time being. It gave the Japanese a breathing space in which to refit and rearm their battle-damaged and work-worn ships in readiness to meet the eventual threat posed by the Russian Baltic Fleet which, renamed the 2nd Pacific Squadron, had since 15 October 1904 been making a painfully slow and misfortune-studded voyage to the Far East under the flag of Rear Admiral Rozhestvenski.

The decision to send reinforcements to the Russian Pacific Squadron had been taken as long ago as April 1904. On the face of it, if the Russian building programme could be relied upon to progress as planned, a useful force of new first-class battleships could be ready by the autumn. There was firstly the *Oslyabya*, the ship which had been on its way to the Far East when war broke out and which, after a long wait in the Red Sea, had been recalled. Another, the *Imperator Alexander III* was completed and ready at Cronstadt. Her sister-ships *Borodino* and

Kniaz Suvorov were expected to be completed in the late summer, while another of the same class would be ready in the autumn.

Four older battleships, the *Sisoi Veliki, Navarin, Imperator Nikolai I* and *Imperator Alexander II*, were undergoing refits which would be completed during the summer. In addition there were three modern light cruisers, *Aurora, Zhemchug* and *Izumrud*, as well as a number of older cruisers and some thirty torpedo craft.

So long as Port Arthur held out and the Pacific Squadron remained 'in being', it could be argued that the addition of an effective new squadron, its arrival timed to coincide with a sortie from Port Arthur and Vladivostok, could completely upset the naval balance of power, and with it the whole Japanese war plan. Even the distant threat had prevented Togo from using his battleships with the vigour which would have turned his partial successes into annihilating victories.

Even to grasp so great a prize, however, there were grave difficulties to be overcome in sending a squadron of those days some 19,000 miles over a route devoid of friendly naval bases. The pounding reciprocating engines of battleships of the pre-dreadnought era were liable to constant defects if run for long periods at anything but slow speeds. Boilers required frequent cleaning, a horrible task for white men in the tropics. The high-grade Welsh coal for their furnaces would need repeated replenishment, which could be procured only by a system of colliers organized in advance to meet them at sea, for legally a neutral might not allow coal to be embarked in his ports by a belligerent. At the end of the voyage the ships would have to go into action needing refit and docking, their bottoms foul after cruising in tropical waters, with only a fraction of their speed available.

Nevertheless the Russian Admiralty decided to undertake this hazardous plan. Rear Admiral Rozhestvenski was one of their best officers appointed to command the force. Difficulties of every sort were encountered during the fitting out of the various ships, owing to a dearth of skilled workmen, the majority of whom had been sent off to Port Arthur and Vladivostok. Trained crews were equally scarce; nor was there time to mould the rough human material available into efficient ships' companies.

However, by 11 September Rozhestvenski's 2nd Pacific Squadron had assembled at Libau, its last Russian port of call. It comprised seven battleships, *Suvorov*, *Alexander III*, *Borodino*, *Orel*, *Oslyabya*, *Veliki* and *Navarin*, two old armoured cruisers *Admiral Nakhimoff* and *Dmitri Donskoi*, four light cruisers, *Aurora*, *Svietlana*, *Zhemtchug* and *Almaz*, seven destroyers and nine transports. Sailing on 15 October, the squadron arrived at the southern entrance to the Great Belt between Denmark and Sweden two days later.

Its quality, moral and material, was at once revealed, as well as the awe in which the Russians held their enemy and the incompetence with which they were equipped to meet him. Fantastic rumours that the Japanese were intending to mine the waters through which the Russians would have to pass, and that they had sent a torpedo flotilla to Europe to attack the squadron, were taken seriously.

Before Rozhestvenski would risk the narrow waters leading out of the Baltic, some of his auxiliary craft were set to sweeping the channel; but after vain efforts to make their sweeping gear function they were forced to give up, whereupon the squadron ventured the passage, arriving safely off the Skaw and anchoring on 20 October.

It was planned for the squadron to get under way again in six groups on the following day, each group travelling independently as far as Tangier. The battleships, too deep in the water for the Suez Canal, would then take the long route round the Cape of Good Hope, the remainder passing through the Mediterranean. All would eventually rendezvous in Madagascar.

Hardly had the squadron anchored when reports reached the admiral from the captain of one of his transports that suspicious-looking craft resembling torpedo-boats had been seen during the night. The alarm was passed to all ships, and orders were given to sail at once.

During the afternoon and evening the fleet got under way and proceeded in six separate groups with the battleships in two divisions in the rear. Throughout the fleet nerves were stretched taut; anxious eyes peered through the misty North Sea night on the look-out for the mythical Japanese destroyers. The *Kamchatka*, an armed merchant cruiser, lost touch with her group; when dim shapes loomed up near by, albeit showing normal navigation lights, they were at once taken for the enemy, and guns' crews leapt into action. First the Swedish steamer *Aldebaran*, then the French sailing-ship *Guyane* and a German trawler came under their fortunately wild and inaccurate fire.

None of them was hit, but the *Kamchatka's* reports made the Russians all the more convinced that an attack was imminent. Already their oganization was breaking down, and the various divisions were bunching up on each other. So it was that when at around midnight the battleships caught up with the *Aurora* and *Donskoi* just as they ran in amongst the British fishing fleet off the Dogger Bank, wild alarm spread. Guns opened fire in every direction, not only at the unfortunate trawlers but at the two Russian cruisers also.

The British trawler *Crane* was sunk, five others hit and many damaged by splinters from near misses. Two fishermen were killed and six wounded. The *Aurora* was hit five times, her chaplain being mortally wounded. Finally the firing died away as the victims were left astern. The battleship divisions steamed on amidst mutual congratulations at the successful repulse of a dangerous attack.

Relations between the British and Russian Governments were not unnaturally strained to the limit by this astonishing affair, but apologies and an agreement to refer the matter to an International Commission prevented an open breach. The disorganization and lack of training which the incident revealed set the pattern for the rest of Rozhestvenski's ill-starred venture. His halting, uncertain progress round the world continued at a funereal pace, haunted by the constant uncertainty of fuel supplies. Indeed had not the neutral countries, particularly France, winked at the breaches of international law involved in permitting long stays in their harbours and the supply of coal to the Russian ships, the 2nd Pacific Squadron would very quickly have had to revert to its previous role of Baltic Fleet.

To reduce the halts for refuelling so far as was possible coal was piled high on the decks, so that not only were the ships permanently bedraggled and filthy with coal-dust, but also the systematic training which the crews so badly needed became impossible.

When Port Arthur capitulated to the Japanese in January 1905, Rozhestvenski's force had reached Madagascar, where it had been lying for nearly a month while fresh contracts for the supply of coal were being negotiated. The British government had stopped the shipment of Welsh coal for the Russian squadron, the German Hamburg-Amerika line colliers had refused to accompany it into the war zone. Not until the middle of March 1905 would Rozhestvenski be able to set forth again.

Meanwhile the state of affairs which had led to the decision to send reinforcements to the Pacific had entirely changed. With the fall of Port Arthur and the elimination of the 1st Pacific Squadron, Rozhestvenski's untrained, disheartened, apprehensive and periodically mutinous squadron would have to face the whole of Japan's freshly refitted fleet manned by war-experienced, supremely confident veterans. Even if the Russians could succeed in brushing aside the Japanese opposition, there was only the port of Vladivostok with its limited facilities for warship maintenance to receive them. Furthermore the supply of steam coal for such a large force presented an almost insoluble problem.

As the Russian admiral lay at Nossi Bé in Madagascar, he and many of his officers and men in ill-health owing to the tropical climate, the question of coal supplies was still unsolved. The government, with an astonishing lack of comprehension of maritime affairs, telegraphed to point out to him that the task of securing command of the sea now lay in his hands alone, offering to send him reinforcements from amongst the ancient and quite unbattleworthy warships still in the Baltic.

It is impossible not to sympathize with the sorely tried Rozhestvenski when he gloomily replied in the following despairing memorandum:

I have not the slightest prospect of recovering command of the sea with the force under my orders. The despatch of reinforcements composed of untested and in some cases badly built vessels would only render the fleet more vulnerable.

Rozhestvenski concluded this frank expression of opinion with a request to be relieved on account of ill-health. Ignoring his request and his warning alike, the Russian government sent the reinforcements on their way on 15 February; museum pieces such as the obsolete battleship *Nikolai I*, an old armoured cruiser *Vladimir Monomakh*, and three small coast defence ships, *Admiral Apraxin*, *Admiral Seniavin* and *Admiral Ushakoff*, as well as seven auxiliary vessels. Under Rear Admiral Nebogatoff they caught up with the main squadron on 9 May at Van Fong Bay in French Indo-China, to embarrass the unhappy Commander-in-Chief with their slow speed and lack of armament.

From this point onwards the story of Rozhestvenski is dominated by an air of inevitable doom. The only practical route for the squadron was through the Korean Straits, and there the Japanese fleet lay, tensed and waiting at their base near Masan, trained to a hair and superbly confident. The Russians coaled for the last time off the coast of China on 23 May, on which day Rozhestvenski's second-in-command, Rear Admiral Folkersam, at last died from the illness which had overtaken him during the voyage. To avoid such an omen further depressing the spirits of his already demoralized crews, Rozhestvenski kept the news from all but Folkersam's flagship, *Oslyabya*, where he ordered the admiral's flag to be kept flying. Again getting under way, the squadron – complete with its embarrassing tail of auxiliaries, including hospital ships – steered to pass through the Straits of Tsu-shima to the eastward of the island of that name.

The force was organized in four divisions. The 1st was composed of Rozhestvenski's flagship *Suvorov* and the battleships *Alexander III*, *Borodino* and *Orel*. The 2nd comprised the *Oslyabya*, *Sissoi Veliki*, *Navarin* and *Admiral Nakhimoff*. The *Nikolai I*, in which Nebogatoff flew his flag, led the *Apraxin*, *Seniavin* and *Ushakoff* to form the 3rd Division, while the eight cruisers formed a separate division under Rear Admiral Enquist with his flag in the *Oleg*.

Rozhestvenski, who lacked nothing in personal courage, whatever may have been his other qualities, had decided that battle must be accepted and even sought. Merely to evade Togo and take refuge in Vladivostok would in no way contribute towards a challenge to the Japanese control of the sea. He had at least to try to inflict some damage on the enemy. Partly for this reason and partly because he feared torpedo attack by night in the narrow waters close to the enemy bases, he adjusted his speed to enter the Tsu-shima Strait at daylight on 27 May.

With time in hand, he steamed at slow speed during the twenty-sixth, and spent some time exercising battle manoeuvres. On account of the old, slow ships in company, all of which were foul with tropical growth and many of which had boiler defects, the battle speed was established as only eleven knots. As the daylight faded he reformed his unwieldy squadron into its cruising order and signalled 'Prepare for action. Tomorrow at the hoisting of the colours, battle flags will be flown'.

Rarely, if ever, can a fleet have steered for a certain pitched battle so hopelessly outclassed by its opponent. Togo's ships, freshly refitted and worked up to a peak of efficiency could await the outcome with total confidence. His main body lay in the Masan anchorage while stretched across the Tsu-shima Straits, south of the island, was a double line of scouts composed of Rear Admiral Dewa's four light cruisers, four armed merchant cruisers and two old cruisers *Akitsushima* and *Idzumi*, and in the harbour of Tsu-shima were four old cruisers of Rear Admiral Kataoka's division.

It was one of the armed merchant cruisers, *Shinano Maru*, which, against the first pale gleams of dawn to the eastward, first sighted the enemy under a dense pall of black funnel smoke. By 0630 Togo was leading his fleet to sea ; circling to the north of Tsu-shima Island he placed himself across the path the Russian ships must follow. With him were the ships of his own division, the battleships *Mikasa*, *Fuji* and *Asahi* and the armoured cruisers *Kasuga* and *Nisshin*, and Kamimura's six armoured cruisers.

Meanwhile the Japanese scouting forces had ranged themselves on either side of Rozhestvenski. As he advanced (while changing from his more compact cruising formation into a battle line composed of his twelve armoured ships with his cruisers, transports and destroyers to starboard), the Russian squadron was ushered towards the Japanese main body as by some ceremonial guard of honour, or perhaps more like a line of stolid oxen to the slaughter.

Knowing that Togo must be somewhere ahead, the Russian admiral now attempted a manoeuvre designed to give him the advantage of being across the enemy's 'T' at the moment of encounter. A thickening of the mist had hidden the watching Japanese cruisers, and he thought he might surprise Togo by advancing in line abreast. A simple turn together would then put him in line ahead across the path of the approaching Japanese battle divisions.

Rozhestvenski's tactical idea was beyond the capabilities of his unskilled, unpractised captains. Long before it had been completed, the Japanese cruisers had drawn into view again. Surprise being lost, Rozhestvenski cancelled the manoeuvre. Thus when at 1339 the Russians were sighted by the Japanese battle divisions at a distance of seven miles, they were in neither one formation nor the other.

Togo had previously decided that he would attack from the enemy's port bow; so when the Russians came in sight fine to starboard, he at once led round to cross ahead of the enemy line at right angles. Then, as he reached the chosen position, he unfurled his battle ensigns and led round in a turn of more than 180 degrees to range himself on a parallel course to the Russians. It was a risky manoeuvre, for his turning-point was well within range of the enemy, who at once opened undisturbed fire. The time was 1408.

The Togo of this day, however, was in a different mood from that of 10 August. Not only was he confident that he had the measure of the Russians, but, with Russia's last fleet in view, he was prepared to exchange blow for blow at killing range even at some cost in ships to himself. There was no longer need to conserve his battleship strength against the possibility of another battle later. As he had signalled to his fleet on sailing, 'The future of the Empire depends on this battle'. He therefore deliberately risked placing himself where he could concentrate on the head of the enemy line, with his strongest ships in the lead to bear the brunt of the shell fire.

The risk had in fact been well calculated; for though the Japanese ships were surrounded by shell splashes as they followed their flagship round, hits were very few, and none of them from the bigger guns. As they settled on their course, one after the other they in turn opened a slow deliberate fire at a range from five to six thousand yards. For a while their shooting was indifferent as they picked their targets from the still-confused Russian line. Then as they found the range, the five leading Russian ships were subjected to a violent battering.

The flagships of the two leading divisions, *Suvorov* and

Oslyabya were particularly singled out for punishment, and were soon set ablaze. As the fire parties struggled to control the flames they were killed or wounded by the storm of shell which swept the decks. Guns became jammed through shell fragments entering by the gun ports and lodging in the mechanism. In the *Oslyabya* the fore turret had been knocked out, and her decks were littered with dead and wounded.

In the midst of this fury of fire, the Russians, still trying to re-form their line following Rozhestvenski's ill-advised manoeuvre, fell into a worse confusion. The *Oslyabya* had to stop to avoid collision with the *Orel*; ships in the rear became bunched up, and also had to reduce speed or stop in consequence.

All the while, the Japanese with their superior speed were drawing ahead, and were thus able to pour a concentrated fire into the confused mass of ships at the head of the Russian formation. Soon they would be crossing the Russian 'T'. To prevent this and to enable all his guns to bear on the enemy, Rozhestvenski led away to starboard and brought the *Mikasa* once again on to his beam.

The Japanese had by no means gone unscathed through the early exchanges. The *Mikasa* had already suffered fifty-four casualties from hits by two 12-inch shells and two 6-inch. The *Asama*, last but one of Kamimura's division, had been hit by a 12-inch shell which had disabled her steering gear and caused such flooding that she had to leave the line for repairs, the first ship on either side to do so. But except for her, the Japanese line was not seriously affected, and still steamed in perfect formation at fifteen knots, all guns fully in action.

From this time onwards the battle became a veritable slaughter of the Russian ships whose own firing became wild and largely ineffective. The first to succumb was the *Oslyabya* which at 1450 staggered out of the line and capsized to sink fifteen minutes later, with the loss of thirty-four officers and 481 men. At 1455 the *Suvorov*, battered to a wreck, swerved away to starboard with a jammed rudder. Rozhestvenski lay wounded and barely conscious with most of his staff killed or wounded.

The leadership of the confused Russian line now devolved upon the *Alexander III* which turned to port to try to escape under the stern of the Japanese line now beginning to cross ahead. But this manoeuvre was countered as Togo's ships turned faultlessly about together, forcing the *Alexander III* back on to a south-easterly course. This brought the Russians a brief respite as they disappeared into the pall of black smoke laid by their funnels, their gunfire and the fires blazing in many of them.

For a while only the *Suvorov*, which had got painfully under way again at a crawl, was in sight; on her Kamimura turned the 8-inch and 6-inch guns of his cruisers, while destroyers closed to launch torpedoes. The crew of the battleship fought back valiantly against these daunting odds, her one remaining 12-inch gun and a few 12-pounders replying defiantly. It was enough to make the destroyers keep their distance; not one of their torpedoes hit. The *Suvorov* was still stubbornly afloat when Kamimura left to follow Togo north-eastward in search of the vanished Russian main body.

About 1600 this came in sight again making slowly northward behind the *Alexander III*, which under the renewed cannonade was forced out of the formation. At a range of barely a thousand yards, Togo's ships poured their fire into the remainder which turned away south. Escape was impossible; but this brought them a temporary respite as Togo withdrew to give his crews a rest and a chance to repair their damage while destroyers were ordered forward to launch torpedoes. In the fog of battle they found only the indomitable *Suvorov* which they failed to hit.

As the Japanese torpedo-craft drew off, the Russian destroyer *Buini* arrived to take off the badly wounded Commander-in-Chief and his staff. It was clear, however, that Rozhestvenski was in no condition to take control again, even if he could have been put aboard one of his surviving battleships. Barely conscious, he could only murmur to the destroyer captain, 'Nebogatoff – Vladivostok – Course N23E'. Another destroyer therefore left to seek Nebogatoff and tell him that the command had devolved upon him.

While the heavy ships on either side had been engaged with their enemy equivalents, the Russian cruisers and auxiliaries, following the battleships, had been fiercely harried by the Japanese cruiser divisions. Several auxiliaries had been sunk; the cruisers *Oleg* and *Zhemtchug* were blazing. Amongst the Japanese ships only Rear Admiral Dewa's flagship *Kasuga* had been seriously damaged, receiving a hit below the water-line which forced Dewa to transfer his flag to the *Chitose*.

At 1800 Togo resumed his assault on the Russian main body, now rejoined by the *Alexander III* which within a short while received such further damage that she suddenly swung away, turned turtle and sank taking with her all but four of the ship's company of 836 who had so gallantly fought to the inevitable end.

Meanwhile the *Orel* and the *Borodino* were both ablaze; Russian guns continued to fire but their aim was wild and uncontrolled. As the sun set, Togo decided to withdraw for the night, leaving his torpedo craft to complete the destruction of the crippled enemy. Even as he did so, a last salvo from the 12-inch guns of the *Fuji* smashed into the *Borodino's* hull. There were two dull explosions in her vitals and a column of flame as her magazines exploded. Swerving away to starboard the shattered ship rolled slowly over, lay for a while bottom up and then slid below the surface. One solitary survivor was picked up three hours later by a Japanese torpedo-boat.

At about the same time the battered *Suvorov*, fighting to the last with her little 12-pounders against the Japanese cruiser squadrons which, one after the other, had steamed slowly past her to smother her at point-blank range, had been given the *coup de grâce* by torpedoes and gone to the bottom with every man of her gallant company.

The Russians had achieved some sort of order before darkness came down. Following Nebogatoff in the *Nikolai*, were the *Orel*, *Apraxin*, *Seniavin* and, at a considerable interval, the *Ushakoff*. A long way behind again were the *Navarin*, *Veliki* and *Nakhimoff*. On the *Nikolai's* port side the light cruiser *Izumrud* had taken station. Abreast the *Navarin's* division and to port of it were the cruisers *Oleg*, *Aurora*, *Zhemtchug*, *Donskoi* and *Monomakh*, under Rear Admiral Enquist, who during the night, with the *Oleg*, *Aurora* and *Zhemtchug*, sheered away to the south westward and vanished from the scene until he reappeared some time later in the Philippine Islands where he delivered his ships into internment at Manila.

Of the remainder the *Navarin* was hit by four torpedoes and sank with all but three of her crew. The *Veliki*, *Nakhimoff* and *Monomakh*, also torpedoed, steered for the island of Tsu-shima and were scuttled to avoid capture. Nebogatoff's five leading ships were rediscovered at daylight. The four heavies were soon ringed by Japanese ships and surrendered. The *Izumrud* was able to use her high speed to escape, only to be wrecked by running ashore near Vladivostok. The *Ushakoff*, *Svyetlana* and *Donskoi* were all sunk in the course of the day. Only the cruiser *Almaz* and one destroyer escaped to Vladivostok.

The final act of the tragedy concerned the fate of Rozhestvenski himself. When it became necessary to scuttle the *Buini*, her crew were taken off at daylight, the admiral and his staff being taken on board the destroyer *Biedovy*. In company with the destroyer *Grosny* she steered north. When sighted by Japanese destroyers near Matsushima, the former, though quite undamaged, at once hauled down her flag and surrendered, while the *Grosny* succeeded in making her escape. Thus the unconscious Russian Commander-in-Chief suffered the shame of falling into his enemy's hands through the cowardly action of his subordinates.

The Russian fleet had ceased to exist. Of the line of battle, out of twelve ships, eight had been sunk and the remainder captured. Of the cruisers, five were destroyed and three interned. Seven destroyers were sunk during the twenty-eighth, one was captured and one reached Vladivostok. All this had been achieved by the Japanese at the cost of three torpedo-boats, one of which was sunk in collision. The Japanese had 117 killed and 585 wounded; the Russians lost 4,830 killed alone.

It was indeed annihilation. With the results of the Battle of 10 August in mind, a realization of the ramshackle material state of the Russian ships and the lack of training of their crews at the end of their seven months painful voyage, such an outcome was always inevitable. But to a western world to which Gilbert and Sullivan's comic opera, *The Mikado*, was a not altogether fantastic concept, the total destruction of a first-class navy by the 'quaint' Japanese was unimaginable. It was suddenly realized that with the countries of Europe moving towards a power struggle that would absorb all their forces in the west and with the United States only just beginning to expand their navy into a first-class force, Japan held the key to sea power in the Pacific.

12

JAPAN'S IMPERIALIST AMBITIONS

The Russo-Japanese War was always strictly a limited one from the Japanese point of view. There could be no question, with their limited resources, of advancing into Russia to impose terms following the capture of Port Arthur and defeat of the Russian armies in Manchuria. As for the Russians, even if the internal political instability of their vast country, and the inadequacy of communications had not prevented a reinforcement of their armies in the east, the final obliteration of their navy in the massacre of Tsu-shima removed any possibility of imposing their will on the Japanese.

President Theodore Roosevelt was thus able to induce the two antagonists to meet at Portsmouth, New Hampshire, where a peace treaty was concluded in October 1905. By its terms Japan obtained sovereignty over the southern half of Sakhalin, assumed the suzerainty over Korea, and took over the Russian leasehold of the Liaotung Peninsula, including Port Arthur, and the railway and economic rights in Manchuria which the Russians had obtained from China.

Naval supremacy in the Far East also now fell into the hands of the Japanese. Great Britain, which had held it hitherto, was faced with the vaulting naval ambitions of Germany in European waters. The far-sighted innovating genius, Admiral Sir John Fisher, First Sea Lord since October 1904, was confidently foretelling war and was carrying out wide-spread reorganization which included the concentration of British naval strength in home waters. The Anglo-Japanese alliance of 1902, renewed and strengthened in August 1905, and a programme of naval expansion begun by the Japanese, allowed Fisher to withdraw the majority of the China Fleet.

Up to this time it can be said that sea power in the Pacific was synonymous with sea power in the Far East, that is, in the waters of the China Sea, Yellow Sea and Sea of Japan. Not only was the Pacific too vast an ocean for any one naval power to dominate in its entirety, particularly in the age of sail when communications between its extremes were so infinitely slow and difficult, but elsewhere than the Far East such sea power as had been exercised had been merely local and temporary. Even before the break-up of the Spanish Empire small naval squadrons or even individual ships either national or piratical, had been able to operate virtually unchallenged along the American Pacific coasts, as witness the several captures of the annual 'Manila galleon'. Russian infiltration on the Pacific coast of North America has been mentioned earlier.

With the westward expansion of the United States and the arrival, during the first half of the nineteenth century, of American settlers on the Pacific coast, the eventual establishment of a first-class naval power there became inevitable. That the United States considered themselves the dominant power of the American continent was made clear by the pronouncement of the Monroe Doctrine in 1823. Their influence in the Pacific was soon spreading further afield. The Monroe Doctrine was invoked in the 1840s to prevent Britain and France from taking over the Hawaiian Islands. Disputes with Britain arose over the frontier delimitation between Oregon and British Columbia and over the right to construct and control a Panama Canal, though both were amicably settled.

During the war with Mexico (1846–8), an American squadron controlled the Pacific coastal waters and in the subsequent peace treaty the United States acquired California. The discovery of gold there in 1849 led to a rapid increase in sea traffic via Cape Horn, mainly by the famous fast clippers under the American flag, with many of the ships going on from California across the Pacific to compete successfully with the British in the trade with China.

Though the United States had as yet neither the means nor the ambition to become a first-class naval power, her growing influence in the Pacific was demonstrated by the expedition of Commodore Perry in 1853 and 1854 which resulted in the re-opening of Japan to intercourse with the outside world. In the course of these operations Perry visited the Liu-chiu Islands and the Bonins, taking formal possession of the latter in spite of the presence of British colonists and similar pretensions by the British government. Perry also recommended the establishment of a protectorate over Formosa. The United States government was not interested, however; his recommendation was ignored and the annexation of the Bonins never ratified. It was not until the last decade of the nineteenth century that a combination of a succession of Republican administrations following an imperialist line in trade policy and bold interventionism in international politics with the persuasive advocacy of the American historian Mahan of a strong American navy led to an upsurge of public interest in naval matters and a programme of naval expansion. The result, though it was not for another decade to reach the status of a first-class navy by European standards, was sufficient to overwhelm the Spanish Navy in the war of 1898. This led to the acquisition of the Philippine Islands and Guam. Hawaii, which had been under United States control since 1893, was now formally annexed as was Tutuila in the Samoa group in 1899. In 1900, Britain was constrained to abandon any share in control of the projected Panama Canal.

In spite of this entry of the United States into the ranks of colonialist powers, she took the lead regarding China, which seemed to be heading for partition between the great powers, in a policy known as that of the 'Open Door'. This stipulated the maintenance of China's independence with equal opportunities for all nations to trade with her. In this a *modus vivendi* was reached with Great Britain who was anxious to co-operate in such a policy. The 'Open Door', indeed, was formally recognized by Britain, France, Russia and Japan. At the turn of the century relations between the United States and Japan took their first downwards turn as a result of moves to restrict the immigration of Japanese into California.

Following a series of restrictive acts from 1882 onwards by the United States Congress, the influx of Chinese labourers into the western states had been halted; whereupon Californian employers had accepted Japanese in their place, the numbers soaring to such a height that demands for the Chinese Exclusion Laws to be applied to them had been raised. The result was the euphemistically styled Gentlemen's Agreement of 1907–8 by which the Japanese government was to grant no more passports to its citizens to settle in the States.

This was a painful humiliation and, followed in 1913 by an

anti-alien law passed by the Californian legislation which discriminated against Japanese, was one source of tension between what were by that time the two most powerful Pacific states. Another, and, in the long run the most consequential, was the dominant position in Manchuria and Korea inherited by Japan as the outcome of the Russo-Japanese War.

A period of apparently good relations had followed the Gentlemen's Agreement, marked by the Root-Takahira Agreement to respect the *status quo* in the Pacific, to uphold the Open Door policy and support China's independence and integrity. An American fleet making a round-the-world tour was warmly welcomed in Japan. Nevertheless, at the same time, Japan was working towards an agreement with her former enemy to perpetuate a joint Russo-Japanese domination of Manchuria and Mongolia. This led in July 1910 to a Russo-Japanese Treaty ostensibly to maintain the *status quo*, but with a secret clause, directed basically against the United States, guaranteeing common Russian-Japanese action should their interests in the Far East be threatened. This was followed by Japanese annexation of Korea, while Russia took steps to establish a virtual protectorate over Outer Mongolia. Finally, when China fell into the throes of revolution in 1911, Russia and Japan took advantage of the situation to sign another secret convention to divide Inner Mongolia into mutually satisfactory spheres of interest.

These steps were clearly an abrogation of the policy of the Open Door. Relations between Japan and America suffered a further deterioration.

When the First World War broke out on 4 August 1914, its origins were mainly European and it was to be fought over the territories and waters of that continent. The naval forces available to the opponents and the supplies and bases on which their effectiveness depended made it inevitable that sea power in the Pacific should come to be wielded by the Allies virtually unopposed, particularly after Japan invoked the Anglo-Japanese Alliance to enter the war on their side on 27 August.

The much inferior German naval squadron in the Far East could contemplate a course of commerce raiding only for as long as their supplies of fuel and ammunition held out; the former depended upon the capture of colliers; replenishment of the latter became impossible owing to the blockade of their only base, Tsingtau, which was promptly instituted by the British Far East squadron. Thus the challenge to Allied control of the Pacific was strictly limited in scope and duration.

While it lasted, however, it was real enough on account of the two fast, modern and well-manned armoured cruisers, *Scharnhorst* and *Gneisenau* which constituted its hard core. By the time Japan had decided to declare war, they, together with the light cruisers *Emden* and *Nürnberg*, two armed merchant cruisers and some supply ships had vanished into the immensity of the Pacific. The German Commander-in-Chief, Vice Admiral Graf von Spee, had in fact taken them to the German Marshall Islands, whence he had detached the *Emden* to raid the shipping routes in the Indian Ocean and the two AMC's to do the same in Australian waters before taking a zig-zag route across the Pacific with the remainder.

The two British admirals in the Pacific, Vice Admiral Sir Martyn Jerram commanding on the China Station, and Rear Admiral Sir George Patey in Australian waters, in the dark as to von Spee's whereabouts, concentrated their forces to cover the most likely points of attack, Hong Kong and the Bismarck Archipelago. It was not until 14 September that von Spee's position became known when he arrived off Apia harbour in Samoa, the German colony recently occupied by New Zealand troops. He found the harbour empty of worthwhile victims for his guns and sailed on eastwards to coal in the Society Islands and bombard Tahiti; then eastwards again via the Marquesas Islands, arriving at lonely Easter Island on 12 October, where he was joined by the light cruisers *Leipzig* and *Dresden*; the former had come from her station off the American west coast, the latter from the Caribbean via Cape Horn, having evaded searches for her instituted by Rear Admiral Sir Christopher Cradock, who had followed her from the West Indies.

The general trend of von Spee's movements so far as they were known, the disappearance of the *Leipzig* from her station, news of the *Dresden's* presence on the Chilean coast and of German colliers in the area all combined to indicate that the German squadron was to be expected off the west coast of America. Dispositions designed to meet the threat were ordered by the Admiralty; the task of directing the forces thus gathered was Cradock's. To what degree either or both of these were responsible for the situation which developed can be decided only by a study of the relevant facts in greater detail than space in this volume permits. It can be said, however, that Cradock had no doubts that his force was inadequate to meet von Spee's concentrated squadron; but imbued with a sense of duty and patriotic self-sacrifice like the heroes of ancient Rome, he steamed north up the Chilean coast and at 1630 on 1 November 1914, with the armoured cruisers *Good Hope* (flagship) and *Monmouth*, the light cruiser *Glasgow* and the armed merchant cruiser *Otranto* spread on a line of search at fifteen-mile intervals, he encountered *Scharnhorst, Gneisenau, Nürnberg, Dresden* and *Leipzig* off Coronel.

Even a 'paper' comparison of the opposing forces reveals the British as greatly inferior in strength. The German armoured cruisers each mounted eight 8.2-inch and six 5.9-inch guns, as compared to the two 9.2-inch and sixteen 6-inch guns of the *Good Hope* and the fourteen 6-inch of the *Monmouth*. But half of the 6-inch braodsides of each of the British ships were mounted so low down as to be operable only in a sea much calmer than that raised by the force 6 wind prevailing. Furthermore von Spee's guns were manned by highly trained crews who had recently won the Kaiser's prize for gunnery efficiency; whereas the *Good Hope* and *Monmouth* had been commissioned with reservists on the outbreak of war and there had been no opportunity since for gunnery practice. The *Glasgow's* armament was superior by two 6-inch to that of a German light-cruiser, but there were three of them to oppose her. The *Otranto* was a passenger liner mounting eight 4.7-inch guns but was no match for a warship.

The fourteen-year-old, pre-dreadnought battleship *Canopus* mounting four 12-inch guns and twelve 6-inch which the Admiralty had sent to reinforce Cradock was some three hundred miles to the southward escorting two colliers. Her captain had reported that engine-room defects had reduced her speed to twelve knots and Cradock had decided that so slow a ship could only be a handicap in the wide-ranging search for the enemy he was expecting.

On discovering the odds that faced him, Cradock could, without dishonour, have avoided action and fallen back on the

Canopus. This, however, would have allowed the long-sought and dangerous threat to the vital American trade to vanish again to turn up no-one knew where. Furthermore Cradock no doubt felt that he could surely inflict some serious damage on the enemy before he himself succumbed to superior gun power. With no dockyard available to von Spee, that would be all that was necessary to bring his cruise to an end. Whatever his reasoning, Cradock did not hesitate ; he concentrated his ships and tried to force an immediate action. Von Spee, to the eastward, his gunlayers dazzled by the setting sun, held off until dusk ; then, with his opponents silhouetted against the afterglow, his own mere shadows in the gathering gloom, at 1900 he opened fire at a range at which the whole of his 8.2-inch were in action opposed only by the *Good Hope's* two 9.2-inch.

Before the British cruisers could close to bring their 6-inch guns into play, they had already been shattered by the accurate shooting of von Spee's crack ships. Within an hour the *Good Hope* had gone down with all hands. The *Monmouth* survived until 2128, when the *coup de grâce* was given by the *Nürnberg*. The *Glasgow* and *Otranto* escaped into the night.

For the time being Admiral von Spee was supreme in the south-east Pacific. But half the ammunition of his heavy cruisers had been expended and could not be replenished. At Valparaiso two days after the battle he received advice from Berlin 'to try and break through with all your ships and return home'. This advice the admiral accepted. After a delay at Mas a Fuera until 15 November – a delay which in the event was to prove mortal – his whole squadron sailed, via St Quentin Bay, where coal was brought in colliers from Chilean ports, for the voyage round the Horn.

How he was surprised and brought to action off the Falkland Islands by a British force which included two battle cruisers, and suffered the same fate in his turn as Cradock, has no place in this volume. The light-cruiser *Dresden* escaped from the Battle of the Falklands to break back into the Pacific to conduct a fruitless campaign in vain search of Allied shipping until run to earth and destroyed nearly three months later at Juan Fernandez Island by the *Glasgow* and *Kent*. Except for occasional incursions by disguised merchant cruisers the naval side of the First World War did not disturb the Pacific from that time onwards.

The preoccupation of the Great Powers with the life and death struggle in Europe, however, presented Japan with the opportunity to attempt to make herself supreme in the Far East. The terms of her alliance with Britain permitted her to enter the war against Germany, ostensibly in support of her ally. But that she had ambitions of her own to serve was evident when she rejected British suggestions that she should confine her operations to defence of Allied shipping in the Pacific.

When she declared war on Germany on 27 August 1914, however, the British were content that the Japanese should undertake the reduction of the German naval base at Tsingtau with the token assistance of a small force of British troops which had been stationed at Tientsin, the old battleship *Triumph* and a destroyer. Other British and Australian naval forces in the Pacific were fully extended by the threat from von Spee's squadron and other forces, which had scattered on the outbreak of war to institute the *guerre de course* against Allied merchant shipping. The Japanese were soon seen to be aiming at more than Tsingtau itself. They were determined to take over the whole German concession of Kiaochow and all the rights and privileges held by the Germans in the Shantung Peninsula, though it was given out that their operations were in support of restoration of Chinese territorial integrity.

Japanese troops were landed on 2 September 1914, some eighty miles north of Tsingtau and occupied the whole peninsula as they moved southwards towards the base near which the remainder of the troops were landed on the eighteenth. A siege of seven weeks followed until 7 November when Tsingtau surrendered. In the meantime the Japanese had seized the strategic Tsingtau-Tsinan Railway; they now made it clear that they had no intention of returning the territory to China. On 18 January 1915 they revealed their ambitions more plainly by the presentation of the famous Twenty-One Demands to China.

Divided into five Groups, these demands in the main called upon the Chinese government to agree to exclusive Japanese inheritance of all German rights in Shantung (Group I); to acknowledge Japan's special position in South Manchuria and Eastern Inner Mongolia, to extend the lease of Port Arthur and the South Manchurian Railway to a period of ninety-nine years and to seek Japanese consent before granting any third power permission to build a railway in South Manchuria and Eastern Inner Mongolia (Group II); to make the control of certain mines a joint concern of the two nations (Group III); not to cede or lease to a third power any harbour or bay or island along the coast of China (Group IV); to employ Japanese political, financial and military advisers, to employ Japanese in the police force and to establish a Sino-Japanese jointly-worked arsenal where fifty per cent of China's requirements of munitions of war would be produced (Group V).

When Chinese objections, particularly to Group V, brought negotiations to deadlock, the Japanese presented on 26 April amended demands, softened by the virtual elimination of Group V and by a conditional promise to return Kiaochow to China at the end of the war. Finally, on 7 May 1915, the Chinese were presented with an ultimatum allowing approximately forty-eight hours after which the Japanese would take 'such independent action as they may deem necessary to meet the situation'. The Chinese submitted and on 25 May a treaty was signed.

The European powers were too engrossed with their own life and death struggle to take any serious notice of these events; even the United States contented itself with a note to the two governments stating its inability to recognize any treaty that impaired the Open Door policy.

The chief immediate consequence of China's humiliation was the birth of a new spirit of nationalism amongst her people, expressed primarily in anti-Japanese feelings and a boycott of Japanese merchants and goods. During the next twenty-one months she was too preoccupied with the internal disruption caused by rebellion against the assumption of the Imperial title by President Yuan Shih-k'ai to pay much attention to foreign affairs. After Yuan's death in June 1916, however, the Republic was restored; and in February 1917, at the invitation of the United States, and with encouragement from the Allies who offered to consider suspension of China's indemnity payments for the Boxer Rebellion and to revise her customs tariffs, the Chinese government followed the United States in severing diplomatic relations with Germany over the question of unrestricted submarine warfare.

The possibility of China entering the war against Germany and eventually claiming a seat at the peace conference now loomed up. The Allies wished to encourage this; but Japan foresaw that it could lead to a restoration to China of Shantung and proceeded to secure a secret pledge from Britain, France and Russia to support her claims to Shantung and to the German islands north of the equator provided that Japan helped to persuade China to declare war and, in Britain's case, backed British claims to retain the former German islands south of the equator.

The influence on the course of the war brought to bear by China's entry was minimal. The country was torn by civil war between north and south. The official government, in the north, turned to Japan for loans which were granted in return for military and naval agreements which put China virtually under Japanese control. When Russia collapsed into revolution and civil war the Japanese moved into northern Manchuria; Allied intervention in Siberia in 1918 was principally undertaken by the Americans and Japanese; and when the former withdrew in 1920, the Japanese remained and it was not until the question arose during the Washington Conference of 1922 that they finally followed suit.

The First World War which had at first left America and Japan to compete for commercial advantages in China, left the latter supreme when the United States declared against Germany and turned all its energies towards her defeat. In November 1917, by the Lansing-Ishii Agreement the United States recognized Japan's 'special interests in Manchuria' with which the former 'did not desire to do anything to interfere'. Although the independence and integrity of China and the principle of the 'Open Door' were reaffirmed, it is not surprising that this agreement was generally looked upon as the granting of a free hand to Japan in the north.

At the Paris Peace Conference, President Wilson tried to remove this impression by proposing that the ex-German holdings and rights in Shantung should be taken over by the Great Powers with a view to their being eventually returned to China. But he came up against an adamant refusal by Japan, backed by the secret agreements of 1915 with the European powers. China was also bound by her agreement in 1915 to transfer

German rights in Shantung to Japan who would then return Kiaochow to China, though retaining the right to establish a concession in Tsingtao. The Japanese demands for the implementation of the promises made to them were met in April 1919 when they were given possession of the islands as Class 'C' Mandates under the League of Nations which conferred virtually unlimited authority over them. And, though Japan announced that her policy in Shantung would be 'to hand back the Shantung Peninsula in full sovereignty to China, retaining only the economic privileges granted to Germany and the right to establish a settlement at Tsingtao', the agreement was a humiliating set-back both to President Wilson and to the Chinese.

Having thus achieved their immediate aims, the Japanese now adopted a more conciliatory attitude in foreign relations which was given expression by their liberal foreign minister, Baron Shidehara. They were thus in an agreeable mood when in 1921, together with the British, French and Italians, they accepted the invitation of the United States government to a conference at Washington the scope of which was to cover Pacific and Far Eastern problems as well as a limitation of naval armaments. A Four-Power Treaty was quickly agreed and signed on 13 December 1921 whereby the Anglo-Japanese Treaty was terminated, the status quo of the Pacific islands was to be respected and the Powers agreed to confer if any dispute in the Pacific should arise. On 4 February 1922 Japan restored the Shantung Peninsula to China, including the Tsinan-Tsingtao railway, and relinquished her special rights. Two days later a treaty between the Nine Powers, mainly concerned with Far Eastern affairs, but excluding Russia, bound them to respect the sovereignty, independence and territorial integrity of China.

It was in this conciliatory atmosphere that the sweeping naval disarmament proposals put forward by Secretary of State Hughes were discussed and a treaty finally signed on 6 February 1922. To appreciate its full meaning it is necessary to examine the shape and size of the three principal navies at that time. The strength of a navy was then calculated mainly by the number of battleships and battle-cruisers it mustered and by this reckoning the British Royal Navy was by far the most powerful with forty-one dreadnought battleships and battle-cruisers, though only one of these, the battle-cruiser *Hood*, was of a design which took advantage of the lessons of the Battle of Jutland, and only thirty were on the effective list. The number in full commission had furthermore been reduced to twenty. Four 'super-*Hood*' battleships were projected but had not yet been approved.

The United States Navy had only thirty-three battleships of which thirteen were obsolete pre-dreadnought types and none were of post-Jutland design. Until 1916 the United States had been content to accept British naval supremacy; but in that year Congress had approved a huge naval appropriations bill for the construction of ten battleships, six battle-cruisers, ten cruisers, fifty destroyers, and sixty-seven submarines. With her entry into the war, she had suspended the greater part of this programme in order to concentrate building capacity on craft required for anti-submarine warfare.

In 1918 it had been decided to resume construction to complete the 1916 programme; but by 1921 the programme for 'a navy second-to-none' had lost much congressional support; money for its continuation was grudgingly and meagrely voted; only one new battleship, the *Maryland*, had been completed, though work on three others was well advanced; on the remaining six, which were about twenty-five per cent completed, work was proceeding very slowly.

Japanese capital ships totalled twenty completed, of which four were pre-dreadnoughts. A programme of construction of eight battleships and eight battle-cruisers had been begun which by 1925 would give her a force of twenty-seven capital ships of which eight would be of post-Jutland design as compared with a United States force of twenty-two with twelve of post-Jutland design and a British fleet of twenty-seven with only one post-Jutland unit.

In the face of this situation, with the British wedded to the 'one power standard' which called for a fleet equal to that of any other single power, and the vocal naval lobby in the United States similarly calling for a 'navy second-to-none', both Britain and America were viewing with dismay the prospect of a ruinous armaments race. In the autumn of 1919 the former British Foreign Secretary, Lord Grey of Fallodon, during a mission to the United States, had explored the possibility of a naval limitation agreement. Though no concrete proposals had been made, the fact that Britain was prepared to negotiate a settlement on the basis of parity had been hinted to the administration of the dying President Wilson. His successor, Warren G. Harding, had been in office only four months, therefore, when he took the initiative to invite delegations from Britain, France, Italy and Japan to the conference at Washington to discuss the limitation of armaments as well as Pacific and Far Eastern questions.

The Conference had been opened by a series of sweeping proposals by Secretary of State Hughes for the wholesale scrapping or abandonment of scores of capital ships built, building or projected by the United States, Britain and Japan which would leave the capital ship strength of the three powers at a ratio of 5 : 5 : 3. After the first shock of these proposals had been absorbed and some subsequent bargaining, this principle was accepted, though Japan secured as a condition an agreement by the three powers that no new fortifications or naval bases should be established in the Pacific islands east of 110 degrees east longitude, except in Japan itself, the Hawaiian Islands, Australia, New Zealand and islands on the American and Canadian coasts.

This condition, which effectively barred the Americans from fortifying the Philippine Islands or establishing a first-class naval base there for their Asiatic Fleet, justified Theodore Roosevelt's pronouncement of 1906 that the Philippines were America's Achilles' Heel. In the years to come, as relations between the United States and Japan steadily deteriorated, this was to exert a vital influence on the situation, encouraging the Japanese to take advantage of the strong strategic position it gave them; particularly as they themselves were secretly to break their side of the bargain and fortify their mandated island groups.

Although the acceptance by Japan of an inferior naval strength entailed an apparent loss of face she had, in fact, secured an excellent bargain. The fleet of her chief Pacific rival not only had to be divided between two oceans, but in any clash that might occur over Far Eastern affairs would have to operate thousands of miles from its nearest base, a disadvantage virtually absolute for a battle force at that time. Thus Japan was left predominant in Far Eastern waters and at the same time was spared participation in a naval armaments race in which she must have found herself outclassed.

Only if Great Britain and the United States were to act in concert would Japan's supremacy in eastern affairs be challenged, a situation which was now to be prevented as an era of Anglo-American hostility with regard to naval strength set in. This state of affairs no doubt contributed to the replacement of Japan's conciliatory attitude in Far Eastern affairs by the 'Positive Policy' adopted under Baron Tanaka, the Premier and Foreign Minister from 1927–9, between Shidehara's two terms of office, and to her eventual embarkation on the fatal course of aggression in 1931 which led to the establishment of the puppet state of Manchukuo in the following year.

13

ORIGINS OF THE PACIFIC WAR

The outcome of the Washington Disarmament Conference and the conciliatory attitude of the Japanese government voiced by their Foreign Minister Shidehara during the next five years seemed to promise an era of stability in the Pacific. Even the strained relations between Japan and Soviet Russia resulting from the former's military adventures, which had taken Japanese troops to the shores of Lake Baikal, were resolved in 1922 by Japanese withdrawal from all Russian territory except northern Sakhalin; and in 1925 withdrawal from the latter was also one of the terms of a Russo-Japanese Treaty of Peking.

Beneath the calm surface of international relations in the Far East, however, the waters were stirring. The main source of the disturbance was a combination of circumstances in Japan which, with the best will in the world, was bound to lead to an outward surge of energy from those overcrowded islands – an industrial revolution of unprecedented speed and vigour in a country whose natural resources were small, accompanied by a population explosion the dangerous effects of which only emigration on a large scale could mitigate. Had such emigration under peaceful conditions been possible the disastrous events that were soon to engulf the Far East might perhaps have been avoided. But both American and Australian regulations barred their territories to Japanese immigrants, while in the vast sprawl of the Chinese Empire there was a traditional hatred and contempt for the island people sustained through past centuries by their refusal to recognize Chinese suzerainty, and by their repeated – and finally successful – attempts to annex the Ryukyu Islands, Formosa and Korea; more recently by the thrusting arrogance of Japanese business men in China, encouraged by the militarism of a growing proportion of the Japanese people based on the *samurai* tradition and the semi-religious tenets of *bushido*.

Exposed to this potentially explosive situation was a China whose military energies were almost totally absorbed by a smouldering civil war between north and south and, in the north, between rival warlords, a state of affairs offering irresistible temptation to a warlike neighbour hungry for territory and resources.

Following the death of Yüan Shih-k'ai in June 1916, after a brief restoration of democratic institutions at Peking, power had fallen into the hands of a succession of warlords, the most prominent of whom were Chang Tso-lin, a one-time Manchurian bandit who had co-operated with the Japanese in the Russo-Japanese War and had become military governor of the Manchurian province of Fengtien in 1911; Wu Pei-fu who captured Peking on Chang's behalf in 1920 and, finding his reward inadequate, set himself up as an independent warlord and drove Chang back to Manchuria in 1922; and the so-called 'Christian General' Feng Yü-hsiang who, coming first to the fore as an ally of Wu Pei-fu, became the third of a trio which, in constantly shifting combinations, held northern China and Manchuria under military dictatorship until 1928.

In south China, although the revolutionary Dr Sun Yat-sen had nominally presided over a republican government since 1917, his Kuomintang (National People's Party) was in disarray and he himself was dependent upon local warlords to keep himself in power. In 1923, however, Sun turned for aid to Soviet Russia whence came political and military advisers under whose guidance the Kuomintang was reorganized on Communist lines and a foundation of military strength laid by the establishment of the Whampoa Military Academy with Chiang Kai-shek as its head and with German and Russian instructors. Communists were admitted to the Kuomintang; Sun published his famous Three Principles of the People, the propaganda force of which for the first time brought mass support for the Party. He was not to live to see its triumph, however. As a first step towards re-unification of the country Sun journeyed to Peking at the end of 1924 to negotiate an alliance with Chang Tso-lin and Feng Yü-hsiang against Wu Pei-fu who controlled the Yangtse valley. He failed to win them over and in March 1925 he fell ill and died in Peking.

The nationalist sentiments that the Kuomintang sought to inspire were much strengthened when, a few months later, a labour demonstration in the Shanghai International Settlement was fired on by the mainly British-commanded police; and in June demonstrators in Canton protesting against this incident were also fired on by the police. Anti-foreign feeling, more particularly anti-British, became widespread, but its most effective and immediate manifestation was in Hong Kong where the Kuomintang brought about a general strike.

The familiar process in revolutionary parties of a contest for leadership between extremists and moderates now developed in the Kuomintang with Borodin, the China-born Russian communist adviser, representing the former and Chiang Kai-shek's Nationalists the latter. A compromise was for the time being worked out and allowed an expedition to march triumphantly north to the Yangtse Valley, capturing the cities of Wuchang and Hankow and destroying the power of Wu Pei-fu.

The split between Communists and Nationalists now reopened; but the dispute was decisively resolved in the latters' favour when the two warlords holding the provinces immediately north of the Yangtse, Feng Yü-hsiang and Yen Hsi-shan, threw in their lot with Chiang Kai-shek. In July 1927 Borodin quit his position as political adviser and, with his mission, returned to Russia. After a further period of internal party wrangling during which there was much confusion Chiang was re-elected party chairman and commander-in-chief in January 1928.

Though this placed the leadership firmly in militarist hands, it was a militarism of a new sort that inspired the party and people, one with a fervently patriotic basis as compared to the self-seeking of the various warlords. It received the full support of the people who had groaned under the extortions of the latter. So, when in May 1928 the Nationalist forces, with the co-operation of Feng Yü-hsiang and Yen Hsi-shan, moved north again they met little opposition. Chang Tso-lin fled Peking on 3 June and, as his train rolled towards Mukden, he was blown up and killed, reputedly at the instigation of the Japanese against whom the old warlord had turned in his old age. His place as ruler of Manchuria was taken by his son Chang Hsueh-liang.

The proclamation on 10 October 1928 of the establishment of the Nationalist government with its capital at Nanking seemed to set China on the road to unification and stability which would enable her to resist foreign aggression. Already the western powers had recognized the Nationalist regime and had agreed to give up the most hated treaty right – that of tariff control. Significantly the last power to do so was Japan. But behind the screen with its display of national stability there was still, in fact, considerable turmoil with petty warlords continuing virtually independent, while in Kiangsi the Communist leaders were establishing a regime of their own. In the north Chang Hsueh-liang was left to lord it over Manchuria and Jehol in return for his recognition of the Nationalist regime.

Thus the Chinese government's ability to bring force to bear upon disputes with foreign powers was severely limited. An example which exposed its weakness was the failure of Nationalist forces in co-operation with those of Chang Hsueh-liang to seize full control of the Chinese Eastern Railway in 1929. By the terms of a treaty of 1924 administration of this was to have been equally shared between Chinese and Russians – an arrangement which had inevitably led to constant friction. Wholesale arrests of Russian officials now led to armed clashes and when the Chinese forces suffered defeat, Russian terms restoring the status quo had to be accepted.

It was, however, from the increasingly imperialistic Japan that the real threat to Chinese sovereignty over Manchuria loomed. From every point of view, commercial, strategic and colonial (as an outlet for surplus Japanese and Korean population as well as a vital source of food and raw materials), Manchuria was coveted by Japan. The Kwantung Army (the Japanese force occupying the leased territory) was officered by firebrand followers of the aggressive militarist political clique. It was only a matter of time before they acted independently of government control.

The occasion arose, or was manufactured, on the night of 18 September 1931 when a mysterious explosion damaged the South Manchurian Railway near Mukden. With the clockwork precision of a pre-arranged plan, Japanese troops occupied Mukden before dawn. The troops of Chang Hsueh-liang offered no resistance. By the end of the year all South Manchuria was in Japanese hands. Meanwhile the League of Nations had made ineffectual protests calling for both sides to withdraw their forces and had decided to send a commission of inquiry under

Lord Lytton, which sailed for the Far East in February 1932.

The United States – not a member of the League – sent notes, refusing in advance to admit the legality of any agreement which might be made by the two combatants with regard to Manchuria which. would affect treaty rights or the Open Door policy.

Ideas put forward for imposing economic sanctions were strongly opposed by President Hoover, who would go no further than the gesture of concentrating the United States Fleet in Hawaii which was ordered in February.

While these verbal broadsides still echoed, Japan announced on 18 February the establishment of the independent state of Manchukuo with the last of the Ch'ing dynasty, Henry Pu-yi, installed as its puppet ruler.

By the publication on 23 February 1932 of a letter from Secretary of State Stimson to Senator Borah, the Chairman of the Senate Committee on Foreign Relations, the seriousness with which the United States viewed Japanese aggression was brought home to them. It was ignored, however, by the Japanese government which had already made its position clear by a contemptuous reply to a League of Nations appeal to cease its attacks on China.

The Lytton Commission's report refuting the Japanese contention that their actions in Manchuria had been in self-defence and recommending an independent Manchuria under Chinese sovereignty was published in October 1932 and unanimously approved by the Assembly of the League of Nations in February. Japan promptly resigned from the League: no League sanctions to attempt to impose its will were concerted; nor did America show any inclination to use force to oppose Japan. Thus for the first time the lack of resolution amongst the western powers to resist aggression was exposed, a revelation which was to encourage Fascist Italy and Nazi Germany to follow suit in due course as well as Japan.

Aggressive Japanese military operations, including a destructive attack on Shanghai in which the navy for the first time co-operated with its carrier-based bombers, and, in the north, a pursuit across the Great Wall into China proper of the defeated Nationalist forces, impelled Chiang Kai-shek's government to negotiate a humiliating truce on 31 May 1933.

A period of uneasy calm followed while Japan sought to cloak its ambitions to subjugate China as a desire to assist the Chinese to liberate themselves from the menace of Communism. This failed to win the co-operation of the Chinese government and in 1935 Japan resumed her aggressive course, taking advantage of incidents to force Chinese agreement to further withdrawals and to set up puppet 'independent' regimes in the northern provinces.

In the United States a new administration under President Franklin D. Roosevelt took office in March 1933 with Cordell Hull as Secretary of State. Beset by the problems of the great depression and with a large body of United States public opinion wedded to pacifism and isolationism as a result of disillusionment with the aims of their European Allies in the First World War, it was no more willing to employ force against Japanese aggression than its predecessor. It had to content itself with repeated statements of American rights and of its policy of non-recognition of any unilateral changes in the Open Door policy. It was, however, ahead of public opinion in its realization that force would in the long run have to be called on to stem Japanese expansion at the expense of China. The announcement was made early in 1934 that the Navy would be built up to its full treaty strength. In the summer of 1935, the fleet, concentrated in the Pacific, held widespread man-oeuvres ranging from the Aleutians in the north to Midway in the west.

Meanwhile in China, repeated inroads into Nationalist dominion by Japanese forces led to a rapprochement between Chiang Kai-shek and the Communists and agreement on a united front against Japanese aggression. The Japanese now abandoned all pretences: taking advantage of a clash between Chinese and Japanese troops at the Marco Polo Bridge at Lukouchiao, twenty miles west of Peking, on the night of 7 July 1937 they launched a full-scale, though undeclared war in the north. A further incident at Shanghai on 11 August led to heavy fighting there and, after the occupation of the city, they advanced up the Yangtse valley.

Nanking fell on 13 December and the Nationalist capital, whence the government had moved to Chungking, was given over to an orgy of sadistic murder and looting by the Japanese troops. During the indiscriminate air raids by the Japanese the United States river gunboat *Panay* was deliberately bombed and sunk on 12 December 1937. Several British gunboats were also attacked.

While Japan had thus been getting ever more deeply involved in what was becoming a war of conquest of China – albeit undeclared and referred to by the Japanese as 'the China Incident' – an act of aggression which clearly called for intervention by the League of Nations and by the United States, the Western powers were exposing their helplessness in that respect. Britain and France, preoccupied with the aggressive defiance of the two Fascist states, Italy and Germany, could not contemplate deploying forces sufficient to confront Japan in the Far East. The United States, its navy still far below treaty strength, was also handicapped in any confrontation with Japan by the vast distances of the operational area from the nearest naval base, Pearl Harbour, which itself was far from completion.

All the major democratic powers were furthermore shackled against efforts to re-arm following the naval 'holiday' imposed by the Washington Treaty and by the pacifism which inspired large sections of their peoples. France had never recovered from the holocaust of her man-power in the First World War and feared a repetition at the hands of the resurgent Nazi Germany. The British, in large numbers, had signed the Peace Pledge; while in America pacifist organizations had spread the false idea that American munitions profiteers, the 'merchants of death', had been responsible for America entering the war.

In contrast, the Japanese had from the beginning chafed under the restrictions of the Washington Treaty and its sequel, the London Naval Conference of 1930, from which they had obtained such concessions as parity in submarine strength and an improved ratio in light cruisers and destroyers. At this same conference the building holiday for battleships had been extended to last until 1936. The assembly of a further conference in 1935 for the purpose of working out a new treaty was also agreed.

When preliminary talks began in October 1934 the Japanese had immediately demanded parity in total tonnage and when this was refused they announced their intention to denounce the

Washington Naval Treaty, a denunciation which became effective on the last day of 1934. They were officially bound by the treaty until the end of 1936 and they gave assurances that they did not seek naval aggrandizement and that they would welcome a new limitation treaty on more equitable terms.

Meanwhile the London Conference between the five major naval powers opened in December 1935. Great Britain and the United States had been wrangling for many years on the subject of cruiser limitation, the former insisting that her need for that class of ship was far greater owing to her world-wide responsibilities and commitments. With Japan about to be freed from the Washington Treaty limitations, Britain had already announced that she would no longer support limitation by the ratio principle.

Japan now renewed her demands for a common upper limit and would not discuss any qualitative limitations without it. When proposals were rejected she withdrew from the conference. A treaty, of which the most notable provision was the limitation of the size of guns to 14-inch calibre, but which was so peppered with escape clauses as to minimize its effectiveness, was signed only by the United States, Great Britain and France. Both Italy and Japan were already planning ships outside the treaty limitations and both refused their signature.

In the Pacific the United States now found herself faced with the problem of ambitious, intransigent Japan, just as Britain and France were with that of Italy and Germany. In neither case were the liberal governments sufficiently supported by public opinion to act with the firmness which might have halted the disastrous course leading inexorably to war. President Roosevelt's administration knew that in spite of Japanese attacks on American missionaries and other citizens, as well as the atrocious behaviour of Japanese soldiers (as they ravaged the Chinese territory they overran) and the indiscriminate bombing of Chinese cities, the American people would not fight on China's behalf. Even the *Panay* outrage was settled by apologies for an 'unfortunate mistake' and an indemnity.

Although the euphemism of 'the China Incident' obviated the classification of China and Japan as 'belligerents' and the invocation of the American Neutrality Acts which would have cut off American aid to China, it also permitted Japan, in accordance with the 1911 Treaty of Commerce, to buy huge quantities of petroleum oils, iron ore and scrap without which her war effort would have been crippled. Only the actual export to Japan of aircraft, their equipment and weapons, and materials essential to their manufacture such as aluminium was stopped as a result of a 'moral embargo' by manufacturers at the request of the President in protest against the bombing of civilian populations. As it was, by the autumn of 1938, after a series of military victories the Japanese were in occupation of large areas of China including most of her great cities, and the whole of her coastline.

Up to November 1938 American actions had been confined to repeated protests based, for the most part, on demands for Japan's adherence to the policy of the Open Door, protests which had been fobbed off by specious denials that American treaty rights had been violated or American interests discriminated against. Now, however, the Japanese threw off the cloak of international legality. In a reply by their Foreign Minister it was stated that Japan was 'devoting its entire energy to the establishment of a new order . . . throughout East Asia' and that old principles were no longer applicable nor would they 'promote the firm establishment of enduring peace in East Asia'.

This unmasking of Japan's ultimate aims was followed in the spring of 1939 by the occupation of the island of Hainan which dominated the Gulf of Tonkin and threatened French Indo-China. The limits had been reached for America to stand inactively by, watching the advancing tide of Japanese conquest. In July the Japanese government was given the six-months' statutory notice of abrogation of the Treaty of Commerce. In January 1940, therefore, the United States would be free to impose sanctions in the form of embargoes on exports to Japan. Nothing in this way was at first done ; but the Japanese, having set up a puppet Chinese government at Nanking under Wang Ch'ing-wei, now turned hungry eyes towards the oil-fields of the Netherlands East Indies and Borneo, as well as toward the rubber and tin of Malaya. At the same time they brought pressure to bear on the French in Indo-China to plug the hole in the blockade of China that traffic through Tonkin represented. The British, too, with Hong Kong a hostage, surrounded by Japanese troops, acceded for a while to demands to close the Burma Road supply route to Chungking. It was known also that Japan was moving towards a military alliance with Germany and Italy.

Not yet did the Roosevelt administration have sufficient backing from the American public to reinforce its verbal protests with effective action. But the President's proclamation of 2 July 1940 which, under the terms of the recently passed National Defence Act, put the export of arms, ammunition and a wide range of items and materials important to any war effort under licence, was the first step in a process which was eventually to force Japan to choose between the abandonment of her imperialistic ambitions or go to war to seize the main sources of raw materials for herself.

On 25 July the key materials, scrap iron and petroleum products were added to the list. The first teeth were given to the licensing system six days later when it was announced that aviation gasoline would be exported to the western hemisphere only. Other restrictions were added piecemeal over the following months. Each brought a protest from Japan firmly rejected by the State Department. They did nothing, however, to halt the steady southward tide of Japanese aggression. In September 1940 the French in Indo-China were forced to allow the Japanese to establish air bases there and Japanese garrisons for them. In the same month Japan allied herself defensively to Germany and Italy in a Tripartite Pact. Thailand became virtually a Japanese satellite in December.

When a new Japanese ambassador to the United States, Admiral Nomura, presented his credentials in February 1941, it was decided that the time had come for a definitive effort to halt Japanese plans for conquest. In a series of conversations Secretary of State Hull once again stated the basic principles on which civilized international arrangements should exist: respect for territorial integrity and independence, non-interference in internal affairs of other countries, support of the principle of equality and the Open Door and rejection of the use of force to change the *status quo*. The Japanese reply, delivered on 12 May 1941, included proposals that the United States should persuade the Chinese to negotiate a peace settlement or otherwise suffer a cessation of American aid; it was clear that the two points of view were poles apart; no compromise was imaginable.

Nevertheless negotiations continued with the Japanese government's total insincerity revealed to the Americans through the breaking of the former's diplomatic code. A number of steps taken by the Japanese government, including the call-up of more than one million recruits and the recall of all merchant shipping from the Atlantic, were evidence of preparations for a major war. And when Japan, in July 1941, announced that Vichy France had consented to a joint protectorate of the whole of Indo-China and proceeded to move forces into the southern half of the country, the Rubicon was crossed.

President Roosevelt now announced the freezing of all Japanese assets in the United States, bringing about virtually a total stoppage of trade between the two countries. Supplies of oil, in particular, from America or the East Indies, were cut off. A term had thus been set to Japan's ability to continue to function, to maintain her industries and carry on military operations against China; after that she would be forced either to abandon her conquest of China and plans for the Great East-Asia Co-Prosperity Sphere, as her enlarged empire was to be known, or to go to war to seize the vital raw materials for herself.

That there was never more than an infinitely remote chance of a Japanese climb-down was demonstrated by the continued mobilization, the reinforcement of Japanese armies in China and Indo-China and the ruthless bombing of the Chinese capital, Chungking. Even that faint possibility vanished when a new Japanese government under General Tojo, leader of the militarist clique, took office in October 1941. And, indeed, detailed plans for military operations to thrust southwards and seize the oil, tin and rubber supplies of the East Indies had been already prepared under the previous administration headed by Prince Konoye. The objective of these plans was the establishment of a zone of Japanese occupation covering all territory within a perimeter which circled from Burma southwards anti-clockwise to enclose Malaya, the East Indies, New Guinea, the Bismarck Archipelago, the Gilbert Islands and thence northwards to Kamchatka.

This involved a military take-over of Thailand, an amphibious invasion of Malaya and the capture of Singapore. The

Philippine Islands were to come under massive air attack in which the carrier-borne and shore-based planes of the Japanese Navy would play the principal part, as a preliminary to an invasion backed by the whole Imperial fleet. The American Pacific Fleet, steaming from Pearl Harbour to the rescue, would be harried by air and submarine attack from the Marshall and Caroline islands before being brought to action in the Philippine Sea. The advance towards the planned perimeter of the Great East Asia Co-Prosperity Sphere would then be resumed with the occupation of the East Indies, followed by New Guinea and the Bismarcks. The achievement of this perimeter, within which lay the territories which would give her economic dependence, was the limit of Japanese initial aims. For all their martial spirit, their superb confidence in their fighting superiority, the Japanese did not envisage an all-out victory over Britain and the United States. They believed, however, that they could defend their perimeter effectively enough to force their enemies to a compromise peace and acceptance of a *fait accompli*.

Geography dictated that any war between Japan and the western powers, particularly against America, would be decided primarily by sea power. With the Japanese Navy potentially weaker than that of the United States even if the latter were acting without the British and Dutch allies it could be expected to have, the basically defensive employment of the main Japanese fleet envisaged by the war plan was orthodoxly sensible. American commitments to the Philippines could be expected to force them to launch their Pacific Fleet, inferior to Japan's Combined Fleet, to the rescue under all the disadvantages of having to fight some four thousand miles from its nearest fleet base, Pearl Harbour. For it will be recalled that under the terms of the Washington Treaty, the United States had agreed not to establish any such base in the Philippines, a restriction to which they had adhered; whereas the Japanese had secretly fortified and equipped bases in the islands which, unintelligibly, the League of Nations had left under their mandate even though Japan had quitted the League in 1932.

Early in 1941, however, the Japanese war plan had come under critical examination by the new Commander-in-Chief of the Combined Fleet, Admiral Isoroku Yamamoto. Unlike the military clique who with their arrogance and narrow, blinkered outlook, were forcing Japan along the road to major war, he realized that his island country, totally dependent for its existence on overseas supply of raw materials and food, yet possessing only a merchant navy quite inadequate for the purpose, could only hope to hold off the American fleet long enough for the perimeter to be established if she could inflict at the outset a decisive and annihilating naval victory. And under his hand he believed he had the weapon necessary for the purpose, the Striking Force composed of six fleet aircraft carriers with their escort of fast battleships, cruisers and destroyers. With the force of nearly 400 aircraft from these carriers he proposed to deliver a surprise attack, simultaneously with the declaration of war, on the United States Pacific Fleet at its moorings in Pearl Harbour.

Yamamoto set his staff experts to planning the operation. In spite of its initial reception with obstinate disapproval by the Naval General Staff headed by Admiral Osami Nagano, who not only insisted that the carriers could not be spared from the attack on the Philippines, but believed that such a thrust across thousands of miles of ocean was too much of a gamble, Yamamoto pressed ahead with preparations. The carrier squadrons were launched on an intensive programme of torpedo and dive-bombing practices against targets in enclosed waters. Air-borne torpedoes were modified so that on being released into shallow water they would not plunge into the mud.

The object of all this practice was not revealed to any but the staff planners until October when, in great secrecy, a scale model of Pearl Harbour was set up in a compartment in the carrier *Akagi*, flagship of Vice Admiral Chuichi Nagumo, commanding the Striking Force. There, all officer-pilots of the air groups were given the electrifying news by Yamamoto himself. The Commander-in-Chief's basic operation order, naming 8 December Japanese time (Sunday 7 December, Hawaii time) as the day of destiny, was issued on 1 November, though it was not for another two days that Admiral Nagano, having persuaded his colleagues of the Imperial Headquarters to approve the change in the war plan, gave his consent.

So, while in Washington diplomatic exchanges continued with each side formulating terms which it knew the other had no intention of accepting but which enabled the game to be played out, granting American industry more time to adapt itself to war and enabling Japanese preliminaries for their treacherous blow to be completed, Nagumo's ships secretly, singly or in pairs, slipped away from their anchorages between 10 and 18 November for a rendezvous in desolate Tankan Bay on Etorofu in the Kuriles. Radio silence was maintained by them while, from Kure, dummy traffic was transmitted for the benefit of American radio intelligence.

Another force which now set out across the ocean comprised sixteen submarines of the Advanced Expeditionary Force, five of them carrying midget submarines which were to be launched in time to penetrate Pearl Harbour simultaneously with the air attack. The remainder were to patrol where they could expect to encounter any American ships that escaped seawards. Finally on 26 November the carrier force, accompanied by tankers from which ships would refuel at sea, weighed anchor and set an easterly course along the 43rd Parallel across a part of the ocean where they were unlikely to be sighted by other shipping. Concealment was further ensured by the foul weather, storms and thick fogs through which they wallowed for the first six days.

American cryptanalysts were meanwhile supplying their government with enough information to make it clear that war was imminent. The exact date could not be deduced, however; nor could the even more crucial information giving the target selected for Japan's initial assault. It was known that widespread movements of troop convoys and warships in a southerly direction were in train. These were correctly judged to be aimed at the Philippines, the Kra Isthmus or Borneo and American naval opinion was unanimous that these would absorb all available Japanese resources. The possibility of so bold a stroke as a carrier-borne attack on Pearl Harbour at a range of nearly 4,000 miles was never imagined. Thus when on 27 November Admiral Stark, United States Chief of Naval Operations, sent a war warning to Admiral Kimmel, commanding the Pacific Fleet at Pearl Harbour, and to Admiral Hart, commander of the small Asiatic Fleet based on Manila, his appreciation made no mention of Pearl Harbour.

Admiral Kimmel, indeed, did order a state of alert which called for a proportion of close-range armament to be kept manned, though ammunition was not kept immediately available. Otherwise the training programme necessary to bring a rapidly expanding fleet up to efficiency was maintained, though at an intensity less than extreme, with all ships in harbour for rest and recreation at week-ends and all-night leave for many of their officers and men – a fact faithfully conveyed to Tokyo in messages from the Japanese consul in Honolulu.

In the small hours of 6 December the latest of these messages reached Nagumo in the *Akagi* as he steered south-eastward to reach a position some six hundred miles north of Oahu. Five days earlier Yamamoto's executive signal for the attack on Pearl Harbour to be delivered at dawn on Sunday 7 December had been received. But now Nagumo learned that though seven battleships of the United States Pacific Fleet were moored invitingly head and stern in Battleship Row and the flagship lay in dry-dock, no aircraft carriers, his top priority targets, were in harbour. In conference with his staff, the admiral decided that the attack should go ahead as planned. It was hoped the carriers might return to harbour during the thirty hours or so remaining until zero hour.

As dusk fell that Saturday evening and the carrier force turned south at high speed for the dawn flying-off position north of Oahu, a solemn dedication was staged on the flight-decks, with emotional patriotic speeches greeted by fervent cries of 'banzai'. To the *Akagi's* masthead was hoisted the historic signal flag used by Admiral Togo before the Battle of Tsushima. The excited crews dispersed to rest and sleep if they could, till the great moment came to launch the air fleet in the morning twilight.

At Pearl Harbour the light-hearted routine of a peace-time Saturday night prevailed. The only signs that a war warning had been issued were the boom defences strung across the entrance, some auxiliary minesweepers getting ready to make a routine sweep of the approach channel and, farther out the duty destroyer *Ward*, on anti-submarine patrol.

14

PEARL HARBOUR — CORAL SEA — MIDWAY

The first small ripple on the sleepy calm prevailing at Pearl Harbour on the morning of 7 December 1941 arose when the patrolling destroyer *Ward* received a message by signal light at 0342 from the minesweeper *Condor* that a periscope had been sighted. The destroyer instituted a search which after two hours had yielded nothing. False reports of periscopes were commonplace and it had not been considered necessary to relay this one to the command on shore. Not until a second periscope sighting by a patrolling Catalina flying boat had led the *Ward* into contact and the destruction of a midget submarine at 0645 were steps taken to raise the alarm which resulted in a second duty destroyer being ordered out to assist. Urgent messages now flooded the telephone system and it was a further forty minutes before the duty officer on the Commander-in-Chief's staff received the warning. At 0750 Admiral Kimmel was on his way from his house to his office when an aerial bomb exploded on Ford Island, the Naval Air Station in the middle of the harbour. The greatest naval war in history had begun.

One hour and fifty minutes earlier, two hundred miles to the northward, Admiral Nagumo's carriers had swung into wind and the first striking force of fifty Nakajima Type 97 bombers ('Kates') each armed with one 1,760-pound armour-piercing bomb, seventy more 'Kates' each carrying a torpedo, fifty-one Aichi Type 99 dive-bombers ('Vals') loaded each with one 550-pound bomb and forty-three escorting Mitsubishi 'Zero' fighters had roared off the decks. A second wave of aircraft – fifty-four 'Kates' with 550-pound bombs, eighty 'Vals' and thirty-six 'Zeros' had been launched at 0715. Led by Commander Mitsuo Fuchida in one of the bomb-laden 'Kates', the swarm had headed south and was soon visible on the scan of a mobile army radar station where a trainee operator, awaiting the arrival of transport before closing down and going to his breakfast, watched with mild curiosity what he assumed to be a flight of bombers due that morning from the States.

Although no inkling of what was about to befall had reached Pearl Harbour, information which, correctly evaluated, might have given grounds for a full alert to be instituted had been circulating at a stately peace-time Sunday pace amongst government and service leaders at Washington since 0915 (0345 Hawaiian Time), when Admiral Stark was shown a decyphered message addressed to the Japanese ambassador. This instructed Admiral Nomura to deliver to the United States Secretary of State, at 1300 Washington Time (0730 at Hawaii), a message finally breaking off negotiations. When this was shewn thirty-five minutes later to the Secretary of State and the Secretary of the Navy Department it was pointed out that this would be about time of sunrise over Honolulu. No alarm bells rang and no warning to Pearl Harbour was initiated until General Marshall, Chief of the United States General Staff, on his return from his morning ride, saw the message at 1130 and by 1200 had drafted a message to his Army commanders which concluded : 'Just what significance the hour set may have we do not know, but be on the alert accordingly'. By the time this reached Pearl Harbour the battle squadron of the Pacific Fleet and the naval and army air forces on Oahu were sunk or in smoking ruin.

Translation and preparation delays in the Japanese Embassy caused the time for the presentation of the Japanese government's ultimatum to be delayed until 1400. Forty minutes earlier, (0750 Hawaiian time) the panorama of Pearl Harbour had come in sight of Mitsuo Fuchida with the seven battleships tethered for the slaughter. To the air fleet he gave the brief executive order for the long practised attack : 'Tora ! Tora !'. And as the torpedo planes slanted down and the dive-bombers plummeted unopposed by guns or fighters he reported to the impatiently waiting Nagumo that complete surprise had been achieved.

For details of the catastrophic events of the next two hours the reader must turn to sources listed in the bibliography. For the purposes of this volume it must suffice to record that when the Japanese air fleet departed to return to its carriers, leaving only nine 'Zeros', fifteen 'Vals' and five torpedo planes shot down out of their total of 354, four battleships had been sunk, one beached and the remaining three severely damaged. Three cruisers, three destroyers and four miscellaneous types had been heavily damaged. The United States navy had also lost ninety-two aircraft with thirty-one others damaged, while ninety-six army aircraft had been destroyed. Altogether 2,403 Americans had died, 1,176 more had been wounded.[1]

There were nevertheless two notable omissions from the list of Japanese achievements. The repair facilities of the naval dockyard and the fuel depot with its fifty-odd tanks brimming with oil remained intact; and none of the three aircraft carriers of the United States Pacific Fleet had come under attack. Had a second attack been launched against the former, as Fuchida and other air group leaders vainly urged, the only base from which American naval operations in the Pacific could have been effectively carried on might have been crippled for many months. As for the carriers, by good fortune the *Lexington* had been absent on a mission to deliver aircraft to Midway Island; the *Enterprise*, returning from a similar mission to Wake Island was 200 miles west of Oahu; the *Saratoga* was at San Diego, California.

Nagumo would not tarry to seek out any of these and, having refuelled his ships, set course for Japan. Thus in spite of the spectacular destruction of the battle force (ships which in fact had already become virtually useless for the type of naval war about to develop in the Pacific), a fleet of three large carriers, sixteen cruisers and forty destroyers, with an intact base in mid-ocean, remained. It was to prove powerful enough to dispute Japanese control of the ocean pending reinforcement by ships transferred from the Atlantic and by the new, faster battleships and fleet carriers that were being hastened to completion in American yards. Furthermore the shock and horror of the treacherous attack which was immediately followed by a declaration of war by Japan's Axis partners, had probably been the one thing able to bring the American people united into war alongside Britain and her allies.

[1] The Japanese submarine force achieved nothing of importance though at least one midget penetrated the harbour and fired torpedoes harmlessly before being destroyed.

British Empire territory had indeed, suffered its first impact of Japanese aggression at almost the same time as Pearl Harbour was reeling under air attack when, at 0025, 8 December (Singapore time) troops from a large convoy poured ashore unopposed at Singora and Kota Bahru in northern Malaya. So, too, had the Philippines where, soon after noon on the same day, massive air raids by shore-based Japanese naval planes from Formosa had begun the process of eliminating American air power, completed two days later. This left the islands open to invasion from the sea, a development which was to take place in the Japanese army's own good time with Manila falling on Christmas Day and the conquest of Luzon being completed on 6 May when the island fortress of Corregidor surrendered.

More urgent for the Japanese was the multi-pronged southward drive to the vital sources of oil, rubber and tin. The first of these, down the Malay Peninsula to capture the British naval base of Singapore, required the establishment of naval superiority in the Gulf of Siam. Had the British been able to deploy a balanced naval force with an adequate air element, this must have involved a naval battle between the Japanese force covering the amphibious operation, the battleships *Kongo* and *Haruna*, three heavy cruisers and a destroyer screen supported by shore-based naval air fleets from airfields near Saigon. In the event, however, all that the British, hard-pressed in European waters at one of the blackest periods of the war against the Axis, were able to send to Singapore were the battleship *Prince of Wales*, the old battle-cruiser *Repulse* and four destroyers to join the China squadron composed of three veteran light cruisers and a few First World War destroyers, the whole constituting a newly-formed Eastern Fleet. Such air support as the Commander-in-Chief Eastern Fleet Sir Tom Phillips, with his flag in the *Prince of Wales*, could call upon would have to be provided by the Royal Air Force units in Malaya which were meagre in numbers, and obsolete in performance. Co-operation with the United States Asiatic Fleet, composed, apart from a strong force of submarines, of two cruisers and thirteen old destroyers and the Netherlands East Indies Force comprising three small cruisers, half a dozen destroyers and sixteen submarines, had been agreed in a series of conferences during 1941; but no unified command was planned and though the

Netherlands Force was to accept British strategic direction, the American Admiral Hart was categorically forbidden to do so.

At the first news of the Japanese landings on the Malayan coast, Admiral Phillips took his two capital ships and a screen of four destroyers to sea with the hope of falling by surprise on the enemy's troop convoys. He was sighted and reported by a Japanese submarine, however, and became the target for a force of fifty-two torpedo planes and thirty-four bombers from Saigon. The Royal Air Force, fully committed to the land battle, could supply no timely fighter cover. Hit by six and five torpedoes respectively, the *Prince of Wales* and *Repulse* were sent to the bottom.

Japanese naval invasion forces now poured southwards in two main streams divided by the land mass of Borneo. With brief pauses at the key ports to secure the surrounding land area and set up air bases, the advance continued unchecked. Opposition by Dutch and American submarines took a certain toll but could not stop the flood. Allied air forces available for maritime operations were too slender to affect the issue. By the end of January Borneo, Celebes and Amboyna in the Netherlands East Indies and Rabaul, key harbour of the Bismarck Archipelago, were in Japanese hands. Singapore surrendered on 15 February. By this time a Combined Striking Force of American and Dutch warships had been gathered under the Netherlands Rear Admiral Karel Doorman at Surabaya. Besides his flagship, the cruiser *De Ruyter*, it consisted of the Netherlands light cruiser *Tromp* and three destroyers, the United States cruisers *Houston* and *Marblehead* and four destroyers. But when this squadron sailed on 4 February to operate against enemy convoys in the Macassar Strait it was heavily attacked from the air: the *Marblehead* was so damaged that she had to limp back to the United States for repairs; the *Houston* had her after triple 8-inch turret demolished and the *De Ruyter's* anti-aircraft control was put out of action. Doorman was forced to withdraw south of Java to avoid further air attack and await the Japanese advance into the Java Sea when an opportunity might arise to strike more effectively at them.

An attempt to oppose the invasion force approaching Sumatra on 15 February was turned back by continuous, un-opposed air attack during which two American destroyers were put out of action and a Dutch destroyer was wrecked on a reef. Japanese forces landed the next day at Palembang. Doorman next mounted a night attack, therefore, on Japanese transports in the Badung Strait as they withdrew after landing troops on Bali. In a confused engagement another Dutch destroyer was lost, the light cruiser *Tromp* and an American destroyer put out of action and the *Java* damaged. In return two Japanese destroyers were badly damaged.

The climax of the Japanese southward drive, the occupation of Java, was now at hand. By 26 February Doorman had gathered under his flag the two heavy cruisers HMS *Exeter* and USS *Houston*, three light cruisers, H Neth MS *De Ruyter* (flag) and *Java* and HMAS *Perth*, three British, two Dutch and four American destroyers. Impressive on paper, it suffered from a lack of joint training, tactical doctrine or system of signals. Its personnel were nearing exhaustion after weeks of ceaseless harrying by the enemy's unopposed air power.

Such was the force that steamed out of Surabaya on the twenty-seventh to oppose the two invasion convoys in the Java Sea. It was met by the Japanese covering force of two heavy cruisers, two light cruisers and fourteen destroyers, not greatly superior in material strength but enormously so in effectiveness. While the troop convoys were diverted clear, the two fleets fought the day and night action known as the Battle of the Java Sea by the end of which Admiral Doorman had gone down in his flagship together with his other cruiser, one Dutch and two British destroyers; HMS *Exeter* had limped away heavily damaged; USS *Houston* had expended nearly all her ammunition and the American destroyers their torpedoes. The Japanese had suffered serious damage only to one destroyer. The catastrophe was soon made total when the *Perth*, *Houston*, *Exeter*, an American and a British destroyer were caught by superior forces and destroyed as they sought to escape through the Sunda Strait during the following days. Thereafter Japanese forces were able to swarm ashore on Java unopposed to complete the planned occupation of the 'Southern Resources Area' in less than three months from the Pearl Harbour attack.

The ineffectual defiance offered by the Allied naval forces to their greatly superior enemy had been mainly an act of self-sacrifice on the altar of national honour. There had been no hope of stemming the Japanese advance; nor, indeed, had it even been appreciably delayed. Elsewhere in the Pacific opposition by the United States Pacific Fleet had been necessarily confined to air-raids on Japanese bases in the Marshalls and Gilberts launched from the three carriers available: *Enterprise*, *Lexington* and *Yorktown*. For the time being the opposing carrier force, following delivery of its thunderclap at Pearl Harbour, was similarly (though with two years of experience in the China War behind it, more effectively) engaged. Wake Island, Rabaul, Amboyna and Tjilatjap (southern Java) had all cowered under Japanese carrier raids prior to their capture; Darwin, and, at the beginning of April, Colombo and Trincomalee in Ceylon, were hammered by Nagumo's airmen swooping almost unopposed to sink the small carrier HMS *Hermes* and the cruisers *Cornwall* and *Dorsetshire* as well as to wreck harbour installations. Both sides were demonstrating that in the vastness of the oceans, fast carrier striking forces were the main key to sea power on which, in turn, the outcome of the war would depend. Inevitably, in pursuit of such sea power, the opposing carrier forces must eventually confront each other in battle. The moment was not to be long delayed.

Had the Japanese adhered to their original war plan and now concentrated on the consolidation and strengthening of their perimeter, this might conceivably, not have been so. But the unexpectedly easy conquest of the Southern Resources Area had engendered what they were later, ruefully, to call the 'victory disease' – contempt for their enemies and an overweening ambition to extend their perimeter to take in the western Aleutians in the north, Midway Island in the east, Samoa, Fiji, New Caledonia and Port Moresby in the south and south-west, thus cutting communications between Hawaii and Australia and threatening them both.

The desire to push the perimeter eastwards to include Midway was intensified by the stunning experience of the sight of American bombers over Tokyo on 18 April. Such a violation of the Japanese homeland had an effect on morale out of all proportion to the minor damage caused by the sixteen B25 United States Army bombers which had been launched from the carrier *Hornet*, newly transferred from the Atlantic. Plans for the capture of Midway were now urgently pushed ahead.

The first operation to be launched, however, was aimed at the capture of Port Moresby. Like other Japanese naval operations of the war, it was over-elaborately planned to be carried out by several separate but correlated expeditions; the failure or even the delay of one could dislocate the whole. Furthermore it was based on the assumption that surprise would be achieved and so give the Americans no guide as to where to concentrate their carrier strength in opposition.

This was the fatal mistake which, on two crucial occasions, was to upset all Japanese calculations: for the Commander-in-Chief Pacific Fleet, Admiral Chester W. Nimitz at Pearl Harbour, was kept sufficiently informed of their operational plans by his code-breakers to make his own dispositions in anticipation. In this case, he knew the main features of the Japanese plan which was to open with the seizure of a seaplane base at Tulagi in the Solomon Islands on 3 May and follow with the despatch of an invasion convoy routed round the eastern tip of Papua to Port Moresby. It was to be given close cover by a squadron composed of four heavy cruisers and the light carrier *Shoho*. More distant cover against interference by the Allied naval forces deployed in the South Pacific was to be provided by a Carrier Striking Force operating in the Coral Sea.

Japanese intelligence placed only one American carrier in the area, the *Yorktown*, forming, with her screen of three cruisers and six destroyers, Task Force 17 under Rear Admiral Frank Fletcher. The others were thought to be at Pearl Harbour, where in fact *Enterprise* and *Hornet* arrived from the Tokyo raid on 25 April and were thus unable to intervene in time. The *Saratoga* had been torpedoed by a Japanese submarine in January and was undergoing repairs and modernization in the States. The Japanese were content, therefore, to restrict their Striking Force to the two fleet carriers *Zuikaku* and *Shokaku* accompanied by two cruisers and six destroyers, so as to allow the remainder of Nagumo's carriers an urgently needed period of rest, recreation and replacement of air crews after their triumphant career from Pearl Harbour to Colombo. Nimitz, apprised of the Japanese plan, was able to rush the *Lexington's* Task Group 11 from Pearl Harbour to join Fletcher. The two carrier groups made rendezvous on 1 May and were joined by a joint American-Australian cruiser squadron on the fourth.

Thus the two fleets were of comparable strength when the two-day Battle of the Coral Sea opened on 7 May with the scouting planes of the carrier forces fanning out in search of their opponents. Both sides made serious tactical errors in the opening stages. At dawn on the seventh Fletcher detached his joint cruiser squadron to intercept the Port Moresby expedition which had been located on the previous day by shore-based aircraft. At the same time he launched an air search for the enemy's carriers. This failed to locate the Striking Force which was shrouded in a belt of rain; but a signal from one of the *Yorktown's* planes reporting the force supporting the invasion convoy was wrongly interpreted as reporting 'two carriers and four heavy cruisers'. Fletcher at once launched the whole of his striking force with a large proportion of his fighter defence to escort them. They located and sank the little *Shoho*; but for this secondary objective Fletcher had left himself perilously open to attack by the Japanese carrier strike planes. And these, indeed, thirty-six dive-bombers and twenty-four 'Kate' bombers with fighter escort were winging their way in his general direction.

Luck was with him, however. Japanese reconnaissance had also erred, mistaking one of Fletcher's supporting tankers for a carrier; and it was on her and her solitary destroyer escort that the Japanese bombers expended their fury, sending both to the bottom. With evening approaching neither carrier force had located its opponent. Fletcher decided to wait for the morrow; but the Japanese Admiral Takagi, with a confidence based on past spectacular successes, launched a force of twelve dive-bombers and fifteen torpedo planes. They failed to locate the enemy and, at dusk, jettisoned their weapon loads and turned for home. Their route took them, ironically, directly over Fletcher's force where they were set upon by his Wildcat fighters, many being shot down. The remainder had difficulty in finding their carriers in the stormy night. All but seven splashed into the sea when their fuel failed. The first day of the battle had undoubtedly gone in favour of the Americans.

On the following morning, 8 May, both sides launched air searches while it was yet dark. Each located the other soon after daylight; each despatched a striking force at maximum strength. By mid-day the *Shokaku*, thrice hit by bombs and set ablaze, was limping away, eventually to reach Japan, heavily damaged, after a hazardous voyage. In return the *Lexington* had suffered two torpedo hits, three bomb hits and several near misses, leaving her listing and on fire. Damage control and fire parties apparently had the situation under control when a heavy explosion of accumulated petrol vapour between decks brought their work to naught. The ship had to be abandoned and sunk. The *Yorktown* had been hit only once, by a bomb that plunged through three decks before exploding. Casualties were severe and damage heavy, but she remained capable of operating aircraft and gathered in a number of the *Lexington's* as well as her own.

In assessing the outcome of the Coral Sea Battle several factors have to be taken into account. The loss of the *Lexington* and damage to the *Yorktown* had occurred at a critical moment when it was known at Pearl Harbour that another massive Japanese naval operation was imminent. On the other hand Japanese losses in aircraft and expert air crews were both more numerous and much more difficult to replace; so much so that the *Zuikaku* as well as the shattered *Shokaku* would be unable to take part in the coming operation. More significant than any simple profit and loss account, however, was the fact that the Japanese aggression had received its first serious check as the Port Moresby operation was abandoned and the threat to the Antipodes countered.

Nevertheless, but for the overriding advantage possessed by Admiral Nimitz in being able to know Japanese plans in advance, the problem facing him of where to deploy the exiguous forces available would have been insuperable. Though a battleship squadron had been allocated to the Pacific Fleet its units were too slow to keep up with carriers in the extended, fast-moving operations that war in the oceans had become. They were retained on the United States west coast, leaving Nimitz with only two battle-worthy carriers, *Enterprise* and *Hornet* (Task Force 16) as the vital hardcore of his fleet, with six cruisers and nine destroyers as their screen. Fortunately, by 10 May 1942, Nimitz knew that the Japanese expedition scheduled to get under way on about 24 May was to have the capture of Midway as its main objective. He decided that the South Pacific could be for the time being denuded of carriers. Task Force 16 was recalled to Pearl Harbour where it arrived on 26 May for last-minute preparations for battle, and, incidentally, to receive a new commander, Rear Admiral Raymond Spruance, in place of the ailing Vice Admiral Thomas W. Halsey. Two days later it sailed to take up a waiting position to the north-east of Midway. The *Yorktown*, arriving on the twenty-seventh, received round-the-clock attention by the dockyard which enabled Rear Admiral Fletcher to take her to sea with the two cruisers and five destroyers making up Task Force 17 on the thirtieth. By the afternoon of 2 June the two forces had joined. Japanese submarines deployed to report their movements arrived too late to do so. Admiral Yamamoto, in command of the apparently overwhelming Combined Fleet, and Nagumo, leading his striking force of four fleet carriers, were left in ignorance of the whereabouts of the American fleet.

In view of the deployment devised for his fleet by Yamamoto this was to be the most crucial factor in the decisive Battle of Midway that was to follow. For Nagumo, operating widely separated from the powerful main body and, indeed, from all the numerous groups of ships advancing to the attack on Midway in accordance with the typically intricate Japanese plan, was charged with two incompatible roles – an air strike of Midway itself to neutralize the island's defences and the location and attack of the enemy fleet. Unaware of the exposure of his secret plans, Yamamoto was confident that the latter could not develop until the former had been completed as he assumed that the United States fleet would be at Pearl Harbour until, at news of the attack on Midway, it would sally forth in defence. It would then be attacked in overwhelming strength by the whole combined Japanese Fleet. The absence of any reports from his reconnoitring submarines confirmed him in this view.

In the event Nagumo was fatally caught on the horns of a dilemma on 4 June when the first, incomplete reports of the American fleet came in to him at the moment that his striking force was returning from its raid on Midway and requiring to land on his carriers' decks, thus inhibiting him from concentrating on despatch of a force to strike the enemy carriers. In consequence he was caught with his decks cluttered with bombers and fighters being re-armed and re-fuelled at the moment that American dive-bombers plummeted down out of the sky to destroy three of his four carriers – *Akagi*, *Kaga* and *Soryu*.

From the sole survivor, the *Hiryu*, two strike-forces were launched which succeeded in crippling the *Yorktown* before she herself was also so damaged and swept by uncontrollable fires that she had to be scuttled. The *Yorktown* meanwhile found herself once again limping for Pearl Harbour. Her luck had run out, however. She was intercepted and sent to the bottom by torpedoes from a Japanese submarine.

Such in brief was the central episode of the Battle of Midway which came virtually to an end when Yamamoto conceded defeat early on 5 June and ordered all his forces to abandon the operation and retire – though pursuit by Spruance's strike planes sank the heavy cruiser *Mikuma* and severely damaged the *Mogami* during that day. Simultaneously with the battle, and intended by Yamamoto partly as a diversionary lure for part of the American fleet, another Japanese force including two carriers bombed Dutch Harbour in the Aleutians and subsequently occupied Kiska and Attu.

The Battle of Midway with its unforeseeable catastrophe for the Japanese carrier force which had amazed the world with its whirlwind career of destruction, must be held to be a major turning point in the Pacific War. Just six months after Pearl Harbour, Japanese naval superiority in the type of ship that had replaced the battleship as the queen of battles had been wiped out. Sea power in the Pacific, hitherto predominantly in Japanese hands, was now in dispute on fairly equal terms. Not yet had the moment come for the Americans to go over to the offensive; but the Japanese advance had been decisively halted. From this time onwards the wealth, industrial potential, ship-building capacity and technology of the western powers would inexorably and at an ever increasing pace overwhelm the Japanese war machine. The warning given by Yamamoto himself to the Premier, Prince Konoye, when the conclusion of the Tripartite Pact had brought the likelihood of war closer, was being clearly justified. 'If I am told to fight regardless of consequence', he had said, 'I shall run wild considerably for the first six months or a year, but I have utterly no confidence for the second and third years.'

15

THE TURN OF THE TIDE—SOLOMONS, NEW GUINEA RECONQUERED

Shaken by the catastrophic outcome of Midway, the Japanese shelved their plans for extending their perimeter except for the inception of a landward thrust towards Port Moresby across the lofty Owen Stanley mountains. The Americans, with their Australian and New Zealand allies, had meanwhile been building up their forces in the South Pacific area. The nucleus of an Allied naval South Pacific Force under Vice Admiral R. L. Ghormley, USN had been assembled with United States Navy and Marine seaplanes and fighter aircraft, United States Army bombers and fighters and some Royal New Zealand Air Force bombers based on island airfields in the chain stretching from Espiritu Santo to Samoa.

Plans for an ambitious advance through the Solomon Islands chain had been under consideration for some time but had foundered on the impossibility of providing fighter cover, the Solomons being beyond the range of the shore-based fighters. Now, however, the Commander-in-Chief Pacific was able to allocate three carriers to the South Pacific, *Saratoga*, *Enterprise* and *Wasp* (recently redeployed from the Atlantic), and orders were given for the enterprise to go ahead, starting with an occupation of the Santa Cruz Islands on 1 August 1942. Before they could be begin, however, news came in of a Japanese air strip being constructed on a grassy plain on the north coast of the Solomon Island of Guadalcanal, virtually the only suitable piece of ground in the mountainous or swampy and jungle-clad group.

That Guadalcanal was the key to control of the area was at once apparent. Plans were hastily revised in favour of an amphibious expedition bringing 19,000 United States Marines to evict the Japanese and occupy the uncompleted air strip as the opening move. The twenty-three transports of the Amphibious Force under Rear Admiral Richmond K. Turner, USN, with a close escort of five American and three Australian cruisers and fifteen American destroyers under the command of Rear Admiral V. A. C. Crutchley, RN was given air cover by the Air Support Force composed of the three carriers, one of the first of the post-Washington Treaty fast battleships, the *North Carolina*, six cruisers and sixteen destroyers. Aided by dirty weather the expedition achieved surprise ; the Marines were already ashore in strength and advancing inland on 7 August to capture the airstrip against feeble resistance before the first Japanese reaction in the shape of a heavy air raid on the anchored transports developed. This was met and successfully defeated by massed fighters from the carriers.

So began a six-months', savagely contested campaign for possession of the fever-haunted island. It was to be fought out among the swamps and jungle of the coastal strip running westwards from Henderson Field, as the air station was named, over the air strip and the anchorage, in the glassy black waters of Ironbottom Sound, embracing the jungle-clad cone of Savo Island between Guadalcanal and Florida Islands and, further afield, in the evenly matched carrier battles of the Eastern Solomons and the Santa Cruz Islands. The outcome was to be decided largely by the degree of success achieved by the two sides in supplying and reinforcing the troops on shore.

Once Henderson Field was established and secured, with a strong force of fighters and dive-bombers of the United States Marine Corps deployed on it, the Japanese, with their nearest air base some 560 nautical miles distant at Rabaul, were in a position of local air inferiority. By day, therefore, the seaward approaches were under Allied control and supply convoys could be brought forward and unloaded. But after dark control went to the navy best trained and equipped for surface night action ; in this the Japanese, in spite of their opponents' advantage in exclusive possession of radar, proved themselves time and again the masters. In a series of night battles they inflicted grave losses in ships and heavy casualties, delivered destructive bombardments on the airfield and its defenders and covered the reinforcement and supply of their troops on the island using destroyers whose nightly dashes earned them the name of the Tokyo Express.

The first of these night actions, the Battle of Savo Island, occurred in the early hours of 9 August while the American troop convoy was still at anchor off Henderson Field. Five Japanese heavy cruisers swept undetected into the Sound to surprise the Allied escorting force, deployed in three separate groups to the south and east of Savo Island. In the course of a single wild hour of gun and torpedo fire with searchlight illumination, they destroyed the Australian cruiser *Canberra*, the American cruisers *Astoria*, *Quincey* and *Vincennes* and damaged the *Chicago* and a destroyer at the cost of light damage to three of their own number. The loss of the cruiser *Kako* later the same day to the torpedoes of an American submarine went only a little way to even the disastrous score.

For the time being the 'Tokyo Express' was able to operate nightly undisturbed. Towards the end of August, Yamamoto tried to draw Rear Admiral Fletcher's carrier force (Task Force 61) into decisive battle with the whole Japanese Combined Fleet which he brought south from Truk ostensibly to cover the landing of reinforcements on Guadalcanal. The Japanese Commander-in-Chief still harboured the delusion that a carrier battle might lead to a situation in which his great battleship superiority could be brought to bear.

News of the sortie of the Japanese fleet reached Fletcher in time for him to deploy his carriers to the northward of the Eastern Solomons by 21 August. Nevertheless he was caught with one of his three carriers, the *Wasp*, absent refuelling some 240 miles to the southward when, during the twenty-fourth a Japanese carrier group was located three hundred miles to the north and steering towards him. This was, in fact, only a decoy group centred on the light carrier *Ryujo*, detached to draw Fletcher's striking force away from Nagumo's main carrier force, the *Zuikaku* and *Shokaku*. This regular feature of Japanese strategy was on this occasion to succeed in its object. As in the Coral Sea battle, Fletcher committed his main strength to a subsidiary target and though the *Ryujo* was quickly overwhelmed by his dive bombers, eventually to sink, the two big Japanese carriers were left free to launch two massive waves of strike aircraft against the *Enterprise* and *Saratoga*.

Fletcher had profited from his experiences in the Coral Sea, however, and had retained a large number of defensive fighters; so that when the attack by the first wave developed the Japanese suffered fearful losses with less than ten of the eighty attackers surviving to get back to their carriers. The *Enterprise* was heavily damaged by three bombs but continued to operate aircraft until the end of the day. The second Japanese strike wave failed to locate the American carriers and the carrier Battle of the Eastern Solomons came to an end as both sides withdrew that evening.

Once again the opposing fleets had fought at a range of some three hundred miles from each other. Japanese battleship superiority had again had no influence on the outcome. Once more, too, in the course of a drawn battle the Japanese had lost large numbers of trained aircrew whose replacement was becoming more and more difficult; whereas on the American side, not only was there a stream of new, fast carriers leaving the building yards but a huge training programme had got under way to provide replacements for casualties as well as to man new carrier squadrons. This was to have a decisive influence on the future conduct and outcome of the war in the Pacific.

For the time being, nevertheless, the South Pacific carrier force, in which the *Hornet* arrived to replace the damaged *Enterprise*, had little advantage over its opponent. In the next few weeks it was to be further weakened by rash exposure to Japanese submarine attack through operating continuously in the same stretch of water in the eastern approaches to the Coral Sea. The *Saratoga* was the first to be torpedoed and put out of action for nearly three months. In spite of a further narrow escape six days later when the *Hornet* and *North Carolina* were attacked on 6 September, the Task Force continued in the same general area and on 15 September the *Wasp* and a destroyer were torpedoed and sunk, the *North Carolina* severely damaged. The South Pacific carrier force now consisted of the *Hornet* alone.

Fortunately over Guadalcanal American air superiority was being maintained from Henderson Field, thus continuing the same divided control with the Japanese surface ships only by night able to use the elliptical seaward approach enclosed by the Solomons archipelago, known as The Slot, to run their reinforcements in. The trickle of supplies this constituted had become inadequate, however, since the Japanese troops on the island had suffered a severe defeat at the hands of the United

States Marines on 12 September. It was decided that transports would have to be used instead of destroyers, even though their slow speed would expose them to air attack during their approach and to inevitable destruction the following morning as they completed disembarkation over the beaches.

The first operation was to be the delivery of troops, heavy artillery and supplies in two seaplane carriers during the night 11/12 October. A covering force composed of the heavy cruisers, *Aoba*, flagship of Rear Admiral Goto, *Kinugasa* and *Furutaka* and two destroyers was shadowed from the air as it ran at high speed down The Slot during the eleventh. An American force of the heavy cruisers *San Francisco* (flagship of Rear Admiral Norman Scott) and *Salt Lake City*, the light cruisers *Boise* and *Helena* and five destroyers which had been hovering to the west of Guadalcanal in anticipation of some such opportunity, was steered to intercept off Cape Esperance, the north-west corner of the island.

Goto's three cruisers in line ahead with a destroyer thrown out on either bow had no radar and were unaware of the presence of an enemy as they steered down the middle of The Slot at twenty-six knots. In Scott's force, which was steering at right angles across Goto's bow in single line ahead with three destroyers in the van and two in the rear, the *Helena* was equipped with the latest radar set and detected the enemy ships when they were still nearly fourteen miles distant. Inexplicably, she failed for fifteen minutes to pass this information to the Admiral so that, unaware of the enemy's approach, he had initiated a complicated reversal of course which was still in progress and temporarily putting his line into disorder when the two forces came together.

In spite of this Goto was taken completely by surprise as the *Aoba*, *Furutaka* and the destroyer *Fubuki* found themselves taken under heavy fire at short range. The destroyer sank; the two cruisers, heavily damaged and on fire, swung away to starboard and steered to escape. The third cruiser, *Kinugasa*, and the remaining destroyer *Hatsuyuki*, turning the other way, encountered and fatally damaged the destroyer *Duncan*. Great confusion had in the meanwhile occurred amongst the American ships as they chased the enemy, during which the destroyer *Farenholt* was crippled by 6-inch shells from the American light cruisers and a number of Japanese torpedoes were narrowly avoided. The cruiser *Furutaka* was limping away in a sinking condition. The *Aoba*, where Goto lay dead, was on fire, but by no means out of action. The *Kinugasa* and *Hatsuyuki* were little damaged.

Lacking radar, the Japanese had been unable to find a clear point of aim for their guns up to this time. But now, the *Boise* switched on a searchlight to illuminate a target detected by radar and was promptly brought under a storm of fire from the two surviving Japanese cruisers. Her fore magazine was set ablaze and only the entry of sea water through her riven hull saved her from blowing up. She was saved from further destruction by the interposition of the *Salt Lake City* which enabled her to stagger away out of action. The chase of the Japanese ships was called off. In the confusion the Americans believed that they had sunk no less than four cruisers and four destroyers and celebrated the Battle of Cape Esperance as a notable victory. The fact was that a most unusual lack of alertness by the Japanese had enabled the Americans to achieve a minor success in sinking the *Furutaka* and *Fubuki* and heavily damaging the *Aoba* as against their own loss of the *Duncan* and serious damage to the *Boise* and *Farenholt*. Most serious, perhaps, was the failure to appreciate the shortcomings of their night fighting expertise which were soon to be painfully re-exposed.

However the outcome of this battle is judged, it is certain that it did not put an end to Japanese domination of The Slot and Ironbottom Sound by night. Nor, indeed, was complete American air supremacy over the region by day maintained in the absence of carrier support and radar-controlled fighter direction. Although a troop convoy bringing three thousand United States Army reinforcements was safely unloaded during 13 October, that same afternoon two heavy, high-flying raids made unopposed bombing practice, churning up the airfield. That night, too, the airfield was subjected to a ninety-minute storm of fire from the sixteen 14-inch guns of the battleships *Kongo* and *Haruna* in Ironbottom Sound, at the end of which more than half the aircraft and most of the petrol supply had gone up in flames. Further devastation was caused by two more air raids during the fourteenth and finally, after the cruisers *Chokai* and *Kinugasa* had fired 752 8-inch shells during the night,

Henderson Field was temporarily neutralized: the airmen could do nothing to prevent the landing of 5,400 Japanese reinforcements and supplies.

Yet another cruiser bombardment delivered during the night 14/15 October led to the conclusion, recorded by Admiral Nimitz that 'we are unable to control the sea in the Guadalcanal area'. To restore morale the colourful thrusting Admiral 'Bill' Halsey was given the South Pacific Command. His arrival coincided with the launching of an all-out offensive by the Japanese aimed at recapture of Henderson Field, which the general in command confidently promised for 22 October. Admiral Yamamoto had therefore ordered the Combined Fleet out from Truk – a force of four carriers, four battleships, fourteen cruisers and more than thirty destroyers under Vice Admiral Kondo – to hold the sea approaches and, as soon as the airfield had been captured, fly in aircraft to occupy it.

The Japanese on Guadalcanal met a gallant and dogged defence, however. General Hyakutake was forced to put back his victory date again and again; fuel in the waiting fleet ran low and on the twenty-sixth when the Japanese offensive was finally and bloodily repulsed, the fleet turned away northwards.

While this fleet had been thus hovering to the north of the Solomons, the American carrier group, hitherto comprising only the *Hornet* and her screen (Task Force 17), had received on the twenty-fourth very timely reinforcement by the *Enterprise*, following hasty repairs at Pearl Harbour, with the fast battleship *South Dakota* amongst her screen (Task Force 16). The two Task Forces, under the command of Rear Admiral Thomas C. Kinkaid in the *Enterprise*, had thereupon circled north of the Santa Cruz Islands and, when patrolling Catalina, flying boats had reported two Japanese carriers 350 miles to the north-west, steering south-east at noon on the twenty-fifth, a scouting force followed by a small strike had been at once launched.

These failed to make contact because the Japanese had temporarily reversed course northwards. During the night Kinkaid pushed on in the same direction and by dawn reports reaching him put the enemy carriers only two hundred miles away. An armed reconnaissance by eight pairs of scout dive bombers from the *Enterprise* was dispatched which at 0650 located and reported Nagumo's carriers, *Shokaku* (flagship), *Zuikaku* and the smaller *Zuiho*.

Nagumo, for his part, had also been probing for his opponents; a report of their position had reached him at about the same time and a striking force was already on its way when out of cloud cover two of the *Enterprise's* planes suddenly plunged vertically to put their two 500-pound bombs squarely on the *Zuiho*, wrecking her flight deck and putting her out of action.

Meanwhile, urged on by a laconic signal from Halsey, 'Attack-Repeat-Attack', Kinkaid had also launched strikes from each of his carriers. The Battle of Santa Cruz Islands thereafter developed on similar lines to previous encounters. On the American side fighter direction was ineffective and the enemy attack which was concentrated on the *Hornet* was met only by gun defences. These inflicted heavy losses but could not save the carrier from hits by several bombs and three torpedoes, which left her burning and immobilized with a heavy list.

The American striking force, unwilling to spend time and fuel forming up, had set out in three separate groups. Passing the Japanese attackers on opposite courses, the *Enterprise* squadron was jumped by a flight of Zeros and lost several of their number. The remainder got strung out and further split up on passage; many failed to find the enemy carriers and expended their force on cruisers, one of which was heavily damaged. Dive bombers from the *Hornet*, however, fought their way through strong fighter opposition to score four hits with 1,000-pound bombs on the flight deck of the *Shokaku*, leaving it a tangle of twisted steel, wrecking the hangar below, where fires blazed up, and reducing her speed to twenty-one knots. The carrier limped away for base and was to be out of action for nine months.

Before this, however, a second strike wave from *Shokaku* and *Zuikaku*, as well as another from the carrier *Junyo* operating with a battleship group, had been sent on its way. That from Nagumo's ships arrived over the *Enterprise* at a time when attention was centred on an attack by a Japanese submarine one of whose torpedoes had sunk the destroyer *Porter*. They thus achieved a considerable measure of surprise and were unopposed by fighters; the 'Val' dive-bombers were already screaming down to drop their bombs when the guns opened up against them. Hardly a single 'Val' survived the hurricane of fire that met them nevertheless; but two bombs hit the *Enterprise's* deck. Her forward lift was put out of action; but her deck was repairable and, with speed and manoeuvrability little affected, she was able to avoid all the torpedoes fired at her. The strike from the *Junyo*, arriving while repairs to the deck were proceeding, achieved nothing of consequence. The *Enterprise's* deck was made serviceable in time to land her planes.

Kinkaid was now threatened by a vastly superior enemy force and his only course was to retire, leaving the *Hornet* to her fate. Bereft of fighter cover she became the target for a number of attacks, being further hit by a torpedo and several bombs. Efforts to salve her were given up in favour of efforts to sink her. Eight hits by American torpedoes and four hundred rounds of 5-inch shell left her still afloat though ablaze from end to end. It was not until four more Japanese torpedoes had also burst against her hull that she finally went to the bottom.

At first sight and in the short term, the Japanese had won a notable victory. In the disputed area they were left with the large carrier *Zuikaku* and the smaller and slower *Junyo* and *Hiyo*, while the Americans had only the *Enterprise* on which repairs were feverishly begun at Noumea. Such a judgement, however, ignores the fact that Japanese losses of aircraft and aircrews had been again far heavier than the American – with the serious long-term consequences mentioned earlier – and less than 100 carrier planes remained with the fleet, sufficient only to operate the two smaller ships.

On Guadalcanal the stubborn Japanese refused to acknowledge the decisiveness of the defeat inflicted on them on 26 October. For a renewed offensive in the following month reinforcements were run nightly down The Slot. So that a convoy of transports with the meagre air escort that could be provided from distant shore bases and the decks of the *Junyo* and *Hiyo* might be safely routed down The Slot during daylight on 14 November, it was planned once again to neutralize Henderson Field using the 14-inch guns of the battleships *Hiei* and *Kirishima*, a light cruiser and fourteen destroyers on the night 12/13 November and by cruisers and destroyers on the following night.

The American South Pacific Amphibious Force anticipated these Japanese moves by arriving off Henderson Field to unload six thousand troop reinforcements and supplies during 11 and 12 November. Air attacks on the transports were successfully beaten off. But then on the twelfth came news of the Japanese battleship force approaching. Though the American battleships *Washington* and *South Dakota* were racing north from Noumea in company with the incompletely repaired *Enterprise*, they could not reach the area until the next day. The transports could and did retire to safety: but Henderson Field could not be abandoned by the Navy. The convoy escort force of two heavy cruisers, three light cruisers and eight destroyers under Rear Admiral Daniel Callaghan steamed back into Ironbottom Sound. In the two forces which were about to meet in the stygian darkness of a calm, moonless, overcast tropical night, basic differences of equipment alone make it unrewarding to try to assess which had the theoretical advantage over the other. The effectiveness of the great guns of the Japanese battleships was offset by the thin-shelled, impact-fused bombardment projectiles with which they had been supplied. On the other hand all the Japanese ships had flashless propellant for their guns, whereas their opponents would be blinded by their own gunfire. The Americans still did not realize that the Japanese possessed a weapon of commanding importance in a night action, the liquid oxygen-fuelled 'Long Lance' 24-inch torpedo with a performance in speed and range many times superior to that of the American torpedo and carrying a warhead of twice the explosive content.

Potentially more important than any of these was the 10-centimetre SG radar fitted in several of Callaghan's ships, enabling a plot of an enemy force's movements to be established at a range of sixteen or more miles. To take full advantage of this, however, called for a close-knit, well organized and trained body of ships with an efficient communications system, which could be compactly manoeuvred during the approach and allowed to exercise initiative to seize opportunities offered them during action. Callaghan's force had none of these characteristics. Neither his flagship, *San Francisco*, nor the *Atlanta*, flagship of his second-in-command, Rear Admiral Scott, victor of Cape Esperance, had the SG radar. It was in a long, unwieldy line with destroyers in van and rear that it was steering slowly westwards through Ironbottom Sound in the early hours of 13 November when the cruiser *Helena* reported radar contact of the enemy between thirteen-and-one-half and sixteen miles distant, advancing south of Savo Island at twenty-three knots.

The Japanese squadron under Rear Admiral Hiroake Abe was formed up with the light cruiser *Nagara* and six destroyers in an arrowhead screen ahead of the two battleships, two other destroyers thrown out farther on the port bow and a group of three, which had lost station in a rain squall, some miles astern. Callaghan ordered his line to turn in succession to pass ahead across the enemy's track at twenty knots. Lacking radar, Abe was unaware of the presence of an enemy who might thus have launched undetected a mass torpedo attack. But poor radio discipline in the American squadron so filled the air with chatter that before orders for it could be passed, the van destroyers on each side came in sight of each other at such short range that the *Cushing*, leading the American line, had to swerve to port to avoid collision.

This caused the squadron to bunch up in confusion while Japanese ships passed on either side. The American commanders waited for orders to open fire ; the Admiral, unable to sort out the confusion or to penetrate the frustrating babble on the voice radio, could not give them. This strange situation was brought to an end in a scene of horror as searchlight beams flashed out, settled on the *Atlanta* which was at once smothered under a hail of shells, one of which killed Admiral Scott and most of his staff. The Japanese, caught initially completely by surprise, had quickly recovered to bring their famed night-fighting techniques into play. The first of many 'Long Lance' torpedoes to hit brought the *Atlanta* to a standstill. The hapless light-cruiser drifting past the advancing American line was mistaken for an enemy and was further shattered and set ablaze by the guns of the *San Francisco*. The horrified Callaghan ordered 'Cease Fire' at the moment that his flagship and the *Portland* had sighted and begun to engage the Japanese battleships. Only in the *San Francisco* and only momentarily, was the order obeyed ; but there, with guns silent under the glare of searchlights, salvos of 14-inch shells from the *Kirishima* shattered her upperworks and bridge, killing the Admiral and his staff.

The battle had become a mêlée in which events piled quickly on one another. In the first clash between the van destroyers, on the one side the *Cushing* and *Laffey* had been mortally damaged and the *Sterett* crippled by gunfire, on the other the *Akatsuki* and *Yudachi* had been fatally hit. The Japanese flagship *Hiei*, pounded by 8-inch and 5-inch guns at point blank range, was badly hurt and circled to port to limp away, barely under control, to the westward. The *Kirishima* and the remainder of the Japanese retired relatively undamaged. In reply the *Portland* and *Juneau* were each riven by the explosion of 'Long Lance' warheads. When the rear American destroyers came into action, the *Barton* was torpedoed and sunk, the *Aaron Ward* and *Monssen* shattered by gunfire.

Dawn revealed the full extent of the American losses. The *Portland* was circling helplessly to be eventually towed to Tulagi for repairs; the *Atlanta* had to be scuttled. The *Helena*, virtually undamaged, led the survivors away: the *San Francisco* her upperworks a tangled wreck, the *Juneau* precariously afloat but able to steam, the damaged *Sterett* and the scatheless destroyers *O'Bannon* and *Fletcher*. One further tragedy was yet to be suffered: the *Juneau*, hit by torpedoes from a Japanese submarine, disintegrated. Survivors had to be left to their fate, only ten being eventually picked up.

Nevertheless, Henderson Field had been spared the planned bombardment; and now naval aircraft from the *Enterprise* which arrived south of Guadalcanal at daybreak, and Marine aircraft from the air base, took revenge on the crippled *Hiei* slowly circling Savo Island. Dive-bombers and torpedo planes hit her repeatedly, but she remained afloat, finally to be scuttled and her crew taken off by Japanese destroyers.

The next episode in the three-day naval Battle of Guadalcanal had already begun with the departure early on 13 November from the Japanese advanced base on Shortland Island of a squadron under Rear Admiral Mikawa composed of four heavy cruisers, *Chokai*, *Kinugasa*, *Suzuya* and *Maya*, two light cruisers and six destroyers. No surface force was available to prevent them delivering a bombardment of Henderson Field that night. But as Mikawa retired south of New Georgia Island he was located by planes from the air base which his guns had failed to neutralize. A torpedo holed the *Kinugasa*, bombs set on fire and damaged the *Izuso*. Planes from the *Enterprise* took up the chase, sent the *Kinugasa* to the bottom and further damaged the *Chokai* and the *Maya*.

Other planes had meanwhile discovered the Japanese reinforcement convoy of eleven transports encircled by a screen of destroyers and covered by a patrol of Zeros from the *Hiyo* and *Junyo*. Throughout the day they were harried by dive-bombers and torpedo planes from the *Enterprise* and Henderson Field and long-range high altitude bombers from the American air base on Espiritu Santo. By nightfall only four transports remained. No doubt relying upon Henderson Field being put out of action by the bombardment group which was also on its way, the tenacious Rear Admiral Tanaka pressed on through the night for Guadalcanal. This bombardment force under Admiral Kondo, composed of the *Kirishima*, the heavy cruisers *Atago* and *Takao*, two light cruisers and nine destroyers had been sighted and reported by an American submarine; to oppose it, Rear Admiral Willis A. Lee's Task Force 64 (the battleships *Washington* (flagship) and *South Dakota* and four destroyers) had been detached from the *Enterprise* carrier group. Lee circled clockwise round Savo Island without discovering the enemy. Kondo in fact had caught sight of him and now steered into Ironbottom Sound to meet Lee in another wild, confused night action between Cape Esperance and Savo.

Once again Japanese night-fighting expertise was evident as all four of Lee's destroyers were shattered by gunfire to sink then or later. In reply only one Japanese destroyer was so damaged as to have to be scuttled later. Lee's battleships, equipped with the latest radar, should have dominated the gun battle; but the *South Dakota* suffered an electrical defect as a result of which she blundered blindly amongst the enemy ships and, though she miraculously evaded no less than thirty-four torpedoes aimed at her, was taken under 14-inch and 8-inch gun fire at point-blank range and must have been crippled had she not been saved in the nick of time by the *Washington*. There the radar-controlled gunnery system functioned perfectly to smother the *Kirishima* and reduce her to a burning, rudderless wreck in a few minutes. Kondo ordered her to be scuttled and her crew taken off in destroyers. The planned bombardment was abandoned. Thus Tanaka's transports, run ashore to avoid being sunk, as well as the disembarked troops and stores, came at daybreak under unopposed air attack from Henderson Field which wreaked fearful havoc and slaughter.

The naval Battle of Guadalcanal was at last over. For all the brilliant and gallant performance of the crews of the Japanese ships and the losses inflicted on their opponents, their own losses were more than the Imperial Navy could afford. They could risk no more heavy ships. From this time onward their troops on the island, restricted to such supplies as could be run in aboard destroyers, were forced on to the defensive, whereas the Americans were able to bring in two fresh regiments of Marines and an infantry division. One month later the Japanese abandoned hope of recapturing Guadalcanal and began preparations for withdrawal.

Although in tactical and material terms they could claim to have had the better of the three days' operations at sea, from the strategical point of view the battle had been an American victory. It was, indeed, another turning point in the Pacific War. The Americans were henceforth to be on the offensive everywhere, with the South Pacific forces working their way up the chain of the Solomons, while General MacArthur's South-West Pacific American and Australian troops, having forced the Japanese back over the Owen Stanley Mountains from Port Moresby, were to take advantage of the newly-secured local command of the sea to make the amphibious leaps which would recapture New Guinea and its offshore island groups. At Pearl Harbour, too, the first of the new generation of fast carriers was to arrive in the spring of 1943 enabling the Central Pacific Force to go over to the offensive and drive in the Japanese perimeter.

Before Guadalcanal was finally secured in February 1943, however, there was to be one more clash between 'Tenacious Tanaka's' light forces and a powerful American squadron in the same sinister waters of Ironbottom Sound off the village of Tassafaronga. Although Tanaka's eight destroyers, their decks cluttered with stores, were surprised by a powerful, radar-equipped American squadron composed of five cruisers and six destroyers, lack of experience and cohesion amongst the American ships and their own superb training added to the advantage of possession of the 'Long Lance' torpedoes combined to bring disaster to the American cruisers. At the cost of one of his destroyers sunk, Tanaka sank the *Northampton* with two torpedoes and left the *Minneapolis*, *Pensacola* and *New Orleans* shattered wrecks as a result of well-aimed 'Long Lances'.

This Japanese victory of Tassafaronga did not, in fact, affect the fate of Guadalcanal, from which the twelve thousand Japanese troops on the island were brilliantly and heroically evacuated by Tanaka's destroyers without the knowledge of the Americans who finally overran their positions on 9 February 1943 only to find them unoccupied.

A pause of several months now ensued in major operations following the expulsion of the Japanese from Guadalcanal and, in the South-West Pacific area, from Papua, while both sides built up their strength in preparation for the next inevitable clash. In the Solomons the Japanese established bases at Munda on New Georgia Island and Vila on Kolombangara. From Rabaul they employed 'Tokyo Express' tactics to reinforce their troops in New Guinea; but at the end of February 1943 they attempted a more ambitious supply effort when they sailed a convoy of seven transports, a collier and eight destroyers, carrying some seven thousand troops. It was set upon by aircraft of the Allied Air Forces of MacArthur's command on the morning of 2 March and during the next thirty-six hours the whole convoy and four of the destroyers were sunk; two thousand Japanese troops lost their lives.

Japanese preparations were now concentrated upon an attempt to re-establish air superiority over the South and South-West Pacific and with it to disrupt the Allied build-up. The campaign was conducted by the Japanese Navy under the direction of Admiral Yamamoto who at the end of March transferred from the fleet carriers to the area ninety-six Zeros, sixty-five dive-bombers and some torpedo planes to reinforce the land-based force of eighty-six fighters, twenty-seven dive-bombers and seventy-two twin-engined bombers of the 11th Air Fleet already stationed there. The offensive which they launched on various Allied bases had only a few minor successes and their own losses were heavy.

American ability to decypher Japanese operational signals, which had repeatedly foiled Yamamoto's plans in the past, now brought about his death. Details of his intention to fly to Buin from Rabaul reached the American command; his aircraft was ambushed and shot down as it was approaching the airfield.

By the end of June, Allied preparations for an offensive were completed; on the thirtieth, South West Pacific forces were transported in landing craft from Buna on the north coast of Papua to Nassau Bay, the first of a long series of such amphibious advances made possible by local American sea supremacy, which was to put them in the next thirteen months in possession of the 1,500 miles of north New Guinea coastline and bring them to the jumping-off position for recapture of the Philippines. On the same date South Pacific forces began their advance up the Solomons by an invasion of New Georgia. These two north-westerly advances were originally aimed at an assault on the Japanese fortress-base of Rabaul; but when the time came it was appreciated that Rabaul could be neutralized and by-passed and left to wither on the vine as numerous other Japanese strongpoints in New Guinea had been by MacArthur's amphibious forces.

As on Guadalcanal, the fighting on shore amid the swamps and jungles was to be long, hard and bitter and Admiral Halsey's surface units were again and again to clash in night battles with the Japanese as the latter strove to reinforce their troops by means of 'Tokyo Express' operations. In these, although the American ships demonstrated their improved mastery of the technique of radar-controlled gunfire, their tactics were still inflexible and exposed them to the 'Long Lance' torpedo fire with calamitous results.

In the first battle – Kula Gulf – on the night 5/6 July 1943, Rear Admiral Ainsworth's squadron of three cruisers and four destroyers encountering seven Japanese destroyers began the action with devastating, radar-controlled gunfire which destroyed the leading enemy ship within a few minutes. Others, however, had launched torpedoes and the cruiser *Helena* was sent to the bottom. With superb aplomb the Japanese destroyers then went on to complete their mission, the delivery of supplies to the troops ashore.

A week later Ainsworth with three cruisers and ten destroyers again encountered the Tokyo Express – four destroyer-transports escorted by the light-cruiser *Jintsu* and five destroyers. A similar sequence of events occurred. The *Jintsu* was smothered under a hail of 6-inch shells, but her destroyers were left free to launch their torpedoes, one of which found a billet in the New Zealand cruiser *Leander* which sent her limping, badly damaged, out of action. The Japanese destroyers, having retired to reload their torpedo tubes, returned to the fight and this time torpedoed Ainsworth's flagship *Honolulu*, demolishing her entire forecastle. Another torpedo sank the destroyer *Gwin*.

That the Americans were nevertheless slowly learning the techniques of night fighting at sea was demonstrated in the destroyer battle of Vella Gulf on the night 6/7 August when a flotilla operated in two mutually supporting divisions of three ships, albeit with the advantage of radar, to overwhelm a Japanese flotilla of four, of which only one survived.

By the end of October, New Georgia, Kolombangara and Vella Lavella Islands had been successively cleared of Japanese. The next to be invaded was Bougainville where the landing in Empress Augusta Bay brought about the last of the long series of night battles. A Japanese force composed of two heavy cruisers screened by light cruisers and six destroyers advancing from Rabaul was opposed by four 6-inch cruisers and eight destroyers.

A night battle of the utmost confusion ensued marked by collisions between ships on both sides which were the ultimate cause of as much damage as gunfire. The Japanese light cruiser *Sendai* was the recipient of the opening salvoes of radar-controlled gunfire and was duly destroyed. Thereafter there was more sound and fury than concrete results from it. For the first time, however, the Japanese 'Long Lances' were effectively countered by the American cruiser column, though an American destroyer which had lost touch with her division ran athwart the track of one and was sunk. With the approach of daylight the Japanese retired, their intention of breaking up the landing frustrated.

A further massive effort was planned, nevertheless, and to affect it six heavy cruisers arrived at Rabaul from Truk.

228

Fortunately Halsey had available a carrier task group composed of the *Saratoga* and *Princeton* from which a strike of twenty-two dive-bombers, twenty-three torpedo planes with an escort of fifty-two fighters took off. They swooped on the enemy cruisers as they were refuelling, so damaging five of them that the squadron was forced to retire to base for repairs.

From this time onwards control of the waters of the South and South-West Pacific lay in the hands of the Allies, a small surface force with massive Allied air superiority being all that was required to support MacArthur's advance. Though this was a prime example of the *exercise* of sea power, to see how, elsewhere, it was being *attained* one must turn to the Central Pacific where, following the Battle of Midway, a state of stalemate had reigned for a year. Though the Japanese, from their numerous bases in the islands and, at first, by reason of their superior numerical strength, could be said to dominate the area, they were not strong enough to contemplate a further effort to expand their perimeter by threatening the Hawaiian Islands; nor indeed, were they able to maintain their hold on the Aleutians from which they were ejected in the summer of 1943.

During this period, however, the United States Central Pacific Force had been steadily reinforced by new carriers, fast battleships and cruisers. The vast increase in mobile naval air strength represented by the ever-growing carrier force offered a new strategic concept for the defeat of Japan. Up to this time the accepted strategy had been MacArthur's plan to concentrate all efforts on an island-hopping approach from New Guinea to the Philippines, a primarily military operation in which the navy would take the ancillary tasks of convoy and transport, shore bombardment and the guarding of MacArthur's seaward flank.

It became apparent now, however, that the Central Pacific Force could conduct its own amphibious advance, with invasion forces covered by carrier air power able to make forward leaps of a magnitude and at a pace which would far exceed MacArthur's island-hopping progress. It was decided, therefore, that though the latter would continue as planned, the main line of advance would be from Pearl Harbour through the island groups of Micronesia to Formosa and Okinawa in the Ryukyus. The vast ocean distances to be covered by the huge carrier fleets and amphibious forces with the complex logistic problems involved were to bring about a new concept of naval warfare.

16

DESTRUCTION OF THE JAPANESE
FLEET

Through the summer of 1943, battle strength of the Central Pacific Force – henceforward referred to as the United States 5th Fleet – was expanding into the greatest force of carriers ever seen with the new, fast battleships and cruisers in support, the whole known as the Fast Carrier Task Force, or Task Force 58. In parallel there was also growing the 5th Amphibious Force under Rear Admiral Turner, rich with experience from the campaign for Guadalcanal. It was divided into Northern and Southern Attack forces; the former, under Turner himself, assembled and trained in Hawaii, and, with troops of the 27th Infantry Division, was assigned to the assault and capture of Makin Atoll in the Gilbert Islands; the latter's troopships embarked the 2nd Marine Division from New Zealand and, after final rehearsals in the New Hebrides, was to assault Tarawa. Each of these attack forces was self-contained with its own squadron of three escort carriers, a squadron of old battleships, as well as cruisers and destroyers, for close escort and bombardment purposes.

While preparations for the capture of the Gilberts were going on, the Fast Carrier Task Force, expanded by September 1943 into a fleet of eleven fast carriers (nine of them new), was 'blooded' in delivering raids on various Japanese island centres. The exploit of one Task Group (*Saratoga* and *Princeton*), operating under Halsey in the South Pacific, which knocked out the cruiser squadron at Rabaul, has been noted earlier. A second Task Group of three carriers lent to Halsey struck there again on 11 November. Working out of Pearl Harbour other Task Groups had hammered Marcus Island, the Gilberts and Wake Island. In the course of these operations they learned to operate groups of carriers in close company inside a common circular screen and under fighter cover drawn from all, but centrally controlled and directed. Such an arrangement made them much less vulnerable to enemy air attack.

Their task in the planned island assaults was to soften up the defences with bomb raids and subsequently to cover the amphibious forces against any attempt by the Japanese Fleet to interfere. But neither during the capture of the Gilberts, which were secured between 20 and 23 November, nor during the assault on the Marshalls which followed at the end of January 1944, was the Japanese Combined Fleet at Truk in any shape to offer a challenge. Its cruiser force had been put out of action by the carrier raids on Rabaul, while its carriers had been sent back to Japan to train replacements for their air groups lost amongst the thousands of naval planes and aircrews destroyed during the campaigns for Guadalcanal and the Solomons.

The Combined Fleet was further reduced and its base made untenable by a two-day pounding of Truk in mid-February by the carrier planes of Task Force 58, forcing Yamamoto's successor, Koga, to withdraw to Palau. When this was seen to be a threat to the flank of MacArthur's advance along the north coast of New Guinea, Palau was given the same treatment at the end of March. The harassed Koga, flying to Davao in Mindanao to set up new headquarters, was killed when his seaplane crashed in bad weather. He was relieved by Admiral Soemu Toyoda who set up his headquarters in Japan, delegating the sea-going command, or the First Mobile Fleet as it was called, to Vice Admiral Jisaburo Ozawa who had relieved the discredited Nagumo of command of the Carrier Force after the Battle of Santa Cruz Islands in November 1942.

With the capture of Eniwetok, the Marianas became the obvious next objective of the 5th Fleet's advance. Loss of them would not only cut across Japan's line of communications with the southern regions; it would also provide a base from which Allied bombers could reach the homeland. At all costs the Combined Fleet would have to offer battle to prevent this. Toyoda devised a plan known as 'A-Go' whereby the fleet's weakness in the air would be compensated for by shore-based air power distributed amongst the Carolines, the Southern Philippines and the Marianas. As soon as the location of the impending battle was known, this air force would be concentrated where it could be brought to bear on the American fleet. Meanwhile the 1st Mobile Fleet was concentrated at Tawi Tawi, an anchorage in the Sulu Archipelago.

Unfortunately for Toyoda's plans, before the Americans had confirmed that the Marianas were in fact their next objective, an urgent call came in for naval and air support for Japanese defenders of the island of Biak, retention of which was vital both for the 'A-Go' plan and as an important air base in the efforts to halt MacArthur's advance. Large numbers of planes from Japan, from the Marianas and the Carolines were rushed to the area where they suffered heavy losses. In an effort to reinforce the troops on Biak, Ozawa detached a force under Vice Admiral Matome Ugaki, composed of the immense battleships *Yamato* and *Musashi* with cruisers and destroyers. It hurried first to Batjan in the Moluccas; but before it could move on to intervene, there came news of heavy carrier aircraft attacks on Guam, Saipan and Tinian in the Marianas on 11 and 12 June and on Chichi Jima and Iwo Jima 650 miles further north in the Bonins.

Ugaki was at once recalled and ordered to rendezvous with Ozawa who sailed from Tawi Tawi when 'A-Go' was activated on the fifteenth upon news of American troops landing on Saipan. The Mobile Fleet was organized in three forces. Force A under Ozawa himself with his flag in the new, large fleet carrier *Taiho*, accompanied by the *Shokaku* and *Zuikaku* with a screen of cruisers and destroyers, provided the main air strength with 207 aircraft. Force B, commanded by Rear Admiral Joshima, comprised the slower *Junyo* and *Hiyo* and the light carrier *Ryuho* which could between them put up 135 aircraft. Its screen contained a battleship, a cruiser and ten destroyers. These two groups operated independently some twelve miles apart. About a hundred miles in advance would be stationed the Van Force under Vice Admiral Takeo Kurita, composed of the four battleships, *Yamato*, *Musashi*, *Haruna* and *Kongo*, four heavy cruisers, a light cruiser and nine destroyers, screening three light carriers *Chitose*, *Chiyoda* and *Zuiho* with a combined complement of ninety aircraft. The object of this disposition was partly to offer a heavily armed and armoured shield to draw the fire of the enemy's air striking forces and partly to extend the range of the scouting seaplanes carried in the cruisers and battleships.

The passage of this fleet (less Ugaki's detachment) from Tawi Tawi through the Philippines to emerge through the San Bernadino Strait into the Philippine Sea on the evening of 15 June, was reported by submarines to Admiral Spruance, commanding the 5th Fleet. Defence of his amphibious Attack Force under Admiral Turner, already committed to the assault of Saipan, was his primary task in accordance with his orders from Nimitz. It would be the duty of Task Force 58, the Fast Carrier Force under Rear Admiral Marc Mitscher, to meet Ozawa's fleet in battle should it advance to intervene. It was calculated, however, that Ozawa could not get within striking distance until the nineteenth; and to avoid any risk of the Japanese using diversionary tactics to get behind him to attack the vulnerable amphibious force, Spruance decided to await the enemy's onslaught within covering distance to the westward of Saipan. In the meantime two of Mitscher's groups comprising seven carriers would complete the interdiction of Iwo Jima and Chichi Jima 650 miles to the north; while the other two groups maintained the air supremacy established over the Marianas, and the battleships of TF 58, as well as those belonging to Turner's force, smothered the island defences with their 16-inch and 14-inch guns. A rendezvous for the whole Task Force, some 180 miles west of the islands, was set for the evening of the eighteenth.

When that time came, Spruance found himself labouring under the grave disadvantage of a lack of knowledge of the enemy's position; the only report received since the fifteenth had been one from the United States submarine *Cavalla*, seven hundred miles west of Guam on the evening of the seventeenth which had sighted part of Ozawa's fleet steering east at twenty knots having spent the day refuelling from his attendant tankers. American shore-based reconnaissance planes had failed to make contact. Scouting carrier planes from Spruance's carriers had reached the limit of their fuel sixty miles short of the Japanese Fleet.

Floatplanes catapulted from the Japanese battleships and cruisers, with their greater endurance, had on the other hand sighted and reported portions of Spruance's four groups of carriers and the fifth group of battleships and cruisers – the 'Battle Line' under Vice Admiral Willis Lee – thrown forward fifteen miles to the westward. While Spruance therefore felt bound to stay within easy reach of Saipan and at dusk turned eastward, Ozawa, his strike planes also enjoying a considerable range advantage over Spruance's, was able to prepare to launch a massive air strike at daylight.

During the night a report of a radio fix of an enemy transmitting 350 miles to the west-south-west of his position reached Spruance. This might or might not be Ozawa. Mitscher urged him to turn west so that a strike might be launched at dawn; but the Fleet Commander, his overriding responsibilities clear in his mind, would not be persuaded. All efforts during the night and the following day to locate the Japanese fleet failed. The great carrier Battle of the Philippine Sea was thus to open at 1000 on the nineteenth when on the radar scans of Lee's battle fleet a swarm of aircraft approaching was detected at a range of 150 miles.

Since dawn, fighters from Mitscher's carriers had been aloft on defensive Combat Air Patrol and to interdict the island air bases where a few survivors of the hammering received in the previous days were caught and shot down as they took off to attack the fleet. Other Japanese planes approaching Guam in reinforcement as visualized in the 'A-Go' plan, were intercepted and more than thirty shot down. The shore-based air element of Toyoda's plan was proving a broken reed. Now, on receipt of the first alarm from Lee, Mitscher recalled his Hellcats from over Guam and turning his huge force together into wind began launching every available fighter.

The strike force which they intercepted when it was still forty-five miles short of Lee's Battle Line, had taken off seventy strong at 0800 from the carriers of the Japanese Van Force. An hour later a second strike almost twice as large had left the decks of Ozawa's Force A carriers. As they were doing so, the carriers steering a steady course into wind presented themselves as perfect targets to the United States submarine *Albacore*; a torpedo struck Ozawa's flagship *Taiho*. The new carrier's design proved sound; the damage caused only a slight reduction in speed and she was able to continue operating her planes. Her petrol system had been ruptured, however, the consequences of which were in time to prove fatal.

In the meantime the waves of Japanese strike planes had met

the massed Hellcats well short of Task Force 58. The former were flown mainly by the hastily trained and recently embarked replacements for the carrier air groups massacred in the Solomons and New Guinea campaigns. The American airmen flying the Hellcats, vast improvements on the Wildcats which had fought in previous carrier battles, were already veterans with double the flying hours of their inexperienced opponents. The outcome was a massacre which the jubilant Americans were to refer to as the 'Great Marianas Turkey Shoot'. Of the first Japanese wave, forty-two were shot down and none penetrated the defence to attack the American ships. About twenty of the second wave pushed doggedly on but failed to inflict damage of any consequence. Barely thirty of the 128 planes that had set out from Force 'A' survived to head back for their carriers.

Meanwhile disaster of another sort had struck Force 'A'. As the *Shokaku* was steaming into wind to recover planes, three torpedoes struck her. They had been fired by the *Cavalla* which, after reporting the enemy on the seventeenth, had been doggedly in chase and had now found herself perfectly placed. Petrol fires blazed up in the carrier, her speed fell away. Her crew struggled to bring the blaze under control but in vain; and at length a final catastrophic explosion tore the ship apart and she sank. At almost the same time in the *Taiho*, where the forced ventilation system had spread gases from her ruptured petrol system throughout the ship, a spark set off a similar explosion, tearing holes in her hull and setting her ablaze. Ozawa and his staff were transferred to the cruiser *Haguro*; but only about 500 of her crew of 2,150 had been saved when, after a further explosion, the carrier capsized and sank.

Two more Japanese strikes, launched from Force 'B' and from the *Zuikaku* were massacred or returned having failed to find their target. By the end of the day, Ozawa had lost 315 aircraft against twenty-three American planes shot down, and six lost operationally. No American ship had suffered any significant damage.

Spruance was still uncertain of Ozawa's position; but on the assumption that news would come in from his shore-based patrol planes, he headed westward during the night 19/20 June to get within striking distance by the following day. But he was again badly served by his shore-based reconnaissance aircraft and, as Ozawa had also made off north-westward to refuel from his tanker force, he was still some four hundred miles distant and so beyond the range of the early morning search sent out by Mitscher. In spite of having lost all but about a hundred planes in his surviving carriers and in the face of advice from his battleship admiral, Kurita, to retire to Japan, Ozawa was determined to renew the battle as soon as his ships had replenished. He believed the stories of his returning airmen who claimed four American carriers sunk and many aircraft destroyed.

Thus it was that at 1605 on the twentieth, a scouting plane from the *Enterprise* at last located him at a range of three hundred miles. It was so late in the day that any American air striking forces would be benighted before they could return to their carriers, and few of the pilots were trained to land on in the dark. Nevertheless Mitscher, who had chafed under what he considered Spruance's excessively cautious tactics, took the bold decision to launch a massive blow while the opportunity offered. Within half an hour, seventy-seven dive-bombers, fifty-four torpedo planes with eighty-five fighter escorts were on their way.

In a frenzied twenty minutes, amidst a spectacular display of multi-coloured anti-aircraft tracers and shell bursts, dive-bombers plunged and torpedo planes streaked in low over the water while Hellcats and Zeros fought aloft. The carrier *Hiyo* was torpedoed and left sinking; the *Chiyoda's* flight deck was mangled; fires blazing in the *Zuikaku* came near to causing her abandonment; the battleship *Haruna* and a cruiser were damaged. Out of his hundred aircraft, only thirty-five finally remained to Ozawa as he fled through the night to Okinawa.

The Americans had lost only fourteen planes in combat but eighty more were lost as they homed through the darkness, some failing to find their carriers in spite of illuminations of every sort, others crashing on deck. Rescue operations, however, reduced the aircrew losses to sixteen pilots and thirty-five others.

Ignorant as yet of the destruction of the *Shokaku* and *Taiho*, the Americans were disappointed at their failure to wipe out the Japanese carrier force and criticism was levelled at Spruance's defensive strategy. But in fact the holocaust of

Japanese aircrews was such that never again would they be able to man their surviving carriers effectively. When next the two fleets met, those carriers would play the role of 'paper tigers' offered as decoys.

With the retirement of the defeated Japanese fleet, external opposition to the American assault forces off Saipan was limited to such Japanese aircraft as could fly up from Truk and Palau in the south and from Japan via Iwo Jima in the north. Repeated interdiction raids by American naval aircraft, some developing into huge air battles in which the inexperienced Japanese pilots were massacred, kept this threat down to a mere nuisance level. The Japanese defenders of Saipan fought heroically to the death, nevertheless, and it was not until 9 July that the island was officially secured at the cost of 3,500 American dead and some 14,000 wounded. The capture of the other islands of the Marianas followed and was completed early in August.

The next move of the two-pronged Allied advance planned was to be MacArthur's amphibious leap from western New Guinea to Morotai and thence up the island chain via Salebaboe and Mindanao to Leyte. The Central Pacific fleet (now nominated the 3rd Fleet since Admiral Halsey had taken over command from Spruance who was to alternate with him, resuming command for the campaign which would follow the invasion of the Philippines) was meanwhile to capture the Palaus, Yap and Ulithi. As a preliminary, Halsey began at the end of August to deliver a series of softening up raids mounted from the carriers of Task Force 38, as Mitscher's fast carriers had become. So meagre was the opposition encountered that Halsey suggested to the Chiefs of Staff that MacArthur's island-hopping progress, each move of which was limited to the supporting range of his own land-based air force, could be replaced by one bold leap from New Guinea to Leyte, supported by the air strength of TF38 and reinforced by the Central Pacific troops earmarked to occupy the Palaus and Yap which could be by-passed.

MacArthur immediately agreed with this bold application of sea power in support of his single-minded determination to return to the Philippines as he had promised to their peoples when he was forced out of Corregidor in 1942. The plan was approved by the Chiefs of Staff, except for the capture of Morotai and the Palaus, which was to go ahead. And so, while these two islands were being secured as well as Ulithi Atoll to make an anchorage and forward base for the 3rd Fleet, the Attack Force which had been on its way to capture Yap was diverted to join the remainder of MacArthur's forces at Manus in the Admiralty Islands to prepare for the 1,500 miles sea advance to Leyte.

The huge armada sailed thence, starting on 10 October 1944. Meanwhile TF38 had begun a series of strikes against air bases to the north from Okinawa in the Ryu-kyus, through Formosa to the Philippines from which interference and reinforcement of the southern air bases could be expected. Japanese reaction took the form of raids on TF38 by large numbers of torpedo planes to make twilight and night attacks. At the cost of more than forty of their number shot down, they succeeded only in crippling two American cruisers. They brought back claims of having annihilated the enemy fleet which led Toyoda, the Japanese Commander-in-Chief, into an error that was to have fatal consequences. Believing that a great opportunity offered and that all that was left to do was to mop up the remnants, he withdrew the newly formed and partially trained carrier air groups from Ozawa's carrier force and sent them to Formosa to join Admiral Fukudome's shore-based air force. In the massed air attacks which Fukudome sent out against Halsey's far from annihilated or even seriously weakened fleet, and in the aerial battles over air bases that developed as Halsey's airmen continued their destructive raids, the Japanese were shot down in droves and achieved nothing. The last hope of manning Ozawa's carriers for the great sea battle that was impending, was dissipated in vain.

While these aerial battles raged in the north, MacArthur's armada steered on undetected and at dawn on 17 October his advance troops spilled ashore on the beaches of Suluan Island in the approaches to the Gulf of Leyte. News of this reaching Toyoda finally pinpointed the next American objective and enabled him to activate the appropriate operational plan: SHO-GO. This called for a complex converging movement by the dispersed Japanese naval forces to fall simultaneously upon the American amphibious fleet.

Kurita's battleship and cruiser force which, since the Battle of the Philippine Sea, had been based on Singapore so as to be near the source of its oil fuel, was to proceed to Brunei in North Borneo, and having refuelled there to advance in two groups through the Philippine archipelago. Force 'A' (under Kurita himself), the battleships *Yamato, Musashi, Nagato, Kongo* and *Haruna*, the heavy cruisers *Atago* (flagship), *Takao, Maya, Chokai, Myoko, Haguro, Kumano, Suzuya, Chikuma* and *Tone* with accompanying destroyer squadrons, was to proceed by the Palawan Passage, the Mindoro Strait, the Sibuyan Sea and the San Bernadino Strait, rounding the island of Samar to approach Leyte from the north. In the absence of any carrier-borne air support, Kurita was to rely upon fighter cover provided by Fukudome's shore-based air force. The remainder, Force 'C', composed of the battleship *Yamashiro* and *Fuso*, the heavy cruiser *Mogamo* and four destroyers, under Vice Admiral Shoji Nishimura, would cross the Mindanao Sea and thread the narrow Surigao Strait to debouch into the Gulf of Leyte from the south simultaneously with Kurita's arrival from the north. Force 'C' would be supported by the 2nd Striking Force composed of the heavy cruisers *Nachi* and *Ashigara* and screen, under Vice Admiral Kiyohide Shima, which was to come south from the Ryu-kyus and, after refuelling in the Calamian Islands, follow Nishimura into the Surigao Strait.

Finally there was that regular feature of Japanese plans, the decoy force composed of Ozawa's four surviving carriers, *Zuikaku, Zuiho, Chitose* and *Chiyoda*, the hermaphrodite battleships *Ise* and *Hyuga*, which had had a small flight deck erected in place of their after gun turrets, and a screen of light cruisers and destroyers. It was euphemistically called the Main Body, though only about a hundred planes with pilots unable to deck-land, were embarked in the carriers. Its role was to sortie from Japan and offer such an apparent threat to Halsey's carrier fleet that the latter would be lured away from the Leyte area at the critical moment.

These complex, interlocking movements began on 18 October when, in response to the executive order for SHO-GO, Kurita sailed for Brunei Bay. The date assigned for the closing of the Japanese pincer on the Leyte assault forces was the twenty-fifth. The sea-borne element of the grand assault on Leyte which opened on the twentieth consisted, apart from the huge array of transports and auxiliaries, of six old battleships, five cruisers and fifteen destroyers of Rear Admiral J. B. Oldendorf's Fire Support and Bombardment Group ; a Close Covering Group of Cruisers (three American and one Australian), and destroyers (five American and one Australian), under Rear Admiral R. S. Berkey ; seven destroyers of a Special Attack Group ; and a Task Group of seventeen escort carriers under Rear Admiral Thomas L. Sprague which, operating some thirty miles apart in three independent Task Units of five or six carriers each on a north-south line to the eastward of Samar and Mindanao islands and each with a screen of three destroyers and four destroyer-escorts, was primarily responsible for providing close air support for the landing forces. These various forces made up the United States 7th Fleet commanded by Vice Admiral T. C. Kinkaid, the naval element of General MacArthur's South-West Pacific Command. Hovering in support also was Halsey's TF38 which of course was part of Nimitz's Pacific Command ; no Supreme Commander had been appointed.

The assault on Leyte had been in progress for three days before the first news came in of Japanese naval reaction. It took the form of a dramatic signal from the United States submarine *Darter* which, in company with the *Dace*, had intercepted Kurita's force 'A' in the Palawan Passage early on the twenty-third and had sunk the heavy cruisers *Atago* – from which Kurita had had to swim to a destroyer – and *Maya* and seriously damaged the *Takao*. On the following day Force 'A' where Kurita had shifted his flag to the *Yamato*, and Nishimura's Force 'C' were both reported by reconnaissance aircraft from Halsey's carriers, the former as it was approaching the Sibuyan Sea, the latter off Negros.

Halsey at once ordered air strikes to be launched from the three Task Groups of TF38 operating in the Philippine Sea (his fourth group, TG38-1, had been detached to refuel, rest and replenish at Ulithi). A day-long series of massed raids ensued during which the giant *Musashi*, hit by at least eighteen torpedoes, was finally sunk. Kurita, whose shore-based fighter cover had failed to materialize, reversed course for four hours in face of these overwhelming attacks but resumed his advance to the San Bernadino Strait before dusk.

The reason that Fukudome had apparently failed Kurita was that the former had decided that the best protection he could give to the latter was by means of attacking the aerial threat at source. His entire resources had been therefore directed against the most northerly of Halsey's carrier groups, Rear Admiral Sherman's TG38.3. There they had met a brilliant defence, a great many being shot down and, except for one lone dive-bomber, those which broke through to drop their bombs failed to achieve anything. The exception succeeded in hitting the light carrier *Princeton* squarely on her flight deck, causing fires which got out of control and the eventual scuttling of the ship.

One of the raids which TG38.3 beat off during the day had, unknown to Halsey, come from Ozawa's decoy force which had been hovering some 210 miles to the northward hoping to be detected. It was not until well into the afternoon, however, that a scouting plane at last located and reported it to Halsey, who was now faced with three alternatives. He could go north with his whole force with the intention of finally annihilating the enemy's last carriers, remain in position to cover the vulnerable 7th Fleet units off Leyte against Kurita when he emerged the following morning from the San Bernadino Strait or divide his force between these two objectives.

His decision to accept the first of these, based on his mistaken belief in his airmen's much exaggerated claims of the destruction they had caused to Force 'A', was to be the subject of fierce controversy, largely owing to a signal confusion which gave Kinkaid the impression that Halsey was leaving the powerful 'Battle Line' to watch the Strait while he hurried north with his three carrier groups. His fourth carrier group, recalled from Ulithi, could not reach the area until late next day.

The consequences were to be very serious and come near to being calamitous. But before that situation could develop, and while Kurita, largely undamaged apart from the loss of the *Musashi*, was threading the San Bernadino Strait under cover of darkness and Halsey was racing north, a separate night battle took place in the western approach to the Gulf of Leyte, the Surigao Strait. There, Nishimura's Force 'C' as it approached the narrow strait through the calm, tropical night, lit up intermittently by lightning, was met by a defence in depth. First to encounter and attack, though ineffectively, were

sections of PT boats. Next to be loosed were twenty of Oldendorf's destroyers which raced forward in small groups hidden
from Japanese eyes or radar by the black loom of the jungle-
clad islands on either side of the strait, to launch their flights of
torpedoes. With an apparently fatalistic view of the suicidal
mission assigned to him, Nishimura steamed steadily on
through the forty-seven missiles fired by the first squadron. The
Fuso staggered out of the line mortally hit and soon to blow
asunder into two burning portions; one Japanese destroyer
blew up, another came to a stop in a sinking condition, a third
retired from the fray with her bow blown off; Nishimura's flagship *Yamashiro* was hit also, but not seriously hurt.

The next squadron to attack scored another hit on the flagship which slowed her down. There now developed a wild,
confused scene as the last squadron of destroyers came in to the
attack at the moment that Nishimura's surviving ships came
within gun range of Oldendorf's cruisers and battleships drawn
up in lines across the exit from the Strait. As the *Yamashiro*,
amidst a forest of shell splashes turned to port to bring all her
guns to bear, the destroyers launched their torpedoes to score
two more hits on her. These and numerous shell hits sealed her
fate and at 0419 she capsized and sank taking with her
Nishimura and all but a handful of her crew. Only the cruiser
Mogami, heavily damaged, and one destroyer now remained to
turn away to escape. Another victim of the American gunfire,
however, had been the destroyer *Albert W. Grant*. Wrongly
identified on the cruisers' radar, she had been struck nineteen
times and put out of action with more than 120 casualties.

All this time, following Nishimura up the strait had been
Shima's two cruisers and their screen. The light cruiser
Abukuma had taken a torpedo from one of the PT boats and
had limped out of action to escape with heavy damage. First
intimation of the catastrophe that had overtaken Force 'C' was
the sight of the two burning halves of the *Fuso*. When the
Mogami, also ablaze, came into sight, Shima wisely refused to
blunder on into the overwhelming storm of shell awaiting him.
He turned to retire, firing torpedoes at random up the strait as
he did so. The *Mogami*, steering to join him, collided with his
flagship, the *Nachi*, damaging her aft and reducing her speed
to eighteen knots.

Dawn in the Surigao Strait revealed the remnants of the southern Japanese force – the cruisers *Nachi* and *Ashigara* with one destroyer escaping to fight another day, the *Mogami* limping painfully away to be finally halted by air attack and scuttled and one crippled destroyer the solitary target for the over-whelming gunfire which finally sent her to the bottom.

Elsewhere, however, dawn had broken over a situation that threatened disaster for a vital portion of Kinkaid's 7th Fleet : Thomas Sprague's TG77.4 of vulnerable, lightly armed escort carriers. The northernmost of his three Task Units – TU77.4.3 or Taffy 3, its voice radio call sign, by which it will be convenienc to refer to it – commanded by Rear Admiral Clifton Sprague and composed of the escort carriers *Fanshaw Bay* (flagship), *St Lo*, *White Plains*, *Kalinin Bay*, *Kitkun Bay* and *Gambier Bay* with the destroyers *Hoel*, *Heermann* and *Johnston* and destroyer escorts *Dennis*, *Butler*, *Raymond* and *Roberts*, was operating to the eastward of Samar. They had begun what they expected to be another day of routine anti-submarine air patrols and missions of close support to the troops ashore, when at 0646 incredulous look-outs reported the pagoda-like top-hamper of Kurita's battleships rising over the north-western horizon. On the natural assumption that the San Bernadino Strait had been under observation during the night, it seemed to Clifton Sprague incredible that no warning of such an encounter had reached him. But as we have seen, Kinkaid thought Halsey was taking care of any threat from that direction.

Taken completely by surprise, Clifton Sprague turned his ships at their full speed of seventeen-and-a-half knots to a course of east on which, though not fully into the north-easterly wind blowing, they could launch their strike aircraft while avoiding a reduction of range from the enemy. Nevertheless splashes from battleships' big guns were soon leaping from the water around the *Fanshaw Bay* and *White Plains* and as soon as the aircraft were away Sprague was infinitely glad to be able to take cover in a rain squall and thereafter edge away to a south and finally a south-westerly course for Leyte and, he hoped, rescue by Oldendorf's battleships.

Fortunately for him Kurita, equally surprised and taking the silhouettes of the little carriers to be those of a group of Halsey's big and fast ships, made a tactical blunder. With his fleet already in disarray as it was changing from its night cruising disposition into the circular day one, he would not wait to concentrate but ordered a General Chase, thereby losing cohesion and control. Even so Sprague's situation was desperate as he emerged from the rain squall; he now called on his screening destroyers to fight a rearguard action. With selfless gallantry they steered out towards the overpowering enemy to attack with torpedoes and guns. The *Johnston* succeeded in torpedoing and blowing off the bow of the heavy cruiser *Kumano*, a deed which, in fact, put two major units out of the battle; for the *Suzuya* stopped to embark the cruiser division commander and never caught up again with the running fight. The *Johnston* paid the penalty of her defiance with heavy shell damage but refused to be driven out of action. The *Hoel* and *Heermann* advancing through a storm of shot which crippled the former, loosed torpedoes which, though they were apparently all avoided, had a decisive effect on the outcome by forcing Kurita to turn the *Yamato* and *Nagato* away for ten minutes and so lose touch with the progress of the battle.

The little destroyer escorts now received permission to join in the wild mêlée during which the *Hoel* had finally to be abandoned and sunk, and the *Roberts* was torn apart by a salvo of 14-inch shells. Their valiant efforts drew the fire of the enemy heavy ships away from the fleeing carriers. And meanwhile aircraft from the neighbouring Taffy 2 as well as from Taffy 3 had been attacking with torpedoes, bombs, rockets and machine guns, even making 'dry-runs' to distract the enemy when no weapons were available. In two of the heavy cruisers, *Chokai* and *Chikuma*, damage accumulated until both became easy targets for torpedo-planes and were sent to the bottom. The *Suzuya*, too, was so bomb-damaged that she was to sink later in the day.

Nevertheless with the surviving Japanese cruisers closing to point-blank range, the situation of Sprague's carriers was fast becoming desperate; and, indeed, the *Gambier Bay*, nearest to the enemy, had to be abandoned and went to the bottom at 0907. A fresh threat in the shape of Kurita's destroyers coming up from astern to launch torpedoes now loomed. Across their path steamed the battered *Johnston*, the fire of whose 5-inch guns forced them to launch prematurely so that their torpedoes were slowing at the end of their run when they reached their targets and were easily avoided. On the lone American destroyer the five Japanese turned their fury, circling and pounding her until she sank.

What now occurred was, not surprisingly, hailed by the hard-pressed Americans as a miracle. At 0915 the Japanese ships, including the cruisers *Haguro* and *Tone* which had closed to within ten thousand yards of the nearest carrier, were seen to reverse course and steam away at high speed. Kurita, out of touch with the battle, harassed by the ceaseless attack of planes which he believed to come from a fast carrier force which had outpaced him, had recalled his scattered units to reform on the flagship.

For a few hours more Kurita pondered the wisdom of pressing forward into Leyte Gulf to get at the assembled transports. He weighed the advantage to be gained against the gathering air and naval force he believed himself threatened by. Soon after mid-day he made up his mind and steered away for the San Bernadino Strait, leaving the 7th Fleet to the attentions of a new form of attack developed in the Japanese naval air force to compensate for the lack of experience and training amongst its pilots. This was the *Kamikaze* suicide dive-bombing attack which Thomas Sprague's Taffy 1 had already experienced, the carriers *Santee* and *Suwannee* being hit and damaged. Now it was Clifton Sprague's turn as the *St Lo* was set alight by one and after a fierce explosion, went to the bottom. A few minutes later the *Kalinin Bay* was the victim of two *Kamikazes* but survived with extensive damage. For the time being the new threat had shot its bolt, but it was to return in ever mounting degree as Japan strove desperately to reduce her enemies' air and naval superiority.

Kurita entered the San Bernadino Strait that evening, thereby missing by three hours an encounter with two of Halsey's battleships, the possible outcome of which, had it occurred, is a subject for interesting, though profitless speculation. How those ships of Halsey's came to be there, however, stems from the controversial chain of circumstances that had begun when TF38 headed north on the evening of 24 October in search of Ozawa, which must be told.

As the three groups of carriers raced through the night, radar-equipped scouting planes kept contact with Ozawa and at 0830 on the twenty-fifth the first striking force, opposed only by the nineteen Zero fighters left in the Japanese carriers, and by the ships' gunfire, swooped to the attack with torpedoes and bombs. What followed was execution rather than combat. First to go was the carrier *Chitose*. By nightfall she had been followed to the sea bed by the *Chiyoda*, the *Zuiho* and the last survivor of the Pearl Harbour force, the *Zuikaku*. The cruiser *Tama*, limping home with bomb damage, was to be sunk by submarine during the night. But, though bereft of all his carriers, Ozawa was able to escape with ten of his thirteen surface vessels. The infuriated Halsey blamed this upon interference from Nimitz at Pearl Harbour which induced him during the forenoon, against his own judgement, to send back to Kinkaid's support one carrier group and the four battleships of Lee's 'Battle Line'. By the time this decision was taken, the threat to Kinkaid's fleet which had led him to send a series of desperate signals calling for help had, as has been seen, been dissipated by Kurita's lack of resolution and the gallant attacks of the air-craft from Thomas Sprague's carriers. Nevertheless in a belated effort to catch the fleeing Kurita, Halsey sent a detachment ahead at maximum speed. It was this force which so narrowly missed an encounter off the San Bernadino Strait.

The vast Battle of Leyte Gulf was over, though pursuit by naval aircraft of the retreating Japanese groups was to inflict further losses. It was the last time, except for a suicidal and fruitless sortie by the *Yamato* six months later, that the Imperial Japanese Navy attempted to challenge American naval supremacy. From now onwards, as Allied forces closed relentlessly on and Allied submarines made absolute the blockade of the Japanese homeland, opposition at sea was to take the form of desperate and costly air attacks, the majority by *Kamikaze* pilots. They came near to forcing a withdrawal of the Pacific Fleet during the hard-fought battle to capture Okinawa. But Japanese air strength was a wasting asset. The American Pacific Fleet, joined in March 1945 by a British Task Force of four carriers, two battleships, five cruisers and ten destroyers, had comparatively limitless reserves. The crisis surmounted, the Anglo-American carrier fleet roamed at will pounding the dockyards and ships of Japan preparatory to the launching of a final invasion.

The detonation over Hiroshima and Nagasaki of the first atomic bombs hastened the capitulation of the Japanese. But sea power, bleeding Japan's life blood, had long before made the eventual surrender certain.

17

THE KOREAN WAR — ITS AFTERMATH

When the Pacific War came to an end with the signature on 2 September 1945 on board the USS *Missouri* of the instrument of Japanese surrender, there was in Far Eastern waters the mightiest deployment of sea power the world had ever seen. Apart from the spearhead of Allied naval strength represented by the United States and British Pacific Fleets, a vast concourse of amphibious and logistic vessels had been under assembly for the invasion of the Japanese mainland planned for November 1945.

By far the largest part of this huge gathering was under the American flag, dwarfing the British Pacific Fleet though this, at any previous time, would have been reckoned a naval force of the first order. Even less significant were the French and Netherlands forces which, having operated under the British Eastern Fleet based on Ceylon, now took part in the recovery of their lost colonial possessions, just as the British reasserted their sovereignty over Malaya, Borneo and Hong-Kong.

That it was American power that totally dominated the Far East seemed unquestionable when the Allies agreed that defeated Japan should not be divided between them for occupation but that the United States should be the occupying power with General of the Army Douglas MacArthur as Supreme Commander. In Chinese affairs, too, the Americans, having provided the main support and advice for the Chiang Kai-shek government and continuing to do so after the Japanese collapse, contrary to the policy of their British allies who more clearly assessed the corruption and mismanagement of the Nationalist regime, were in a far more favourable position than other foreigners. The British, in particular, anxious to play their part in the re-establishment of prewar trade relations, found themselves cold-shouldered in their efforts to repatriate their interned nationals and even obstructed by their American allies when they sought to send men-of-war to Chinese ports for the purpose.

American hegemony in the Far East, based on their immense sea and air power seemed to be the pattern for the future. But two developments which were eventually to disrupt this state of affairs were already in progress when the war came to an end. At the Potsdam Conference, amongst other agreements which put postwar advantages into the hands of the Communists, it had been decided that Russia, having entered the war against Japan a few days before its end, should occupy North Korea down to the 38th parallel, while the United States would occupy South Korea. On 10 August 1945 Russian troops crossed the border between Manchuria and Korea.

Although there had been no agreed intention that by this arrangement Korea should be divided into two countries, the Russians at once began to organize and train a North Korean army and Soviet agents to set up a Communist regime. The 38th parallel became a frontier closed to American officials and when the United Nations appointed a commission to supervise free elections in 1948, neither the members of the commission nor of the Democratic Party of Korea headed by Kim Koo and Syngman Rhee were allowed to cross into North Korea. The outcome was the establishment of a Republic of Korea under the presidency of Syngman Rhee with its capital at Seoul but with no jurisdiction north of the 38th parallel, where a People's Democratic Republic of Korea held sway with its capital at Pyongyang. Russian and American troops were withdrawn in 1949. The efficient North Korean army left by the Russians and the lack of any effective equivalent in the south left a dangerous imbalance and the likelihood of an eventual aggression by the Communists. American military assistance to South Korea, including the equipment of an army of 65,000 men and a naval coastguard force, was to continue and a military advisory group was to supervise the training of these forces; but this programme was still in its early stages in June 1950, when the eruption occurred.

Meanwhile in China, lavish American aid had failed in its object of bolstering the Nationalist regime in opposition to the Communists. The latter, under Mao Tse-tung and controlling a large part of North China, had fought the Japanese with considerable success as ostensible allies of the Chungking government. Some of the weapons with which they fought were captured from the Japanese; others, however, were American arms which had been supplied to Chiang Kai-shek but passed on by corrupt officials. When the two Chinese factions failed to achieve a united China at the end of the war, the race between them to take over from Japanese occupation forces was on.

The American Air Forces were employed to transport Nationalist armies to seize key points; United States Marines were landed in North China, officially to supervise repatriation of Japanese troops. Thus the Nationalists were enabled to take over the cities, railways and ports. Elsewhere, however, the Communists successfully exploited their tactics of infiltration to take over the countryside and conducted a guerilla war. Efforts by the United States Ambassador, General Patrick Hurley, to bring about reconciliation and unity failed; so, too, did those of General of the Army George C. Marshall, who was sent by President Truman to exercise his acknowledged talents as a negotiator. Peace negotiations and conferences to draft a constitution were held at intervals but no compromise between the Nationalists and Communists was achieved.

Lavish American aid and supply of armaments to the Nationalists were denounced by the Communists as 'American imperialism' and the government as the 'Nanking puppets'. A National Assembly which finally met in November 1946 was boycotted by the Communists. In January 1947 Marshall departed to become United States Secretary of State. From this time onwards the Nationalists began to lose ground – politically as their corrupt and repressive regime became more and more unpopular, militarily as the Communist guerilla tactics gained them control of increasing areas in North China. By October 1948 all Manchuria was in Communist hands; during 1949 the People's Liberation Army poured southwards, crossing the Yangtse and capturing the Nationalist capital, Nanking, at the end of April. Canton surrendered on 15 October and on 8 December the Nationalist government fled to Formosa with the remnants of its armies and set up its capital at Taipeh.

On 15 February 1950 Mao Tse-tung's government signed a thirty-year pact of 'friendship, alliance and mutual assistance' with Soviet Russia. China withdrew behind a 'bamboo curtain' into isolation from the West, with which trade shrank to a tiny trickle. American policy in regard to China had suffered a resounding defeat. Reaction to this was reflected in statements by President Truman and Secretary of State Dean Acheson in which it was declared that the United States would not provide military aid or advice to the Chinese in Formosa. This was, no doubt, an indication of the degree to which America had burnt her fingers in supporting the corrupt Nationalist regime. That it was intended to avoid a similar involvement in Korea was also made clear when the Secretary's statement went on to outline a defence perimeter that was 'essential under all circumstances' to the United States, running from the Aleutians to Japan, the Ryu-kyus and the Philippines – a line that pointedly, and unrealistically, omitted Korea and Formosa. Aggression there, the Secretary stated, would have to be opposed by the United Nations.

Four months later this policy received the acid test when on 25 June 1950 the North Korean army crossed the 38th parallel to begin an unprovoked and unheralded invasion of South Korea.

The United Nations Security Council acted with speed and resolution. In an emergency meeting on the next day, boycotted by the Russian delegate and so saved from a Soviet veto, they condemned the North Korean act as a breach of world peace and called for military sanctions. Direction of military operations was to be undertaken by the United States with General MacArthur in supreme command.

Admirable as this was, it could not have prevented the North Korean army overrunning the whole peninsula and occupying the key south coast port of Pusan had there not been readily available a large American naval and amphibious force to transport troops of the occupation forces from Japan to reinforce the troops of the South Korean army. Taken by surprise and outnumbered, the South Koreans had by 5 July been driven helter-skelter southwards. On that day advance elements of the United States 24th Division, transported by air, came into action with greatly superior enemy forces eight miles south of Suwon and were joined two days later by the sea-transported remainder of the division. By the fourteenth another Division had also been landed. Four days later the United States 1st Cavalry Division was landed at the east coast port of

Pohang by an American amphibious force just in time to check the headlong North Korean advance down the east coast towards Pusan.

For a time it remained doubtful whether the American and South Korean forces, outnumbered as they were, could retain a foothold in the peninsula. MacArthur appealed for massive reinforcements from the United States and these began to reach Pusan on 2 August. Gradually the North Korean advance, at the end of its long supply lines, was slowed and finally halted and by mid-August the American troops had stabilized a wide perimeter round their supply port of Pusan. On 29 August the first United Nations ground troops other than American or South Korean, arrived at Pusan. These were two British battalions from the garrison of Hong Kong, transported in the cruiser HMS *Ceylon* and the auxiliary aircraft carrier *Unicorn*. This was the first of the contributions of ground troops, all on a scale minute in comparison to the United States forces engaged, that were to be provided by Great Britain, Australia, France, Turkey, the Netherlands, Greece, Thailand and the Philippines.

More immediately available to assist the Americans in carrying out their United Nations task was the British Far Eastern Fleet. On 29 June, the Admiralty directed the Commander-in-Chief, Admiral Sir Patrick Brind, 'to place the Royal Navy at present in Japanese waters at the disposal of the United States Naval Commander for Korean Operations, in support of the Security Council resolutions'. As a result, during the next two days the cruiser *Jamaica* with two frigates joined the American Task Group which was blockading the Korean east coast, while the cruiser *Belfast*, the carrier *Triumph* and two destroyers joined the American Task Force centred on the carrier *Valley Forge* and by 3 July aircraft from both carriers were engaged over enemy airfields in North Korea.

From this time onwards a sizeable British naval force, including ships of the Royal Australian, Royal Canadian and Royal New Zealand Navies and comprising always one aircraft carrier, cruisers, destroyers and frigates, and supported by tankers and other logistic ships of the Royal Fleet Auxiliary formed a permanent element of the United Nations Fleet. Carrier planes were employed to provide fighter patrols over the land battle and on interdiction tasks along the North

Korean army's supply lines as well as on strafing attacks on enemy airfields. Cruisers, destroyers and frigates patrolled the coast to prevent enemy attempts to land troops or agents by sea and were called upon as necessary to deliver bombardments in support of the troops ashore.

The influence of sea power was most clearly demonstrated, however, when the whole military situation was transformed and the hitherto triumphant North Korean Army found themselves encircled and trapped as a result of a huge and brilliantly executed amphibious landing operation far in their rear. A force of 55 major warships (16 of them British Commonwealth), one French, the remainder American), 22 minor craft and 169 transports, landing ships, store ships and so on was organized; after capturing the off-shore islands on 15 September, some seventy thousand troops were landed at Inchon and struck inland, cutting the road running south from Seoul along which most of the enemy's supplies were transported. At the same time the only other supply route, down the Korean east coast, was interdicted by naval forces. Seoul was recaptured two weeks later and Syngman Rhee's government moved back into the capital. Meanwhile on the sixteenth the United Nations forces within the Pusan perimeter had launched a fierce offensive. The North Koreans, cut off in their rear from their sources of supply, crumbled in the face of this assault. By the twenty-sixth United Nations forces advancing northwards had joined hands with those landed at Inchon. All that remained to be done to liberate South Korea was a mopping-up operation which killed or captured more than half the North Korean Army.

The vexed question now arose as to whether the United Nations forces should cross the 38th parallel to complete the annihilation of the North Korean Army and prevent it regrouping and recovering to repeat its aggression at a later date. Amidst the opinions voiced by the majority of delegates to the United Nations that this should be done, was heard the warning of Pandit Nehru of India that this might bring Chinese armies to the rescue of their fellow Communists. It was ignored, however, and MacArthur's armies were launched northwards towards the Manchurian frontier up two routes, separated by eighty miles of mountainous terrain virtually unpenetrable by the highly mechanized United Nations forces. They were not impenetrable, however, to the mobile Chinese light infantry, trained in infiltration and guerilla tactics, which made up the majority of the People's Liberation Army. Taking advantage of their mobility even in the bitter winter weather that by the last week of November had gripped the countryside, they brought the United Nations advance to a halt and then to a retreat so rapid that only great skill and courage prevented it becoming a rout. The westerly column was forced back beyond Seoul, which once again fell to the Communists, before it could stabilize a new line across the peninsula. On the eastern side the United States Marines, with No. 41 Royal Marine Commando incorporated with them, fought their way out of the ring of Chinese armies that had surrounded them, to conduct a retreat through extremes of cold and snow and through greatly superior enemy troops amounting to eight divisions on whom they inflicted vast casualties. With their vehicles, tanks, guns and equipment they finally reached the port of Hungnam where they were embarked under the guns of the United States 7th Fleet.

The war of movement virtually ceased after this, to be replaced by a war of attrition, though in the process the Communist army, suffering heavy losses, was gradually forced back over the 38th parallel. The United Nations enjoyed an immense superiority in weapons and its air power was virtually unchallenged. Nevertheless the limitless Chinese manpower which the Communists so ruthlessly expended and, above all, the security of their bases beyond the Manchurian frontier, where MacArthur was forbidden to attack them, could delay a decision almost indefinitely.

MacArthur's efforts to have the rules altered, his heated advocacy for a blockade of the Chinese coast and for Chinese Nationalist troops to be employed, led to fears that he might take action that would spread the war beyond Korea. When these views, contained in a letter to the minority leader in the United States House of Representatives, were read out on the floor of the House on 5 April 1951, President Truman regarded it as insubordination on the General's part and summarily relieved him of his command.

Efforts to bring about a cease-fire in Korea had been under way in the United Nations Assembly since December 1950, only to be repeatedly repudiated by the Chinese Communists. On 30 January, however, Red China was branded by the United Nations General Assembly as an international aggressor. At length, at a Russian proposal that armistice talks should be held, General Ridgway, the new United Nations Supreme Commander, invited the enemy to meet United Nations representatives to discuss a cease-fire. The talks began on 10 July 1951 : they were to drag on for more than two years during which the fighting never ceased. An armistice was finally signed on 27 July 1953 by which a demarcation line roughly on the existing battle zone was agreed, with a neutral buffer zone between the opposing sides.

The war thus ground to a halt without a clear-cut victory for either side. It had been waged between a purely land power and a mainly maritime one ; the former's supply lines had been entirely over land owing to the latter's absolute control of the sea. They had been subjected to incessant air attacks and, on the east coast to smothering naval bombardment, and though ingenuity and the use of vast manpower to make repairs prevented them from being decisively cut, the Communist armies had been restricted to a scale of weaponry far less than that of their opponents who could be lavishly supplied from the sea. Some figures will speak for themselves : 54,000,000 tons of dry cargo and 22,000,000 tons of oil and petrol, amounting to 99.63 per cent of all cargo delivered to the United Nations armies, was carried there in ships.

Sea power, however, cannot of itself bring about a decision in war. It can only ensure a situation within a limited distance from the sea in which the armies of its own side can fight under advantageous conditions, by maintaining their supplies and providing, where necessary, superior mobility (as for instance in the Inchon amphibious assault behind the enemy's lines). In Korea it could not enable a United Nations army decisively to defeat the almost inexhaustible manpower of the Chinese armies ; but it could, and did, give them the support necessary firstly to prevent them being overwhelmed and then to inflict such unacceptable casualties that the Communists agreed to relinquish the aims for which they had gone to war.

Sea power, in fact, had demonstrated its influence on maintenance of the *status quo* in face of the Communist strategy of nibbling at the perimeter of the non-Communist world. When Red China, frustrated in Korea, shifted its attention to Formosa and the smaller off-shore islands held by the Nationalists, it was the flexibility and mobility of sea power that once again brought their plans to a halt.

The American policy of non-intervention should Formosa be attacked which was enunciated in 1950 had been immediately discarded when the North Korean aggression occurred. President Truman had ordered the United States 7th Fleet to prevent any attack upon Formosa. From time to time since then the Peking government had fulminated threats that they would capture the island. Not until January 1955, however, did they make any overt move; and then it was directed at one of the many small off-shore islands, Yikiangshen, which being some 215 miles north-north west of Formosa and only twenty miles from the China coast, was not easily defensible and fell to an amphibious assault. The nearby Tachen Islands against which threats were also made, were equally indefensible; the 7th Fleet therefore evacuated their population.

President Eisenhower now obtained Congress authority to use American military forces as he saw fit to defend Formosa and the Pescadores. Nothing was said, however, about the numerous off-shore islands, the most important of which were Quemoy off Amoy and Matsu to seaward of Foochow.

Over the next three years the Red Chinese established airfields and batteries of siege guns on the mainland opposite and within range of Quemoy where there was a garrison of sixty thousand Nationalist troops. During August 1958 tension rose as Communist and Nationalist fighter planes engaged in dogfights over the island; and on the twenty-third the siege guns opened a tremendous bombardment. Invasion seemed imminent. At once, from distant quarters of the Pacific, United States naval forces converged on the area, with carriers coming from Hong Kong, Japan, Pearl Harbour and the Mediterranean. The powerful carrier fleet thus assembled, as well as United States Air Force reinforcements to Chiang Kai-shek's Air Force on Formosa, gave the Red Chinese cause to reconsider. Quemoy was left in peace and today more heavily protected with howitzer batteries it, and Matsu, are still under the Chinese Nationalist flag.

An ancient political pattern has thus recurred in the Far East, with China the exclusive, contemptuous 'Middle Kingdom' firmly established on land and laying claim to, or at least casting a possessive eye towards, the tributary states on her borders but unable to control her own sea areas. Tibet has been reabsorbed into the Chinese Empire : Communist rule over all Vietnam is likely soon to be firmly established as a result of Chinese aid, when the country will be a satellite of China. Thailand, Burma and Malaya lie under a similar threat. In the south, Indonesia had come near to falling under Chinese Communist domination and thus to becoming another tributary satellite when the anti-Chinese uprising of 1966 suppressed the Communist Party. As in the days of the ancient Javanese kingdoms of Singhasari and Majapahit, lack of sea power has forced the acceptance of Indonesian independence of Chinese suzerainty for the time being.

If history is indeed repetitive, the present situation may be the recurrence of the early period of a Chinese dynasty, with the ruler still preoccupied with terrestrial security or aggrandizement to the neglect of maritime effort. At the increased pace of political change of present times as compared to earlier historical eras, it may not be long before Communist China finds itself enjoying such security and stability on land that resources and effort can be spared for maritime expansion. If China then becomes a strong naval power the way will be open for her to support the teeming Chinese overseas population in Malaysia, Indonesia and other island groups in the Pacific in taking over the government of the countries in which they have settled and established themselves in commercial and financial leadership.

How far the Western powers, with their 'obligations' to their ex-colonies, would go to prevent such an expansion of Communist rule is a matter for speculation. The disastrous example of Vietnam must make intervention on land most unlikely. The lesson has been painfully learned that in territory which cannot be defended by sea power ruthless insurgency operations cannot be defeated by military means. In pursuit of the aim of 'containment' of Communism, the Manila Pact brought into being the South East Asia Collective Defence Treaty (Seato) between the United States, Great Britain, Australia, New

Zealand, France, Thailand, Pakistan and the Philippines. The driving force behind the Treaty as a whole is the United States which supplies arms and advisers to the South-East Asian signatories. But although by a protocol to the treaty, the 'Protocol States' of Cambodia and South Vietnam (and until recently Laos) may by invitation or with their consent receive Seato assistance in the event of armed attack or should their integrity or political independence be threatened, the consequences of the United States' and Australian involvement in South Vietnam under this protocol have made future continental intervention unlikely. The maritime implications of Seato remain valid nevertheless, and much effort is expended in integrating the naval forces of the signatories to enable them to operate together. Ideally, for the purposes for which the treaty was negotiated, Malaysia and Indonesia should become members, a development which does not at present belong to practical politics. Great Britain, on the other hand, is playing an important part in setting up defence arrangements for Malaysia and Singapore by the Five Powers – Britain, Australia, New Zealand, Malaysia and Singapore. The British naval contribution will comprise six frigates or destroyers and a submarine, based east of Suez, supported by a number of long-range maritime reconnaissance aircraft of the Royal Air Force.

Japan, another Pacific state which is the object of Chinese Communist ambitions, renounced the making of war 'for ever' in the peace treaty following the end of the Second World War. Such armed forces as she retained were designated 'self-defence' forces. Her 'Self-Defence Fleet', nevertheless, though it contains no ship bigger than a 4,700-ton destroyer, has been expanding steadily under a series of five-year Defence Build-up Plans. By 1971 it had become a sizeable navy with a strength of:

10 submarines (diesel-powered)
27 destroyers (including one guided missile ship)
13 frigates
20 fast patrol vessels
 2 minelayers
 2 training ships
35 coastal minesweepers
10 motor torpedo boats

4 landing ships

93 support ships and service craft

Thus it may be seen that although China can, if she cares to expend the effort, expand the frontiers of her empire on the Asian mainland with little fear of opposition, if she wishes to expand overseas she will have to acquire a first-class navy. This she has as yet shown little ambition to do, though before her break with Soviet Russia she obtained thirty-three large diesel driven submarines which are now obsolescent.

Meanwhile Soviet Russia, which hoped initially to wield sea power in the Far East by equipping satellites such as China and Indonesia, has been frustrated by the break-away of Chinese Communism and the suppression of Communism in Indonesia. Though she has startled the world with her construction of the second biggest navy in existence and by her ever-widening naval presence, she has so far confined her expansion to filling the power vacuums caused by the withdrawal of British sea power from the Mediterranean and the Indian Ocean. It seems possible that so long as the United States and her allies maintain a powerful maritime presence in the Far East and no oriental satellites of Russian Communism emerge there, she will refrain from a naval challenge in those parts.

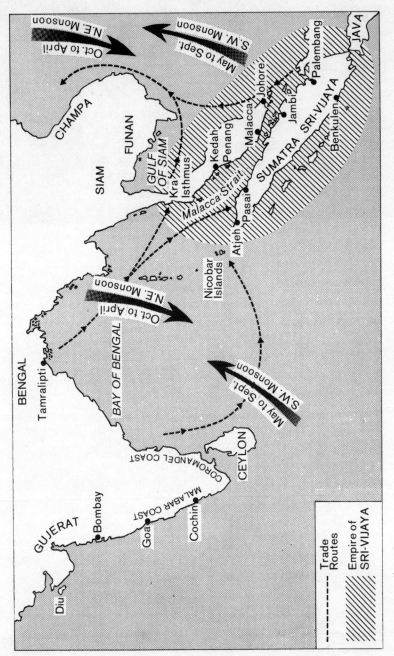

India, the Malay peninsula, Sumatra and Java

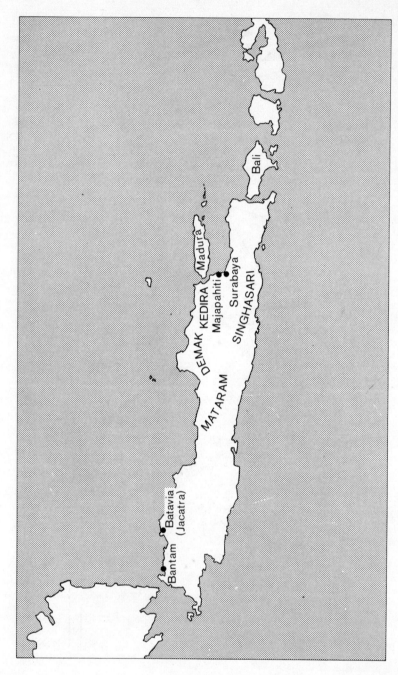

Bali

Madura

DEMAK KEDIRA

Majapahiti

Surabaya

SINGHASARI

MATARAM

Batavia
(Jacatra)

Bantam

Java

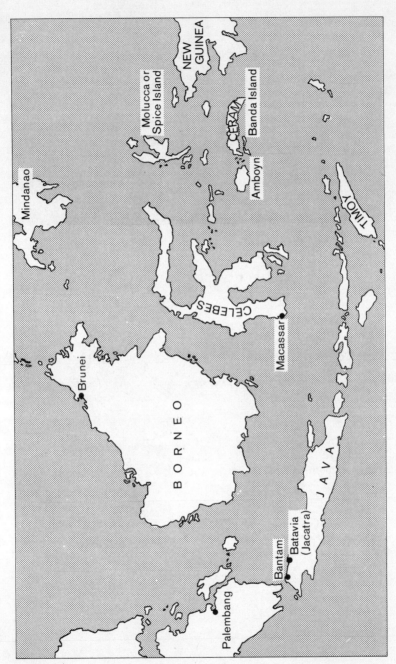

The Indonesian Archipelago

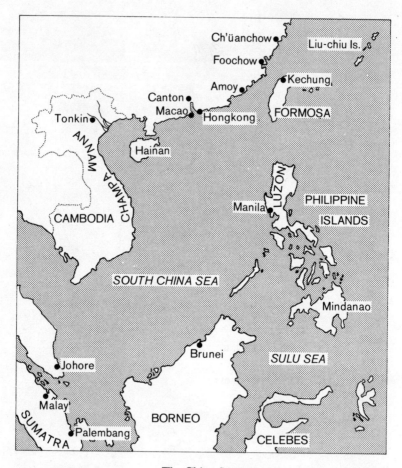

The China Seas

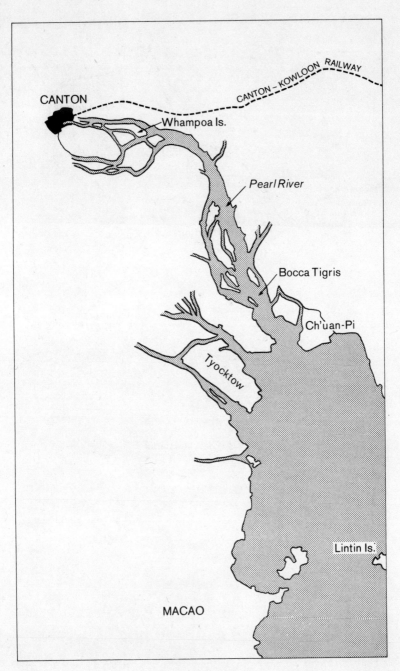

The Pearl river estuary

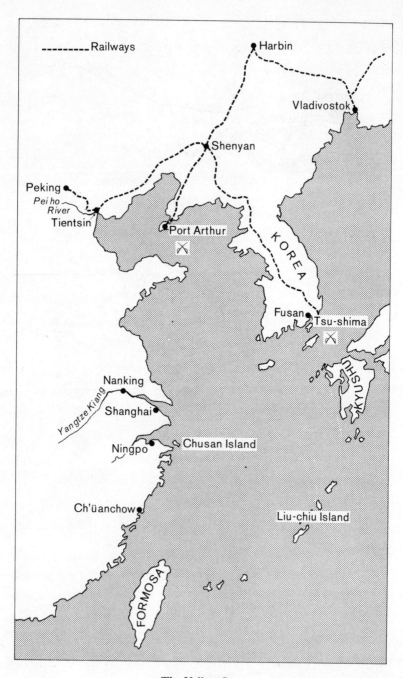

The Yellow Sea

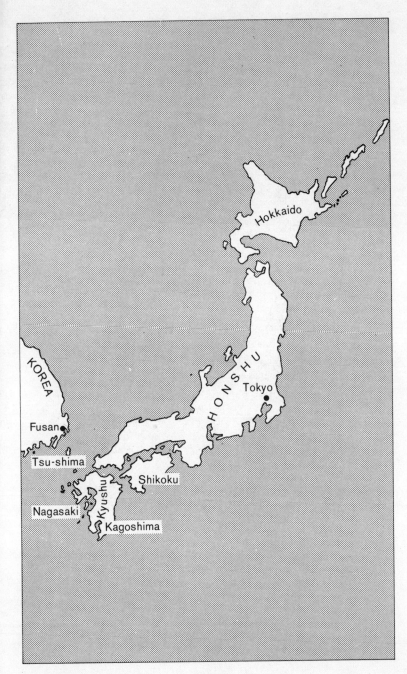

Japan

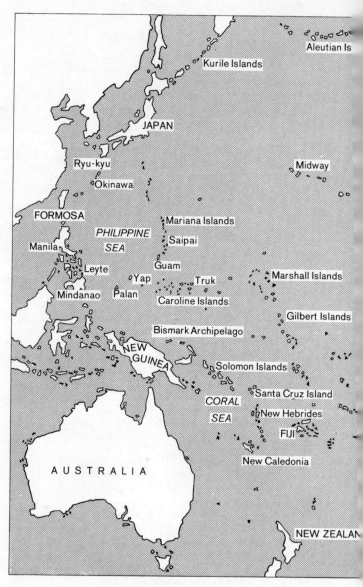

Central and South Pacific

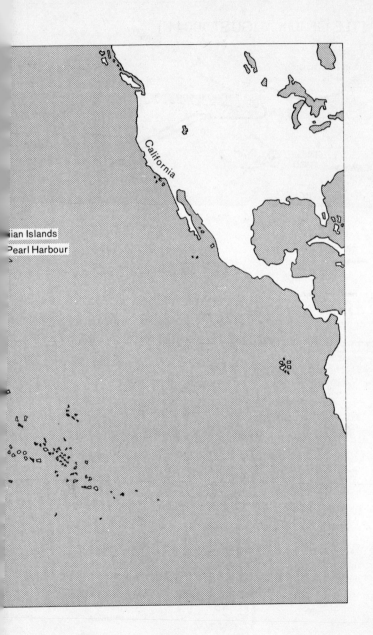

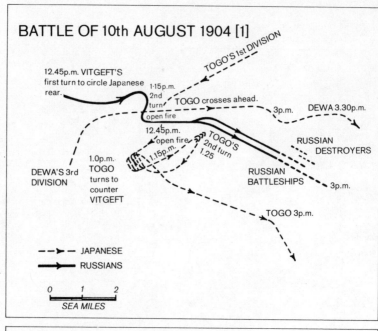

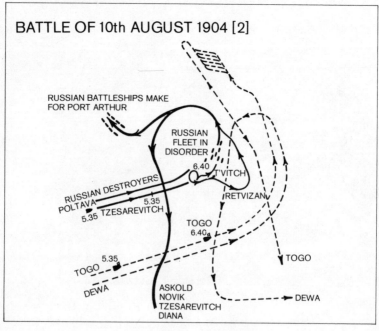

Battle of 10th August 1904

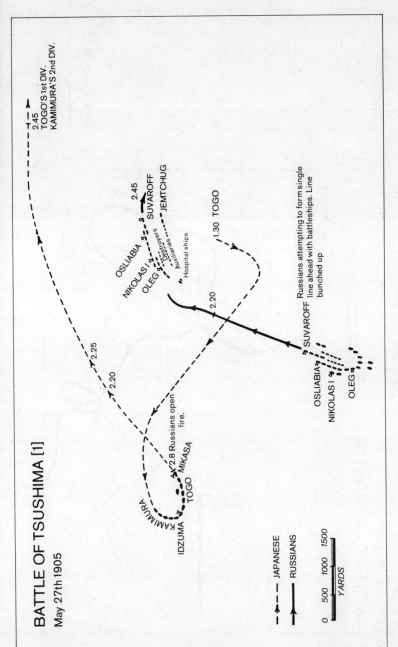

Battle of Tsushima

BATTLE OF TSUSHIMA [2]
May 27th 1905

JAPANESE
RUSSIANS

5.00
5.10
5.20
4.53
4.35
6.20
5.50
4.20
5.50
KAMTCHATKA
sunk 7.5
SUVAROFF
sunk 7.20
URAL
sunk 5.50
5.5
5.20
5.20
6.20 ALEX III sinking.
BORODINO on fire.
4.00
ALEX III
leaves the
line.
3.10
Togo turns his
ships simultaneously
to head off the Russians.
3.00
Russian attempt
to turn north.
2.45
3.10
SUVAROFF
leaves the line.
OSLIABIA sunk 3.5
2.45
2.25
3.40
4.00

0   2   4
SEA MILES

Battle of Tsushima

BIBLIOGRAPHY

Bienstock, Gregory, *The Struggle for the Pacific* (London 1937)

Buchan, John (ed.), *The Nations of Today – Japan* (London 1923)

Cameron, Mahoney, McReynolds, *China, Japan and the Powers* (New York 1952)

Collis, Maurice, *Foreign Mud* (London)

Costin, W. C., *Great Britain and China 1833–1860* (Oxford 1937)

Hsü, Immanuel C. Y., *The Rise of Modern China* (Oxford 1970)

Hulbert, H. B., *History of Korea* (London 1962)

Hurd, Douglas, *The Arrow War* (London 1967)

Hyma, Albert and Wahr, George, *The Dutch in the Far East* (Michigan 1942)

Parkinson, C. Northcote, *War in the Eastern Seas 1793–1815* (London 1954)

Potter, E. B. and Nimitz, Chester (eds), *Sea Power* (New York 1960)

Soothill, W. E., *China and the West* (Oxford 1925)

Vlekke, Bernard, *Nusantara* (Harvard 1943)

INDEX